The Watchman Guide to Privacy

Reclaim Your Digital, Financial, and Lifestyle Freedom

Gabriel Custodiet
watchmanprivacy.com

Text copyright © 2020 Gabriel Custodiet
All rights reserved

Version 1.8 Published 5 September 2022

No part of this book may be reproduced and/or distributed in any form or by any electronic or mechanical means, including information storage and retrieval systems, without permission in writing from the author.

The information presented herein represents the view of the author as of the date of publication. This book is presented for informational and entertainment purposes only.

Quis custodiet ipsos custodes?

Table of Contents

Introduction Does Privacy Matter?..9

Chapter 1 First Steps to Privacy...15
   First, Do No Harm...15
   Think Through the Flow of Information...18
   Be Self-Sufficient..20
   Don't Rely on a Single Company or Service..22
   Use Cash for Everything...25
   Communicate with Private Messengers...26
   Tone Down Social Media...27
   Get Your Digital Life in Order...30

Chapter 2 Physical Privacy..31
   Separate Name from Home Address..32
   Improve Your Locks and Cover the Basics..35
   Appearances Matter..37
   Neighbors and Security Cameras..39
   Car Privacy...42
   Shred Your Life..44
   Your Computer: A Physical Thing?...46
   Choose Location Carefully...47

Chapter 3 Online and Digital Privacy (The Basics)...................................51
   Our Road Map...53
   Find Physical Solutions to Digital Problems..53
   Three Rules of Computer Use..57
   How to Use the Internet...58
   Additional Tweaks to Firefox...61
   VPNs..62
   Email..65
   Passwords and Two-Factor Authentication..70

    Protect Your Identity..76

Chapter 4 Online and Digital Privacy (Intermediate).....................79
    Linux..80
    Acquire Things Secretly Online..85
    Avoid "Always Online" Services and Rental Culture..................89
    File Encryption..91
    Tor..93

Chapter 5 Phone Privacy...97
    Part 1: The Basic Approach to Phone Privacy..........................99
    Interlude: Buying a Phone..103
    Part 2: The Serious Method...105
    The MySudo-iPod Touch Solution...108

Interlude A Brief History of the Death of Privacy.........................111

Chapter 6 Financial Privacy..119
    What is Your Wealth and Do You Own It?...............................120
    First Keep a Low Profile...122
    Use Cash, While You Can...123
    Private Online Shopping..129
    Gold, Precious Metals, Collectibles..133
    Cryptocurrencies..138
    How to Acquire Bitcoin Privately..142
    Other Private Payment Methods...147
    Self-Employment aka Earning Money Privately.....................148
    Offshore Banking?...151
    Accounting and Taxation...152

Chapter 7 Traveling Privacy..155
    Internet While Traveling..157
    GPS Navigation...158
    Driving..159
    Air Travel..163
    Alternative Ways to Travel...166
    International Travel..167
    Hotels and Accommodation..168

  Moving, and How to Do it Privately..170

Chapter 8 Advanced Privacy..173
  Spreading "Lies" with Disinformation...173
  Data Removal Online...174
  Privacy and the Family..175
  VPN: Advanced Use...179
  Temporary Operating Systems (TAILS).......................................180
  Online Fingerprinting...182
  Becoming an International Nomad...184
  LLCs, Trusts, and Other Legal Structures..................................189
  Medical/Health Privacy..192
  Virtual Machines..193
  Fighting Facial Recognition...195

Chapter 9 Privacy and the End of the World....................................199
  Privacy During COVID-1984...200
  Cancel Culture and Censorship...205
  The Upcoming Socioeconomic Collapse.......................................210

Chapter 10 Defending Privacy..215

Resources...223

Everything Else...225
Index...235

Introduction
Does Privacy Matter?

Facebook's Mark Zuckerberg claimed in 2010 that privacy was "no longer a social norm."[1] Three years later he paid $30 million to buy the four estates surrounding his Palo Alto house.[2] One year after that he spent $100 million to buy a private island near Hawaii for his family.[3] In other words, Mr Zuckerberg craves privacy for the reasons we all do: protection, peace of mind, and revivifying solitude. Privacy is essential to human thriving.

Why do so many decry the importance of privacy? *If you have nothing to hide you have nothing to worry about. Security is more important than privacy. Privacy is for criminals. I'm not special: let them watch.* I recall a propaganda poster in the authoritarian world of *Bioshock Infinite* where a giant mechanical bird patrols the city. The poster reads: "The true patriot has nothing to fear from the songbird." Such illogical and fatuous statements were once found only in dystopian fiction. Today they're on the lips of the average person.

Privacy needs no defense, and all defense is a form of weakness. But for those who need a wake-up call—a reason to fear the death of privacy—then this introduction is dedicated to you.

---

[1] https://www.theguardian.com/technology/2010/jan/11/facebook-privacy
[2] https://www.nbcnews.com/businessmain/mark-zuckerberg-spends-30-million-four-homes-ensure-privacy-8C11379396
[3] https://www.forbes.com/sites/erincarlyle/2014/10/11/confirmed-facebooks-mark-zuckerberg-paying-more-than-100-million-for-kauai-property

Do you remember reading as a school kid about Anne Frank, a Jewish girl who hid in an attic during the Holocaust? I don't think anyone needed to convince the Franks about the value of privacy. Privacy is the best protective mechanism we have, and infinitely more secure than any policing agency (the Franks were hiding *from* the police). Your potential adversaries, of which there are many, can't harm you if they don't know where to find you or whether you even exist. You have no enemies and nothing to hide? Let me offer a few ideas.

If you bought this book with a credit card then there's a permanent record of your purchase. If you're ever convicted of a crime—not unlikely living in today's legal-industrial complex—and your Amazon purchasing history is subpoenaed, you can enjoy explaining to the emotionally-driven jury deciding your fate why you bought a "guide to hiding illicit activities" (the lawyer's words—not mine). It's none of their business what books you buy? Exactly what a guilty person would say.[4]

How about some numbers? These represent Americans, but apportion them to your own country. Eleven percent of people will be stalked during their lives.[5] Ten percent will fall victim to life-stalling identity theft.[6] Ten million will be abused by partners, some of whom will flee.[7] A small percentage will be pursued by personal enemies—likely psychopaths—who make up two percent of people but account for fifty percent of violent crimes.[8] Do you think such numbers will decrease or increase during the next decade of social and economic collapse?

The Internet has worsened these dangers while adding new ones. Today you might be called out by an online mob fueled by sensationalist media and quick-fix social media forums. In 2020 in the "free world" you could be called out and arrested for not wearing a piece of cloth across your face. The COVID hysteria is simply a recent and enlarged version of everyday authoritarianism. Do you remember the dentist from Minnesota who hunted Cecil the lion and

---

[4] To buy this book privately on Amazon, create a new account from public Wi-Fi. Pay for the book with an Amazon gift card purchased in cash. Have the item delivered to a nearby Amazon pick-up location.
[5] https://www.cdc.gov/violenceprevention/pdf/nisvs_executive_summary-a.pdf
[6] https://ncvc.dspacedirect.org/bitstream/item/1228/CVR%20Research%20Syntheses_Identity%20Theft%20and%20Fraud_Brief.pdf
[7] https://ncadv.org/learn-more/statistics
[8] See Martha Stout, *The Sociopath Next Door* and Robert Hare, *Without Conscience*, both of whom discuss these disturbing statistics.

got crucified throughout the media for doing so? A Wikipedia page of the event is so biased it reads like a murder plot. And if you didn't catch the end to the story, his personal and business lives were devastated. Another lady made a stupid joke about AIDS to 170 Twitter followers only to discover hours later it had become a national headline. Her life was blown apart.[9] Today more than 60 percent of people support companies based on their political beliefs,[10] many of whom find great sport in calling out, getting fired, and otherwise ruining the lives of those who would disagree with them.

Indeed, in today's scandal-starved world journalists and busybodies have ample time to track down what you've said. Screening software such as FAMA catalogs the controversial social media posts of prospective employees. One man shared his results: all three hundred pages' worth.[11] Perhaps you're an electrician whose hand accidentally formed a "white power" salute while cracking his knuckles,[12] or a J.K. Rowling who made a single politically incorrect statement. Perhaps you've supported the wrong political candidate and had your address posted on Twitter. Maybe you're gay, live in one of eleven countries where being gay is punishable by death, and use a website like Facebook which can out your sexual identity in minutes based solely on your "likes." You have nothing to hide? I'm just getting started.

As legal minefields engulf Western societies constraints get added to constraints. The moment you leave your house—the moment you start your computer—you risk breaking millions of laws that exist to punish you and enrich their creators and defendants. The average American commits three felonies per day,[13] and one in twenty Americans will spend time in jail, many for victimless crimes.[14] Today's judges do not perform justice as much as inflict punishment: the federal conviction rate stands at 90%.[15] In case you're curious, the original American Constitution names three federal offenses. But what can you expect from a place home to one million lawyers, law-happy

---

[9] https://www.nytimes.com/2015/02/15/magazine/how-one-stupid-tweet-ruined-justine-saccos-life.html
[10] https://www.edelman.com/news-awards/two-thirds-consumers-worldwide-now-buy-beliefs
[11] https://twitter.com/kmlefranc/status/1221869659139366912
[12] https://thehill.com/blogs/blog-briefing-room/news/502975-california-man-fired-over-alleged-white-power-sign-says-he-was
[13] See Harvey Silverglate's book *Three Felonies a Day*
[14] https://www.bjs.gov/content/pub/pdf/Llgsfp.pdf
[15] https://www.pewresearch.org/fact-tank/2019/06/11/only-2-of-federal-criminal-defendants-go-to-trial-and-most-who-do-are-found-guilty/

politicians, intelligence agencies with budgets the size of small countries, and police who have traded in peace-keeping for "law enforcement"? As the ancient Roman historian Tacitus put it, "the more corrupt the state, the more numerous the laws."

The Internet of Things—connecting all devices—is a fuse instantiating the nuclear winter for privacy. Insurance apps report location and drivings habits (about that liquor store visit...). Payment apps (Venmo) publicize transactions by default and congeal into huge searchable databases (cannabis emoji in a region where it's illegal?). Casual hackers gather data breaches to blackmail and steal, causing 6 trillion dollars of cybercrime across the world each year.[16] Politicians and central bankers push for federal digital currencies they can monitor, flag, and shut off.[17] [18] With little reason for doing so humanity frantically seeks to connect everything, not stopping to process the exposure inherent to the hive-mind organism. One young family got their IoT wake-up call the hard way when their three-year old daughter starting hearing strange voices speaking to her directly from a Wi-Fi-enabled baby monitor.[19]

Privacy secures one's self and property, but also protects free thought. In the United Kingdom, which has taken its own George Orwell as inspiration rather than warning, the government has begun to punish its flourishing thoughtcrime. Manchester police tweet out threats against "spreading hate,"[20] and Scottish politicians push for laws to punish "hate speech" occurring in one's own home.[21] One northern English police officer confronted a man about a "no crime hate incident" Twitter poem before telling him that "we need to check your thinking."[22] Another girl in Liverpool understands all of this, but only after being arrested for the unforgivable "hate crime" of posting Snoop Dog lyrics on Instagram.[23] Just be careful how much hate you feel when reading these examples: that feeling will soon be illegal as well.

---

[16] https://cybersecurityventures.com/annual-cybercrime-report-2020/?web_view=true
[17] https://www.weforum.org/agenda/2018/04/from-dollar-to-e-sdr
[18] https://finance.yahoo.com/news/yellen-signals-interest-backing-digital-164843289.html
[19] https://www.nbcnews.com/news/us-news/stranger-hacks-baby-monitor-tells-child-i-love-you-n1090046
[20] https://reclaimthenet.org/uk-police-conspiracy-theories/
[21] https://www.thetimes.co.uk/article/hate-crime-bill-hate-talk-in-homes-must-be-prosecuted-6bcthrjdc
[22] https://www.telegraph.co.uk/news/2019/01/24/man-investigated-police-retweeting-transgender-limerick/
[23] https://www.bbc.com/news/uk-england-merseyside-43816921

Meanwhile, across the globe China offers a glimpse of our future. Social credit scores rate behavior—one dare not cross on red or play too many video games—to determine whether one can bank, use buses, or even leave the country. Chinese schools monitor students' enthusiasm with cameras and personal trackers, ensuring they never learn the most important lesson: skipping class. Chinese cash is all but gone—beggars hold out smartphone QR codes—and smart cities are under construction planning to lay out all of this tracking at scale. How do you say *Nineteen Eighty-Four* in Chinese?

The death of privacy means the death of human freedom. Imagine a world of complete neural connection: of shared thoughts and feelings. People begin to organize and gain access to impressive knowledge. Equality and Unity rule the day. Division and strife seem as though they will end. But soon, as with all non-private systems, things go wrong. Coercive minds dominate others. Minority thinking is literally wiped out. Variety and quirkiness smooth to dull conformity. Harassment, thought impossible, begins to flourish; innovation and imagination, needing isolation to develop, slow to a crawl. Unique thoughts dissipate as minds sync-up to the buzz of sameness.

Psychologist Arnold Modell puts it like this:

> Solitude is a necessary part of our daily lives. For it is in states of solitude that we extend the domain of the personal over the impersonal. When alone, we are free to experience what is idiosyncratic in us ... we reestablish contact with the private self.[24]

This fact has hardly been controversial throughout history. From Buddhist meditation to Saint Augustine's *Confessions* to William Hazlitt's essay "On Going a Journey," the importance of solitude—of privacy—has been abundantly clear to anyone with eyes to see. Only in recent decades as governments and tech companies have waged war on the private sphere have we been tricked to question something that is beyond questioning.

Privacy is nothing short of our greatest means to preserve physical and intellectual freedom, individuality, and life itself.

Now let's do something about getting it back.

---

[24] *The Private Self*, Harvard University Press, 1993, pg. 122

Chapter 1
First Steps to Privacy

Everyone thinks of changing the world, but no one thinks of changing himself.

- Leo Tolstoy

Most people searching for privacy solutions want easy answers. They want to know which software to download, which products to purchase, and which businesses to patronize. While these are all important, it is imperative first and foremost that you recognize and change your behavior. Your privacy is at risk because of *you*. Because *you* continue to give out information thoughtlessly to the world. Until you correct that behavior you will remain exposed. This chapter will help you to build a mentality that sees the world more completely and skeptically and recognize where your information is leaking out. Only after you develop this introspection will offensive privacy measures make sense.

First, Do No Harm

Former Google CEO Eric Schmidt once estimated that 5 exabytes of information had been created by humans "between the dawn of civilization through 2003."[25] As of 2003, he claimed, that much information was being created every two days. Two decades later we are pumping out even more data, and all of it reveals something about ourselves.

---

[25] https://techcrunch.com/2010/08/04/schmidt-data/

The first privacy lesson is a negative one: teach yourself to stop giving out your data.

Years ago when people were more trusting and didn't believe, as Robert Frost put it, that "good fences make good neighbors," we wouldn't hesitate to tell our local shop owner all about ourselves. Today things are different. In 2021 Jana from Fourth-Tier Furniture is probably asking where you live so she can shovel it into a database that links to corporate headquarters, which will get hacked seven months later and posted on the Dark Web. Your data might also simply stay in the local database and prove easy pickings for private investigators and law enforcement. Don't blame Jana—that's simply part of her duties.

Oh, but They've already got all my information. Why should I bother?

Because good habit is good habit. And this "They" you refer to isn't the same group of people. By exposing your data to increasingly wide audiences with repeated poor decisions you increase the odds that one of these mess-ups will come back to bite you.

There are several problems with giving out your information. First, data has become a commodity and whoever you give it to will likely sell it to someone else. Second, when you trust your information to Company X you are also trusting its employees, contractors, and partners (including the government) with it as well. There is no such thing as a "trusted third party." All third parties are a vulnerability. Third, this data will be leaked or taken at some point. Let's say you give Store X your phone number, email, and credit card simply because they asked you. You assume that this large company invests heavily in cybersecurity, but that's not the problem. Companies have moving parts, including human ones, which can easily break down or be manipulated. One missed update there, a bit of human error on the side, and *wham:* a bad actor or curious person finds a weakness and grabs a few gigabytes worth of names and numbers. This has happened to Apple, Twitter, Microsoft, and numerous government agencies. It doesn't matter how big the company: expect any information you give them to be stolen at some point. Assuming, of course, that they aren't selling your data to others already based on that obscure user agreement you confirmed when you signed up for the service. Your goal should be to withhold as much information in the first place as you can.

You should be very hesitant to surrender the following pieces of information except to government types who can punish you for withholding it:
- Real full name
- ID (for anything more than quick verification)
- National ID number (social security number, etc.)
- Home address
- Primary email address
- Real phone number
- Credit card or other payment information

If the barista at Starbucks wants to know your name, use a fake one. Likewise, if your car mechanic demands an address attached to your account, you can make one up on the fly. It gets tricky with more serious situations such as medical services, which I cover in Chapter 8. But here are some basic ideas to avoid hemorrhaging data:

1. *Reject by default*. When asked for personal information, say "I'll pass on that" or "I don't give out that kind of information." When in doubt, ask, "Am I required to give this information?" For the online world, this means pressing the submit button first and seeing what categories are mandatory.

2. *Choose services* that don't require information about you. "Zero knowledge" services, which are becoming more common in the privacy business world, tend not record much, if anything, about you.

3. *Give fake information* as often as you can.

4. *Use partial information* such as yours initials instead of your full name, or an address in the area of your real one. But only if absolutely necessary.

There's no quick fix to protecting your information. But it does begin by developing an antagonism toward any request to give it out. Your data is precious, so don't be so eager to expose it to the world.

Think Through the Flow of Information

For the experienced know the 'that' ... whereas the skilled have a grasp of the cause.[26]

- Aristotle

Our data becomes compromised in part because we fail to understand or appreciate the systems we use. Whenever you give out information to someone in person or trust it to the vast stretches of the Internet, ask the following essential question: *why do they want this, and how will it be used*?

Let's take an example. You send a document to the printer at your workplace. The document is a photo of your daughter's state ID number, which you need for an upcoming medical appointment (note you are already compromising on giving out information). You go and pick it up from the printer right away. No harm, right? Not so fast. Let's unpack this system before we make that determination.

Your company probably has its own Internet connection monitored by your administration, and your tech team. It's very much within their reach to see this photo and frankly, all of the data you send on their network. But that's just the beginning. What is a printer, exactly? It's a computer, which means it has a storage drive that records all of the page images ever sent to it. This means your daughter's sensitive ID does not vanish upon printing but remains in the printer's hard drive. Thus, your company's technician, a savvy coworker or intruder, or your company administration could have access to it from the printer as well. But it doesn't end there. Think about what happens to printers at companies. When they get old, they get sold, and many organizations don't bother wiping them. So now in a few years when Susie the 75-year old auction-goer (or the strategic professional identity thief) buys that old printer, she just might have the means to see your daughter's number as well. If you think this scenario unlikely, you can read about the six thousand copiers and printers with confidential data from New Jersey police offices that were sent across the world after an auction.[27] *Bon voyage*.

The point of this example is not to make you paranoid about printing at your office. Instead I want to get you to think through the way information flows

---

[26] *Metaphysics* (1998), Penguin, translated by Hugh Lawson-Tancred
[27] https://www.cbsnews.com/news/digital-photocopiers-loaded-with-secrets/

all around you. If you're not the master of the systems you use, then you're the slave.

Let's try another example. Large industries increasingly collect your data as their business model. This is true of tech companies but also of the traditional sellers of commodities. Did you know that the cheap "smart" TVs you've seen lately are possibly *losing* money for their companies? Why would TV manufacturers do that? Pause for a moment to consider.

Here's one answer. Since smart TVs are connected to the Internet, they can scoop up your viewing data (Netflix, YouTube, etc.), your location (through your IP address), your neighbors via their Wi-Fi, and possibly other choice information.[28] They sell this data to other companies who can use it and thus offset the loss of the TV itself. This is a nifty profit model that can potentially earn recurring revenue. As the new adage goes: if you didn't pay for the product, then *you* were the product. If you don't believe me, believe a chief revenue officer at Vizio: "We make money when we sell a TV and we make money every time a TV gets turned on."[29] The consequences of this TV scenario might not seem so dire, but think about it this way: if a company wants your data so much, then it's more valuable and revealing than you might think.

So what's the solution in these two cases? For one, buy a printer for yourself at work and print strictly to it through a wired connection. Or save sensitive printing such as ID cards for home. Next, when getting rid of any electronic item such as a printer, look into how to wipe its data (see the "Everything Else" appendix). Though some electronics that contain hard drives you should never sell. As for TVs, look for older "offline" models, which might involve searching on Facebook Marketplace, Craigslist, Swappa, eBay, etc. If you want to stick it out with your current TV, try to disconnect from the Internet as much as you can, or diversify your exposed information by connecting an external media player (such as a Roku) instead of the TV's built-in smart features. You can also connect a laptop to the TV with a cable and project the laptop screen to it. Indeed, that's what I tend to recommend.[30]

---

[28] https://www.protocol.com/china/chinese-smart-tvs-have-hoovered-up-data-without-telling-anybody

[29] https://www.wsj.com/articles/tv-maker-vizio-goes-public-as-company-sets-sights-on-ads-and-software-11616694980

[30] Be careful what is on your laptop screen; it is theorized that smart TVs can take snapshots.

More fundamentally, thinking through the flow of information is nothing short of beginning to see the world in a fuller sense. It is essential for anyone who aims to retain privacy and control over their life. Think about the systems —digital, physical, social—that you use daily and develop curiosity about how they work. It's been said that there will only be two types of people in the upcoming digital age: those who give instructions to computers, and those who receive instructions from computers. It is in your interest to be the former.

Be Self-Sufficient

Opportunity is missed by most people because it is dressed in overalls and looks like work.
- Thomas Edison

Most privacy invasions happen because you offloaded a task to someone or something else. If you learned to do your taxes yourself, you wouldn't have to send your sensitive information to a tax company. If you learned JavaScript online then you wouldn't have to pay a university to suck up your personal info (and money) to sell you a degree in "Computer Science." If you always paid with cash you wouldn't have to share the purchase of your pregnancy test kit with the local pharmacy, with VISA, and with your bank (to say nothing of the government). And if you learned how to fix the drain under your sink instead of bringing in a plumber, you'd keep your name and address out of just one more database that could compromise you. Being private means doing more things for yourself and having fewer third-parties intrude into your life.

Here are some basic ideas for self-sufficiency:
- Consult the Internet for house fixes. Slowly build up your knowledge as well as your tool kit: good screwdrivers, a drill, Channellock pliers, a couple of solid plastic buckets. Make it a weekly challenge with your family to fix something around the house.
- Learn to change your own oil—you'd be surprised how invasive garage chains can be when it comes to recording (and reporting) your vehicle identification number, license plate, and odometer.

- Don't use an app for anything you can do in person with cash: buying groceries, ordering pizza, etc. Suck it up and make that short trip yourself.
- Take a few minutes during the week to scan receipts and documents instead of offloading that work to an accountant or funneling it into QuickBooks.
- Learn WordPress, basic HTML, or a website builder instead of outsourcing your website creation. It's not as tricky as you think.
- Learn how to exist without your phone. Don't take it everywhere you go.
- Work on your memory and study maps instead of relying on GPS applications.
- Take physical notes instead of having "Alexa" or "Siri" remember for you.
- Invest in a good bike or a cheap car instead of taking Uber around town.
- Take time to learn the basics of how to fix your body, your house, and your computers.

The mindset of self-sufficiency especially applies to your work. I believe everyone should strive for self-employment. Working for yourself means many things—tax savings, freedom of time and location, greater profit potential—but it especially means greater privacy. As an employee you go into various corporate records and have to dish out your name, state ID number, and address. You might have to schmooze on LinkedIn and plaster your photo on websites. These days you might have to go through a background check or reveal your social media accounts to your potential employers. In short, you must expose yourself to get a job and expose yourself further once you have the job. On the contrary, when your run your own business, you decide how much information you give out. With a sole proprietorship or a basic business entity (an LLC, for example), you can do the exact same work you're doing now as a contractor without the compromise in personal data exposure. People who seek privacy move in one direction, and that is self-employment.

Finally, a disciplined financial saver is the hallmark of self-sufficient private person. With cash on hand you're not relying on online systems to get what you need. But you're also not relying on loans and can thus make faster and more private transactions. For example, with saved cash you can buy a used car in a private sale as opposed to surrendering myriad information to a car dealer. Some used car companies even attach trackers to their vehicles so if you get behind on your payments they can send repo men to come snatch it from you. Remember that if you purchased something through a loan—a car, a house—you don't own it. The bank owns it. And they can take back their property very, very quickly with the ample mandatory information that you will have given them.

Don't Rely on a Single Company or Service

As a privacy enthusiast I'm in the habit of criticizing Google, but let me start by complimenting them: they're too good. They've gotten to the point where they know everything about you and do everything for you. *Google for calendar; Google for email; Google for documents; Google for online searching; Google for Android phone; Google for video streaming; Google for entertainment and research; Google for cloud storage; Google for airline search; Google for hotels; Google for phone service; Google for translations, Google for marketing analytics.* Even more significantly, Google has been skilled at linking all of these data points together. If you use even a handful of Google products, then Google possibly knows more about you than your family does.

As a privacy-seeking person you should never trust a single digital company—Google, Amazon, Apple—for so many of your needs.[31] This is especially the case with "free" services, which almost certainly remain "free" by trading in your data. So-called Big Data is the operating model of many large tech companies and governments today. Big Data wants more inputs from you because it creates richer algorithms from them. Google wants you to use the same Google account to check your email and to watch YouTube and to run your translations because by doing so they collect a wider range of your business and personal interests.

There's a fundamental privacy problem in linking things together, since privacy is inherently decentralized. Centralization is alluring, since a hive organism seems to work incredibly efficiently. It knows what each of its components is doing and can send signals at blazing speed to accomplish things much more efficiently than an individual. That's the main idea behind

---

[31] Or your government, for that matter, which is the ultimate monopoly. See Chapter 8 "Becoming an International Nomad"

new services like Zapier, which does nothing more than link and automate your various accounts. The problem, of course, is that privacy is impossible in a hive organism, or a planned society, or an interconnected digital space.

It used to be the case that Google was the best by a wide margin with most of their offerings. But that advantage has eroded in recent years. Here are some alternatives today that work comparably to Google's services:

Google Product	Alternative
Gmail	ProtonMail; Tutanota
Google Chrome	Firefox; Brave Browser
Google Search	DuckDuckGo; Startpage (replicates Google); Qwant
Google Drive	Proton Drive; SpiderOak One; Nextcloud
Google Documents	LibreOffice; Standard Notes
Google Calendar	Tutanota Calendar; Proton Calendar
"Okay Google"	Okay, just do it yourself
Chromebook	Cheap laptop
Google Maps	OsmAnd Maps; Magic Earth
Google translation, airlines, hotels	Plenty of alternatives exist provided you seek them out

The Chromebook is the foremost symbol of a centralized digital life. At first glance these "laptops" are incredibly cheap and can perform most tasks for most people. But any very cheap product deserves our skepticism. Sure enough, the Chromebook runs on its own Google operating system and restricts you from using anything but Google services. In other words, you can expect when using a Chromebook for Google to know absolutely everything about you, including (possibly) which keys you press and how quickly you press them. Anyone even mildly concerned about privacy should avoid "all-in-one" solutions. Instead of a Chromebook, get a cheap laptop, keep your data offline as much as possible, and learn how to use a real computer.

Here are more ideas to help you remain unbeholden to a single company:

- Be skeptical of convenience. Don't link your phone with your laptop just because you can. Don't use "Google sign-in" or Apple "log-in" on a new website just because you can. Each new account should have its own log-in credentials (see Chapter 3).
- Indeed, don't sign in to anything, whether that is Apple ID (not needed on Macs), Google Chrome, Windows 10 (Microsoft account) unless it is mandatory.
- Diversify your brands and products. If you're an "Apple person" and love MacBooks, consider purposefully buying a different brand for your phone. If you have all VISA cards, try getting something different such as Discover or American Express.
- Learn to buy outside of Amazon and make it a goal to wean yourself off of Bezos' baby.
- Don't participate in rewards programs.
- Avoid bundling services and products. Buy your phone separately from your service; TV separate from Internet service, etc.
- Have multiple investing, checking, and savings accounts, all from different banks.
- Spend time researching alternatives to popular products and services. Sometimes they're even better than what you're using, and often they're cheaper. The free software movement is great place to begin.[32]

TAKE ACTION: YOUR FIRST FOUR STEPS

Now that you're finished plugging the holes, you can start taking proactive measures. But only if you've taken time to digest what you've read so far. Here are the first four things you should do.

---

[32] The FOSS (free and open source) movement is crucial for privacy; free meaning freedom and not no-cost. More on this later.

Use Cash for Everything

Cash gives financial privacy. There are few things as pure in the privacy world as handing over a few cash bills and receiving a good or service. You just have to do more of it. The digitization of finances has proven to be a serious affront to privacy. If you have a credit or debit card, log on to your account right now and look at your purchases. Does that list of shops and services say something about you? Keep in mind that the credit card company can see even more than you can: where you were when you made the purchase (even if online), etc. Your purchases show enough to embarrass you and even to convict you of something which you might not now be aware of.[33]

A war has been raging against cash for a very long time and every excuse has been made for its extinction. *Cash is for criminals and terrorists. Cash can't be traced. Cash transmits disease. Cash is for old people. Cash is suspicious. Cash is insecure. Cash doesn't earn interest.* The list goes on. I urge you to take the cash oath: for the sake of the future of private purchasing, give up your credits cards today and use cash wherever and whenever you possibly can. Make no excuses. You'll be helping humankind while solving your own privacy problems.

I discuss cash at length in Chapter 6, but I'll leave you with some introductory thoughts. The main thing to note is that you must plan things out in advance. You probably can't take out more than a few hundred dollars or its equivalent from an ATM. This can be more than an inconvenience. Let's say you want to buy a used car for $10,000. That means you need to visit an ATM every day for multiple weeks. You could call your bank and ask for an increase to daily ATM withdrawals, but they won't increase it by much. You could also go to your bank directly, of course, but it's always possible they will assume you're a criminal if you ask for your own money in bulk. I wish I were joking. Start keeping cash around your house—considering pitiful interest rates you might start storing much of it on your property anyway. Take all necessary precautions (see more in the next chapter). But honestly, for the sake of all that is good in this world, just start holding and using cash more often.

---

[33] "Did you drive across the border to New Jersey or Delaware to save on taxes when buying back-to-school clothes for the kids? Your cell-phone and credit card receipts document your tax evasion." *Future Crimes*, Marc Goodman, pg. 72.

Communicate with Private Messengers

We kill people based on metadata.

- Michael Hayden, former director of CIA and NSA

Stop using SMS (standard text messaging) and your default phone calling application. These communications are old, insecure, and can easily be monitored by third-parties. Instead, rely on Internet-based ("data") apps. The market for private messengers and voice chat is robust, so you will have no problem finding one that suits you.

I'll suggest specific messenger/calling services in a minute, but it's more important to know the features you're looking for in a private messaging app:

- Text and voice service (not just text).
- *End-to-end encryption.* Only you and the recipient receive the info.
- *Zero-knowledge.* This goes hand-in-hand with encryption but is the more important of the two. Basically it means that the encryption is airtight and even the owner of the service cannot view your account.
- *Open-source.* This means the code is not hidden ("proprietary"), but rather is available to the public; thus you can be more certain that no shenanigans are going on behind closed doors.
- *Expiring messages.* Optional but recommended. With most messaging apps the messages stay on your friend's phone when you send them to her. This is a serious vulnerability, because now your entire conversation exists permanently on her phone as well as yours. Apps such as Signal and Wire allow you to set hourly, daily, or weekly expiration dates for messages.
- *Reputable company.* The company that makes the messenger should be outspoken and transparent about their privacy mission and ideally independent from big tech companies.
- *No personal details.* You shouldn't have to give up your information when signing up for a secure messaging app. Otherwise you're defeating the point. Some messengers don't require your phone number to work and these are obviously preferred.

Don't forget that, unlike an SMS message or an email, the person you're messaging with a private messaging app must also have the application installed on their phone in order to interact with you. For this reason many people end up using the app most commonly used by their friends and family.

Private messengers that you might look into include Signal, Wire, Element, Threema, and Session. There are all kinds of these things but again, if your recipient does not also have the app/program, you're out of luck.

You may also have noticed that I didn't list your favorite messaging app: WhatsApp, Facebook Messenger, etc. These programs either don't have the features I just mentioned or, as in the case of WhatsApp, are owned by Facebook, collect metadata, and are not deserving of my trust.[34]

The great thing about internet-based messengers is that unlike regular phone calls and SMS, you can use them wherever you have Internet access—they can also be used straight from your computer if that company provides a computer version. In other words, you could travel across the world without your phone and talk to your friends on your laptop via Signal or Wire. All without needing a phone.

Unless you want your private messages to be out there in the ether, you should switch to a private messenger and bring along your friends and family. Go download one today.

Tone Down Social Media

Considering what we've discussed so far, do you really think social media is a good idea? The consequences of remaining on social media are more dire than you think. Consider just one story for starters.

In early 2020 a man known as "Eric the Jeweler" set up shop in a hotel room in Miami in preparation for the Super Bowl. He posted an Instagram video showing off a hotel bed littered with almost two million dollars worth of gold watches, rings, and necklaces. Thieves caught onto his activities and, finding his location based on other social media posts or through some phone calls to

---

[34] https://faq.whatsapp.com/general/security-and-privacy/what-information-does-whatsapp-share-with-the-facebook-companies

hotels, broke into his room and stole the entire safe.[35] The thieves apparently had a habit of stalking celebrities in the area by monitoring their social media posts.[36]

Your groups, likes, photos, and friends tell viewers quickly where you live, what you like to do, and where you might be next. Private investigators and stalkers love social media because it allows them to download buckets of data about you. Entire databases exist of collected social media information, conveniently drawing together your name, email address, locations, likes and interests, and whatever else they can get on you. Many of these companies sell your information or share it with scam artists and policing agencies. Indeed, let's not forget government agencies, and especially tax agencies, which no doubt use Facebook to target their victims. Photos of your vintage car collection will ensure you're meager tax returns get a thorough looking at. New York is recently requiring people to show social media history to see if their "character" is such that they will be allowed to have a concealed carry gun license.[37] Social media is the first choice for stalkers, blackmailers, kidnappers, and anyone else who would do you harm. Your social media accounts are also increasingly scrutinized as you enter new countries, especially as a new resident. In other words, what you put on social media can cost you your job, your money, your freedom, and your future.

I understand that social media for many of us is a comforting drug and for a much smaller group might actually be necessary. For any diligent privacy enthusiast the simple solution is to get off of all social media. That might sound extreme, but let me assure you it is quite possible. I erased any personal social media presence I had years ago and my life has only improved and become more social as a result.

If you choose the deletion path, there's no magic wand that can wipe out your accounts. Everything that you've ever posted is backed up to the company's servers, possibly for the long-term. Still, it's good practice to erase as much of the account as possible and sabotage the rest of your information—fill it in with nonsense—before finding the relevant "close account" sections and

---

[35] https://www.local10.com/news/local/2020/02/05/miami-man-accused-of-trying-to-sell-custom-ring-stolen-from-hotel-room-of-famed-jeweler/

[36] https://www.theledger.com/news/20200218/high-tech-miami-jewel-thieves-stalked-rich-including-ny-yankees-star-cops-say

[37] https://www.msn.com/en-us/news/us/new-gun-law-to-require-applicants-to-submit-social-media-accounts-in-ny/ar-AA11k1oi

proceeding. Many regularly-updated guides and videos exist to help you eradicate your accounts and I suggest you check them out. In case you're worried about losing all the information you have accumulated, you'll be happy (or disturbed) to know that you can usually download all of that before you go. Otherwise, download and save what you need and say goodbye to the rest.

Now, assuming that you're not going to quit social media, let's talk about how you can at least minimize your exposure through it. Consider the following:

- Reserve social media for your computer and not your phone. Phone applications like to share their information with neighboring apps. As one example, a *Wall Street Journal* report in 2019 found that eleven popular apps, from menstruation calendars to property investment apps, contained Facebook code to share with one's Facebook app.[38]

- When you use social media on your browser, make sure that you don't contaminate your other browsing. For example, if you use Firefox for your browser, then you might reserve a Chrome browser for your social media and your social media alone. We'll discuss how to lock down your browser in Chapter 3. Don't search the Internet on the same browser you use for logged-in accounts.

- Visit your privacy settings and start switching on or off anything that sounds good. I have little confidence in these settings, and they change constantly, but you may as well do it. Pay particular attention to "tagging"—don't let others tag you without your permission, and look for options to prevent people from searching and finding you.

- Use a slight variation of your real name on your profile—or use your initials—if you must use your real name at all.

- Avoid putting a personal photo on your profile. A crazy cat is much better than your face. No offense. The website www.thispersondoesnotexist.com uses AI to create fake faces from a combination of publicly-available photos. Pretty creepy, but highly useful. Download a few dozen while they still exist.[39]

- Don't reveal your location on social media for any reason. Turn off all GPS and location settings immediately.

---

[38] https://www.wsj.com/articles/you-give-apps-sensitive-personal-information-then-they-tell-facebook-11550851636

[39] If recommendations in this book are no longer available, find alternatives. Be adaptive.

- Consider erasing your current account and creating a new one with minimal information about you. This route is for people who want to become passive observers, since these new accounts might get linked or flagged as duplicate if you invite all the same friends as before.
- Send private messages outside of social media as much as you can. Don't message someone on Twitter or Facebook if you have a different way to get in touch with them.
- Consider browsing sites like Twitter without being logged into your account. Use bookmarks for your favorite YouTube channels. You don't need an account to access this stuff.
- Consider alternatives to social media. *Nitter* replicates Twitter without the tracking elements; *Invidious* works similarly to YouTube (though it gets taken down often). Be on the lookout for more private communities in which to be social. See episode 8 of my podcast.
- Let it be known to your friends and family that you do not wish to be tagged ever, for any reason, on social media.

I'll leave you with one parting thought on social media. I include as social media online forums, Reddit, Discord, and "leave your comment" sections on websites. It should go without saying that you should never embed real information on these services. But also be aware that you can build an online footprint by using these services too often. Instead, why not use the Internet as a passerby? You don't have to interact with everything you see and you don't have to have an account for every website. Read what is says, form your own opinion, keep it to yourself, and move on.

Get Your Digital Life in Order

Privacy can be distilled in the following dictum: practice minimalism. Minimalism says that you are the master of your world, not the things and the services in it. A minimalist does not purchase or download more products or programs than are necessary. He uses basic tools instead of "high tech" and "always online" ones. He learns to do things for himself and talks to real friends in real life instead of fake ones online. A minimalist lives life instead of recording it through a lens. A minimalist gives up very little and has very little that can be exposed. A privacy-seeking person is an aspiring minimalist.[40]

---

[40] See The Watchman Privacy Podcast for more about privacy as a lifestyle

Chapter 2
Physical Privacy

A man's home is his castle.

- Sir Edmund Coke

On rare occasions the populist online forum Reddit provides a drip of wisdom. One afternoon I was perusing the Privacy subreddit and found an article requesting a "privacy evaluation." Basically, a person asks for candid feedback about their privacy lifestyle so that the polite and constructive commentators of Reddit can get to work. I scrolled down. There were some holes in the strategy, for sure, but it seemed solid enough. But then the first comment put things into their fullest perspective: "How secure are your physical computer and documents at home? If someone breaks in what will they find?"

This question is really at the crux of privacy. I'm astonished that so much of the advice out there has little if anything to say about physical privacy. Sure, your life can be devastated purely through digital means, but your physical body and your physical assets cannot be harmed solely by anything in the digital realm.[41]

We must also remember, as this Reddit post made clear, that even the most digital thing in your life has a physical origin. I'm sure you've seen a dramatic action thriller where the hacker of the group says: "If you can get me inside to the mainframe, I can do anything." In some sense it's true. That's because physically connecting to a computer gives you immense access to its contents. I recently "hacked" into a friend's Internet router simply by plugging in an Ethernet cord to his modem and using the standard password, found online. I

---

[41] Though as I write this the first so-called death by cyber attack occurred during the shut down of a hospital in Germany: https://www.securitymagazine.com/articles/93409-first-ransomware-related-death-reported-in-germany

could also have simply pressed the reset button on the device and changed it to whatever I wanted. Equipment assumes that a person in physical proximity is deserving of special status. My advice? Before you go out into the world, make sure your physical world is safe behind a layer of privacy. This chapter will help.

Separate Name from Home Address

Loose lips sink ships.

- WWII propaganda poster

You may have heard the term "doxing" related to some privacy story in the news. The concept is simple. We all leave a trail across the Internet (or the real world) that can trace us back to the place we sleep at night. Have you ever taken a photo with your phone near your house? You might be troubled to know that by default many phones record the geolocation of that image, which it embeds in its EXIF data: basically data about the photo.[42] Now let's say you upload that photo to your personal blog, or some website that doesn't strip out this information (most big websites do). Any stranger could backtrack the photo and deduce where you live. They could also make this information public for others to threaten or scare you. Doxing happens every day to all manner of people for all kinds of reasons. I interviewed one such person, Jameson Lopp, on episode 24 of my podcast.

There are many more ways that you expose your home address to the world. One Japanese stalker found his victim, a singer, based on the train station info that reflected off of her eye in a photo.[43] He simply showed up and waited for her the next day, and then sexually assaulted her. Ever left an Amazon package with the label showing in your car or in the trash bin? Published a photo near your house with identifiable terrain? Showed the unique name of your Wi-Fi network—maybe named after you—on your YouTube video to be tracked down on Wigle.net (which publishes most Wi-Fi networks on the planet)? Do you reveal your city on an online forum or on your PlayStation Network profile? The consequences of doing so might be more severe than you think.

---

[42] Remove EXIF data by finding removal websites online such as Ver EXIF, then turn off GPS photo settings

[43] https://www.bbc.com/news/world-asia-50000234

If doxing is bad, then "swatting" is pure evil. Arnaud hates Theresa because she hasn't paid him back for a bet and he has the savvy to find out where she lives (she's not very good at hiding it). He calls the local police reporting a hostage situation at her house. Minutes later, a SWAT team busts down the door and, with military weapons and itchy trigger fingers, shoots down the nearest frazzled person, who they assume is the aggressor. Sound ridiculous? This happened in 2017 to a man in Wichita, Kansas over a disagreement while playing the latest *Call of Duty* video game.[44] It's been known to happen to unlucky famous streamers who expose themselves to the world. Meanwhile, on the other side, police officers are routinely targeted at their home addresses and even killed in retaliation for their work, especially as support for policing agencies dwindles.

In case you think these examples extreme—perhaps you've grown up in a country where this kind of thing doesn't happen—just remember that things can change quickly. In the summer of 2020 in the United States the mayor of St. Louis read off the names and addresses of some of the "Defund the Police" protesters live on TV.[45] The threat behind doxing is obvious: I know where you live and now everyone else does too. The summer of 2020 in the United States will likely go down as the most tense in that country in some time and things are only going to get worse. In the months since that summer Americans have been approached by mobs and had their houses and businesses destroyed. For others this targeted aggression is commonplace: people in South Africa or Northern Ireland need no reminder of the value of keeping their home address private. Make no mistake: as the world slowly devolves into a more chaotic state in the upcoming decade, the benefits of keeping your house to yourself will become abundantly clear.

Let me be blunt: you have no business revealing to anyone where you live for any reason. Your home address—the place where you sleep at night—is the most precious piece of information you can protect. *Your home address should never pass your lips. No exceptions.*

Start with the simplest stuff. If you live in a country (such as the US) where you can have a package delivered in any name, then create a fake name for shipping and never use your real one again. Or have your mail delivered to a postal box, preferably the next city over. Postal boxes are an extraordinarily

---

[44] https://www.kansas.com/news/local/crime/article192111974.html
[45] https://www.msn.com/en-us/news/us/st-louis-mayor-reads-names-and-addresses-of-protesters-who-want-to-defund-police/ar-BB16Is3X

useful tool. You can and should use them for as much mail in your life as you can. Depending on your country you might have various options for postal boxes, some of which are considered more legitimate as addresses for banking and other accounts. Treat your postal box as your new home address. And if organizations or websites don't accept PO boxes as your address, then try rearranging the text. PO Box 743 now becomes 843 Elizabeth Street # 743, where the first part is the street address of the post office itself. You can also use "Apartment 743" or other variants. Just test this new format to make sure it goes through by sending an empty envelope to the name and address.

Consider some other options for protecting your address:

- Use a fictional address. Your mechanic, and most others, don't need to know your real address. For more legitimacy, learn by heart the address of a hotel nearby (or far away). This is "your" new address when asked.

- When using GPS apps, never input your real address. Select a business in the area and find your way home from there.

- Give your visiting friends and family the address of a nearby shop, and tell them you'll come around the corner to guide them when they arrive. The goal here is to keep your address out of GPS systems and troublesome apps like Uber, which does serious logging of information.

- Have your Uber driver pick you up and drop you off a short distance from your home.

- Instead of delivering packages to your house, deliver them to a store drop-off location (think Amazon Locker) or an alternative address that you have access to.

- Make use of a friend or family member's address, or find a local church or shop and ask to rent their address informally for your own purposes. You would be surprised how willing to help your local community might be. This can be especially useful if you're not in a position to take out a post office box, which itself requires a lot of personal information.

- If you can't afford a postal box call your mail service and ask what they do for homeless people. Often they'll allow packages to remain in their building for such people and you would simply have to show ID (or not) when accepting the package.

Unfortunately, your address—especially if you are an American—is likely already available online from people search websites such as truepeoplesearch.com. You will have to remove them first (see Chapter 8 "People Search Website Removal"), and for the most protection find a new place to live and be more cautious about what you reveal in the future. More advanced techniques of private house ownership and renting require planning and the use of legal entities, which are described in Chapter 8.

Improve Your Locks and Cover the Basics

Your house, apartment, or room is your sanctum. It is the first and foremost barrier between you and the world. Try something with me. Stop reading this book and take a quick survey of this space. Imagine you were locked out. If you were desperate, how would you get in? Come back to the book when you've done this.

Now that you have taken note of weaknesses, let's discuss the minimum requirements for a secure home:

- Cover all windows so that no one can see in, especially at night.
- Close your curtains when you leave your house.
- Don't assume that your apartment on the 27th floor is immune to such invasions—among other possibilities, long-distance photography and drones have ruined that illusion.[46]
- *Privacy film* or *privacy curtains* are see-through and prevent others from peaking in during the day, while allowing the sun to come in and you to see out decently well.
- Make sure window locks are strong. An object is only as strong as its weakest point.

Now take a step back. Are you the first person to ever hold the key to your house? If not, consider changing the locks on your doors. When you install new locks, or even if you decide to stick with your current ones, reinforce them with longer screws of at least 7 centimeters or 2.5 inches. This slows down your door from getting kicked in. You can probably get away with 8

---

[46] Even mobile phones are moving toward "long-zoom" periscope cameras (https://www.androidauthority.com/periscope-camera-iphone-1140402/).

centimeter (3-inch) screws: just be mindful of how much wood you have to screw into. Replace the screws of your door hinges with these longer screws as well.

All locks are improved by using longer screws, but they still may be vulnerable to a kick-in attack. The next step is to buy a *strike plate* and install it using some of your new long screws. You might also consider a *door reinforcement lock*, which have been known to hold strong against kick-in attempts. The *reinforcement lock* is for when you're at home, and the *strike plate* helps you at all times. But before you buy a fancy new device, go get longer screws for your current lock and hinges. Put them in *today*.

If your door has a *dead bolt lock*—the stronger lock above your handle—be sure to use it even if it takes a few more seconds. Make that habit non-negotiable. One morning I stepped outside in early-morning zombie mode and returned to my side door to discover I had locked myself out. Since it was only the handle lock, I searched around my shed for a skinny aluminum sign, slid it into the crack of the door, and kept pushing until *POP*—it opened right up. Always lock the *dead bolt*.

Doors are simply the most obvious entrance to your domain. When I felt locked out that morning I seriously considered breaking a window to get in. Breaking glass is noisy and not a burglar's first choice of entry, but it is easily the weakest point of your house:

- Consider replacing your windows with *double-pane glass* or something fundamentally stronger such as plexiglass.
- If you're short of money, reinforce your current glass with a layer of *security film*. This is essentially an enormous translucent plastic sticker that adheres to your glass and greatly boosts its physical integrity. I won't lie: this film is a real hassle to put on, but also a hassle to break through.
- Avoid doors with glass in the center, as this makes breaking in that much easier, to say nothing of the ease of peering in.
- Avoid glass sliding doors, but if you have one, ensure that you have proper security measures in place, beginning with a *security bar*.

Finally, if you're quite concerned and have some money to burn, consider more serious tools. Get some privacy shutters, window bars, commercial grade locks immune to "lock bumping," and steel doors. These days they're not as ugly as you would think, and they certainly get the job done.

Appearances Matter

Prepare a face to meet the faces that you meet.

— T. S. Eliot

If you suspend your newspaper subscription for two weeks, guess what your shady delivery person is going to know about you? If you leave the box to your new 4K TV by the road for trash services, guess what you've just advertised to burglars? (If you live in TV-license-obsessed Europe, expect an extra visit from the government.) Make use of garages, box cutters, and consider disposing of confidential items far from your home. Anything in your trash can give away your lifestyle, your interests, and anything else about you. In other words, arrange your external affairs so they give no hint of internal reality.[47]

Here are some initial ideas:

- End your physical newspaper subscriptions today in favor of an electronic version and have all mail and packages sent to a postal box far away. At the very least suspend your mail if you'll be gone for a while to prevent junk mail from collecting and revealing your house's state of abandon.
- Ask a friend or trusted neighbor to watch your house or park their car in your driveway while you're gone (for weeks or even just for work).
- Leave a low-watt LED light on in your living room for your entire vacation.
- Consider installing a *programmable timer* that turns on and off your lights at set hours to make it seem as if someone is home.
- Hire a lawn care service to keep your house well-manicured while you're gone. This will help to ward off thieves, or worse: city code enforcement and homeowner associations.

---

[47] If you think I'm over-emphasizing trash, do some quick research on the training that trash collectors receive to report suspicious items for rewards. WM's Waste Watch, for example.

- Make your house seem occupied when it isn't and reveal nothing about what it contains.

Invaders are opportunists looking for the low-hanging fruit. You only need to *appear* less vulnerable than the next house when the thieves come looking for goodies. Motion detector spotlights, cameras, security service signs, wires, thorny hedges, and "beware of" signs can deter would-be thieves. Deep-voiced dogs are a perennial blessing, and large pre-chewed dog toys will do equally good work. Too advanced of a security system will advertise that you have much to hide. Nor do these have to be real; there's a cottage industry of fake security stickers and fake cameras that look quite convincing. The reformed thief who wrote *Secrets of a Superthief* suggests hanging signs such as "Knock all you want. We don't answer" to psychologically exploit would-be thieves, who are always supremely nervous and on edge. It's hard to over-do it here. Just remember that most thieves will approach via the darkest part of your property—usually from the back—so focus most of your attention here.

If you rent a place then you have more concerns to deal with. The landlord, repair crew, and anyone else the landlord brings in have access to your "private" space 24/7. Plan around this fact. As a renter you should be even more cautious about what you have lying around:

- Scan your important physical documents and photos and destroy the real ones. Be ruthless.
- Diversify your items in a storage facility or at a friend's house.
- Use the attic and/or acquire a locked box for private items.
- Consider putting a camera that is *offline* in or outside of the house to record what your landlord is doing when she turns up. You could even make it visible so they're aware of being watched.
- Change the locks while you're renting and deal with the consequences. *Why did you change the locks?* is countered with, *Oops, I wasn't thinking: now what were you doing in my apartment?* Always be ready to pick up and leave if you are a renter.
- Establish in your rental contract that the landlord must give you 24-hour notice before showing up.

Hide your valuables wisely. A giant safe performs well but is expensive and flashy. It's cheaper, easier, and often just as helpful to hide things subtly. On Amazon you can find hollowed-out fake soda cans, clocks, and other gizmos.

You can build your own secret wall outlet container that pulls out to reveal its treasure. Nor does it have to be so fancy. A dusty box in the corner of your attic with old photographs on top is unlikely to be examined. A cleaned-out lotion bottle with rolled-up cash in the corner of your cabinet is fairly safe. Precious metals buried in the yard works wonders, as does cash hidden in junk mail envelopes. Often the best hiding spot is the most boring one. The savvy author of *Bye Bye, Big Brother* recommends storing certain items "well wrapped in a plastic container marked 'Boiled Mackerel' in your freezer.[48] You could hide valuables at the bottom of a potted plant, or hollow out a piece of wood, fill it with goodies, and nail it to your attic rafters. You could bury it in a big bag of rice or tape it under an old office chair with Gorilla Tape. Of course, the more recommendations you see for something the more you should seek to come up with your own ideas, since thieves study those suggestions as well. Above all, diversify your hidings and take action today.

Appearances matter more than ever in the era of Internet politics. I discussed a few pages ago the importance of separating your name from your home address. I'll reiterate that point now. Politics has replaced religion in the West as that thing people are willing to kill for. Be careful about your political affiliations and how you expose them to the world. Public information such as donations should be made without revealing your name and home address—if this is not possible, consider supporting that cause in other ways. It should go without saying that few people and institutions, if any, should know where you live. Your bank accounts should direct toward your postal box address. Your cheques should have only your first initial and last name (J. Johnson)—if that. Food delivery is to be avoided; at minimum use a fake name. Social media should not speak of or show your house: inside or outside. The same is true for websites such as Craigslist. Question everything that you publish to the Internet.

Neighbors and Security Cameras

Think twice before putting up a recording device such as *Amazon's Ring video doorbell*. At Watchman Privacy we ruminate often on the balance between security and privacy, as should you. The *Ring* system uses a camera on your front door that surveys the area in front of it. It connects to your phone and when someone approaches, it detects them, shows you the footage,

---

[48] Boston T. Party, *Bye Bye Big Brother*, pg. 225

and let's you communicate with them. This is convenient, isn't it? But think about the flow of information. Where are those videos kept and who has access (answer: Amazon servers; likely many thousands of employees)? What does Amazon do with these videos? How long before this database is hacked? What about your neighbor across the street who is being recorded at a distance every time it turns on? These questions especially apply for inside cameras. Who is listening on the other end? We already know that *Amazon Alexas* are listening at all times,[49] and that police (in the US) have received permission from courts to listen to them.[50] What have you said in the privacy of your home that you wouldn't want a jury to hear?

More traditional alert systems such as ADT are likewise a mistake. One ADT employee tuned in to "intimate moments" of customers for nearly five years before he was caught.[51] Others are doing it right now and may never be caught. But here's the dirty truth about alarm systems. Because they have so many false alarms, they aren't exactly a high priority for police agencies. If you have a security system for safety, you can probably get as much (or more) safety through the means I've already described. For all that these online security camera systems provide, they risk your privacy too greatly and I cannot recommend them.

Emergency scenarios (hiding from stalkers) aside, I think the only solution to a privacy-starved world is to return to a society in which people in small communities take care of things themselves, and where there is no need for top-down surveillance systems. You might form a coalition with your neighbors to look out for each other. Just make sure you actually create these solutions. And be careful about getting too heavily involved in "neighborhood watch" Gestapos, or highly invasive online social media scams such as *Nextdoor*, which attempts to harvest neighborhood data by offering up online communities that quickly devolve into complaining and petty surveillance. We want to be civil with our neighbors, but never to encourage nonsense like this—or license plate scanners, for that matter.

We need to discuss Nextdoor because it is likely the future: social media for neighborhoods. The sad reality is that people love surveillance, especially

---

[49] https://www.bloomberg.com/news/articles/2019-04-10/is-anyone-listening-to-you-on-alexa-a-global-team-reviews-audio

[50] https://www.nbcnews.com/tech/internet/prosecutors-get-warrant-amazon-echo-data-arkansas-murder-case-n700776

[51] https://abc7ny.com/adt-tech-home-security-hacker-video-hack-internet/9903489/

when it is used against their neighbors. Nextdoor appeals to these impulses. Allow me to share with you a rather sinister message that an acquaintance recently received from Nextdoor (with my added commentary):

Hi [Street Name] Neighbors [this is from the company and not neighbors],

Our neighborhood [again, not neighbors] is now using a free [because you are the product] app called Nextdoor [AREA NAME] and you should join us. It's the neighborhood hub for useful information such as local business recommendations [spam], emergency preparedness information [snitching], lost pet notifications [I'll take my chances], safety updates [complaints] and much more [oh joy].

It's also a great way to connect neighbors in need with those who can help.

It's 100% free [aside from your soul] and private [...] - just for our neighbors.

Please go to www.nextdoor.com/join and enter this code to join us: [REDACTED]
(This code expires in 7 days) [sure it does]

Your neighbor,

[REDACTED NEIGHBOR NAME], [STREET]

P.S. There are already over 900 posts on Nextdoor [AREA NAME], including posts about safety issues in the neighborhood [lovely].

This corporate email is supposed to come off as a warm neighborly welcome: I'm surprised they didn't try to couple it with a plate of fake cookies to match its tone. But I hope you can see right through this nonsense. Nextdoor is using all the tricks in the advertising book, including making it mandatory for you to send a letter to a neighbor after you sign up. They even have a map showing which despicable anti-social neighbors haven't yet signed up. Once you're signed up, they'll want information such as the names of family members, their email addresses, and more. Who knows what they'll do with that information, but I have a few guesses. Ironically, Nextdoor might be the greatest argument for cultivating a real neighborhood relationship. By talking to your neighbor in person you root out all the Big Tech and Big Government trickery. You can use this opportunity to explain the serious downsides of such services.

Oh, and surveillance: welcome to the neighborhood.

Car Privacy

Apply similar strategies to your car as you would your home. Cars are more readily targeted because thieves know they are much less likely to risk their lives breaking in.

- An empty vehicle deters thieves; keep it empty!
- Never leave your registration and insurance cards in your car. Fold them and place them in your wallet.
- Park near residential buildings, in well-lighted areas, and on corners of intersections that get more traffic than secluded areas.
- Make a garage a serious consideration the next time you move—or consider building one this weekend. In addition to protection from thieves, they hide your planned trips and ensure that no one knows when you are away from home.

Look at your car and summarize what it reveals about you and your finances. If you drive a Mercedes Benz you're asking to be robbed or sued (imagine the gleam in someone's eye when you "bump" into their 2005 Ford Fiesta). Especially in the litigious United States, lawyers salivate at the mere idea of a car wreck.[52] Following the theory of "extended liability," these blood-suckers simply keep searching until they find someone with deep enough pockets to sue. You might ultimately decide, like many wealthy people, not to drive at all. If you do drive, choose a common car model with a plain color and spend your money on something else.

Consider also what you put on your car. If you have the wrong political views displayed on bumper stickers you risk having your car vandalized. You also risk being identified around town or pulled over by a police officer with a quota to fill and a power trip to complete. If you have a parking permit of

---

[52] You may have noticed billboards in the US of lawyers promising to "take the hammer" to anyone who has harmed you or your car—even if you are the one fundamentally at fault. The legal-industrial complex is one of the gravest threats that Americans face today.

some kind think about what information that number traces back to. Could I call the university you work for and figure out who the owner is? Very likely. Ideally you would choose a parking area that doesn't require a permit; alternatively you could attach the permit to a piece of paper—not your glass—and remove it from your car as soon as you leave work.

Incidentally, as I write this section I have a friend dealing with a car that was broken into. One thing I've concluded is that her mid-range Toyota was too well-maintained, too new-looking and probably gave the impression that its driver was wealthier than than she is. In other words, she failed to look plain. Moving forward I suggested that she tone down her OCD cleaning tendencies to make it appear more run-down. She should also park nearer a light source and avoid a windshield sun-blocker, which may have offered cover for the lowlife. My friend didn't report the incident to the police, and in most places that is legal. Nothing was taken of substance, the damage was fixed within two hours, and she was not interested in appearing on a police report or insurance incident.

Finally, I'm sad to say that a new horizon of car-invasion looms: license plate readers. Start-up companies like Flock Safety pride themselves on rooting out neighborhood crimes with their plate cameras. I have no doubt they succeed, and I'm reminded in moments like this of a pig-headed argument from former NSA consultant Ed Giorgio: "privacy and security are a zero sum-game."[53] I'll let Dwight D. Eisenhower respond to that: "If you want total security, go to prison." Security is only valuable when it enhances your personal freedom at the expense of no one else. Privacy is its own security. More importantly, freedom and privacy, not security, are the highest values a society can aspire toward.

At any rate license plate scanning is a seriously booming industry that promises to use the data connected to plates (registered owner's name, address, etc.) for policing, marketing, and other targeted harassment. Make no mistake: your information is available. In 2017 the Department of Motor Vehicles in the state of Florida sold the information of Floridians to marketing firms to the tune of $77 million dollars,[54] and that's just one of many ways your car registration is exposed. Police are one step away from gathering this information, and in case you're having difficulty imaging how this might harm

---

[53] https://www.newyorker.com/magazine/2008/01/21/the-spymaster

[54] https://www.abcactionnews.com/news/local-news/i-team-investigates/i-team-florida-dmv-sells-your-personal-information-to-private-companies-marketing-firms

you, consider the case of a man who was extorted by an officer who found his car outside a gay bar and threatened to contact his wife.[55]

You can fight against the ample threats of license plate scanning, hopeless as it may seem. You should obviously begin by speaking with neighbors, employers, and anyone you can about privacy. Give them a copy of this book. Then, take matters into your own hands:

- Back up into parking spaces so that scanners see the front and not the back of your vehicle.
- Park around the corner from your real destination.
- Purchase tinted covers for your plate that make it more difficult to casually spot.
- If you go for car maintenance or car washes—avoid chain stores if you can—remove your plate when you arrive so they don't know who you are.[56]
- One person I knew in a snowy area observed that it was acceptable to have your license plate obscured by snow during the winter months.
- Similarly, if mother nature—a bit of mud or other dirt—was to block out even a single number of your plate, it would be more difficult to identify you.
- Privacy extremist Michael Bazzell admits to using a magnetic plate holder and removing it even before entering his neighborhood—he says he will deal with the consequences if police were to question him about it on that final stretch.[57] These things actually work.
- You could simply take it off when you arrive home to achieve partial privacy.

See Chapter 7 for privacy techniques specific to travel.

Shred Your Life

Some of your financial and legal institutions will insist on sending you paper materials. Avoid these at all cost by selecting "paperless" and "green" options,

---

[55] See Duncan Long's book *Protect Your Privacy*
[56] Big franchises have been known to share data about your car
[57] Michael Bazzell, *Extreme Privacy*

and otherwise calling each of these institutions and demanding they cease their mailing. If they don't respond you might take the mail, write a note on it in bright red ink (or by using a rubber stamp) that says "Return to Sender: Not at this Address", and drop it into your nearest post office. For what remains, purchase a cheap document scanner (the Epson WorkForce ES-50 is a good option and tends to work on Linux), digitize your files, and destroy them. Make sure to store them securely on your computer in encrypted folders (Chapter 4).

Soon you will have no paper coming to your house but instead going to a postal box. For some bills—mortgage statement, utility bills—this might not be possible. For these stragglers, consider the following:

- Every paper no longer needed should be scanned and destroyed. Your digital back-up process must be well-developed (Chapter 4).
- Shredding is great. While it does leave a trace, it makes it much less likely that a casual snooper will pick up something out of the recycling bin with something revealing.
- Buy either a *cross cut* or *micro cut* shredder. Micro cut shredders turn papers into tiny particles that are extremely difficult to reassemble. They are slightly more costly and sometimes can't handle staples, credit cards, or large quantities of paper. A cross cut shredder is a healthy alternative, especially if you plan to burn the pieces anyway.
- As you look for things to shred, don't forget any package labels and junk mail with your name and address that might otherwise end up in the trash. My friend told me a story of putting recycling bags in the nearest bin (which wasn't his) only to return home and find a passive-aggressive neighbor had returned them to his doorstep based on the packaging address. Considering other circumstances in play, if the angry neighbor had instead called the landlord, my friend may have been kicked out based on this incident.
- Consider shredding all of your documents—important or not—to increase the paper mass that thieves have to sort through to find anything good.
- Mounds of shredded documents signal to curious passersby that important documents have just been chewed up. You might burn the shredded paper or separate the papers into different bins and dispose of them over the course of weeks. Paper burns best when put atop a wire grate to allow for oxygen; take care that it doesn't fly away. Burn

at night to hide smoke and give the illusion of having a bonfire with friends.

Your Computer: A Physical Thing?

Too many people spend hundreds of dollars on fancy encrypted cloud storage and malware protection without realizing that none of this matters if someone—a petty robber, a private investigator, or a state actor—breaks into your house and takes the unencrypted data sitting on your computer.

It turns out that your *hard* drive is a physical thing. We'll get more into encryption later on (Chapter 4), but let's cover the bigger picture here. Your hard drive, or solid state drive, is the most revealing piece of hardware on your computer. It can also be copied physically on the spot in such a way that you would never know (Celebrite, a phone technology, makes a near-instant copy of your phone's contents and is often used by police—some speculate it can bypass your phone pass code). Hard drives can also simply be removed and plugged into another system to reveal your information. Take care what you bring with you on a journey, even across town. Keep a close eye on your computers and don't bring them with you when you don't need to. It's becoming common for thieves to grab your laptop while you go to the toilet at a coffee shop. Never leave your items unattended and remember that thieves today don't look like what you're expecting them to look like. Don't leave electronics in unattended hotel rooms.

Old hard drives, solid state drives, and <u>any</u> storage drive should never be sold or given away. Either reuse them or destroy them. Deletion and "recycling bins" on your computer are an illusion; the files are still there. Destroying hard drives involves at minimum drilling a hole through the disc itself (yes, hard drives have a small physical disc inside). There is some debate as to whether this goes far enough; talented engineers could recover parts of the disk that remain intact. If you're really concerned simply chop the drive into little bits or sand it into oblivion, focusing on the actual disk and not its container. Solid state drives, which are becoming the norm, don't have physical disks, but are vulnerable to (very) powerful magnets and the usual assortment of power tools. You can make it up to the environment and your wallet in other ways.

Choose Location Carefully

You might be overwhelmed by this chapter, so let's take a step back and view the big picture. The best solution for physical privacy is ultimately to go somewhere where privacy is more easy to come by. You can evaluate this in various ways. It might be as simple as buying a house instead of renting to gain more control over your environment. Or it might involve moving from a city to escape overbearing police,[58] surveillance systems, and rat-swarms of city officials. Cities, regions, states, and countries differ in their respect for privacy. The United States on paper has some of the strongest admiration for personal freedom and privacy, and that might be true in some regions still. In practice, however, what you'll find is an overreaching military-style police, a huge chance of getting arrested or taken to court, spy agencies with budgets the size of small countries, and a steady erosion of support for individualism. Meanwhile, in supposed crime-ridden places in Latin America, you can actually have a much greater chance for privacy and freedom. In places like Mexico and Argentina governments tend to be more overbearing (on paper), but in reality they exert little sway over the people, who prefer to take cares of things by themselves. I'm painting in very broad brushstrokes here, but my point is to start thinking about this more than you have been.

Start by traveling. Go only to non-touristy spots and always try to make acquaintances in that country. What's the crime rate and aggressiveness of the police? Is there unrest, racial tension, history of protest or political drama? Is its economy tanking and bringing in new crime and surveillance? What is it like at night? Then start reading the news. Countries like Australia have outlawed encryption, and the EU is considering it. Having a passport from a Caribbean island offers tremendous freedom, but living within its borders subjects you to very strict regulations. Some places in the Middle East often don't respect your freedom to be private, to say the least: even more cosmopolitan places like Dubai. India is leaning totalitarian and China is a privacy disaster. Meanwhile, Argentina and Canada have immense open space (if not the best laws). The EU, despite wanting to ban encryption, has one of the most prominent privacy laws in place: the GDPR. Switzerland and Iceland can be great places for legal privacy or protection from the state. There's a whole world out there with a lot of options. Don't assume the country you were born in has all the answers. Read widely, travel extensively, and realize that sometimes you need to change your environment in order to improve yourself.

---

[58] The Atlas of Surveillance project documents police technology in US neighborhoods

Final Thoughts

There is even more we could say about physical privacy, but I'll leave you with some parting ideas to get the wheels turning:

- Use common sense with addresses. Don't provide a return address on letters or packages. Don't put your home address on your luggage; if you must provide some address, tuck the tag into the bag. Don't give your address to an automatic key-cutting machine (a very bad idea).

- Don't sell your DNA to anyone. If not for your own sake then your family's and your children's. That includes the heritage kits that are making the rounds. And while you're at it try not to lick envelopes: use tape or buy pre-sticky ones. If you've already sold your DNA to these companies, plead with them to have it destroyed. Also note that funeral homes increasingly have options to save and sell DNA. Make sure to ask questions in that most stressful of times.

- Mind your utilities. Abnormally high electricity bills could be a signal to your service provider that you're up to something. In a perfect world you would live outside of any power jurisdiction and use solar panels, a water well, and maybe something like Elon Musk's do-it-yourself satellite internet service called Starlink.[59]

- Take your house number off of your house and mailbox.

- Be careful when returning packages not to leave on the previous label.

- Be wary of anything that has a personalized label on it: including prescription drugs in your cabinet. What do they say about you?

- Don't open your door to anyone you aren't expecting. Some private investigators or police—undercover or not—use a knock to test if people live there. If you accidentally open the door, don't respond to any question and don't give your name out. If someone asks your name, respond by asking their name.

- If you hire a cleaning person, consider ending their service. Think about the profound access that a maid has to your stuff. If you make use of a maid, then at the very least ensure you have valuables well hidden or locked up. Treat them as nicely as possible and invite them to join particular family events.

---

[59] https://www.wsj.com/articles/elon-musk-and-amazon-are-battling-to-put-satellite-internet-in-your-backyard-11616212827

- For physical defense, consider at least a can of pepper spray and add one to your car, your purse, your pocket, and your nightstand. Learn to use it while in a hurry. Suffice it to say learning other defense techniques are well worth your time—when you need them it will already be too late.

Chapter 3
Online and Digital Privacy (The Basics)

Man created the atom bomb, but it was created to destroy him.

- Author Unknown

In his book *How to Be Invisible* privacy enthusiast JJ Luna takes a firm stance on the online realm: avoid as much of it as you can.[60] This is good advice. But today we also rely on online tools for banking, business, entertainment, and communication. Could we do more of this in the real world? Absolutely. Could we do *all* of it? Possibly. But the reality is that most of us are not willing to give up the online world. I'm not. The Internet is what helped you discover this book in the first place; it allows me to share the importance of privacy to billions. The Internet will become more central to human behavior every day, and I want to take part in shaping it and mastering it—if not cordoning it off to a suitable place in my life. My assumption in these chapters is that you would like to participate in the Internet to (most of) its fullness while taking precautions to preserve privacy along the way.

Before proceeding I want to frame the difficulty ahead very clearly. The Internet was not built for privacy. It was built for sharing and exposure. Nor can you hope to fully master it. The complexity of the hardware, networks, and programming that undergirds it all has become so intricate and arcane that one person has no hope of understanding even a fraction. Making matters worse is the fact that the online realm is a moving target: it evolves

---

[60] I conflate in this chapter the digital realm and the online realm, since the digital realm has limited use without connectivity.

every second, and at times Internet advice is outdated the moment it is given. For that reason I have decided to focus on fundamentals. I want to arm you with frames of mind and instill in you a curiosity and adeptness that will allow you to achieve self-sufficiency in our online present and future.

While on the topic of fundamentals, I want to begin by explaining what the Internet is. The Internet is simply the wired—and increasingly wireless—connection between each participating computer on earth. Millions of physical cables drape across the planet, stretching across continents and oceans and buried under mega-cities and rural towns. These cables are filled with slivers of glass that facilitate the beams of light transmitting data across the planet in the blink of an eye. Along the way massive cables divert to regional Internet Service Providers (ISPs), and then to individual houses and apartments. When they arrive, small machines called *routers* disperse these signals throughout the building, and computers with storage drives called *servers* collect some of this information, which otherwise would evaporate into a flash of light. Increasing amounts of satellites and cell towers obviate the need for physical connections, penetrating previously-barren parts of the world, slipping past the walls of our homes, and aiming to replace cables with dimensionless connectivity. The ownership of such an amorphous system is complicated. Since these vast networks—physical or satellite—cross local and international jurisdictions, large companies and governments tend to own them, not individuals. This means that spy agencies like the NSA can step millimeters outside of national boundaries to tap into these data-rich cables legally, and bizarre scenarios can transpire whereby sending a message to your friend two meters away might route it to a different continent before sending it back to her phone. This is, in short, what we mean by the Internet.

I hope that clarifies our challenge. In the same ways that the Internet connects us, it also exposes us. When you connect to the Internet you are connected to *and exposed to* billions of other computers across the globe. If not encrypted, this information could be accessed at any step along the way. This exposure benefits greedy governments and their spy agencies, but also a new class of private malicious actors who can sit in front of a keyboard and change world events or interfere with individual lives. Today cybercrime is estimated to cost the world six trillion dollars in damage per year, an amount that has doubled in just half a decade.[61] Your first instinct, and the goal of this chapter, is to limit and take great caution in how you use the awesome tool that is the Internet.

---

[61] https://cybersecurityventures.com/cybercrime-damages-6-trillion-by-2021

Our Road Map

In this chapter I pretend as if I was sitting down in front of you and your devices for the first time. We will begin by talking about changing your behavior—your "digital hygiene"—which you can practice immediately. We will then move to specific software, products, services, and settings that you should consider.

Here is the progression of steps we will take in this chapter:

1. Reconsider the role of Internet in your life
2. Internalize basic rules of computer use
3. Choose and lock down your Internet browser
4. Browse more wisely
5. Use a Virtual Private Network (VPN)
6. Learn password management and secure log-ins
7. Choose better email
8. Protect your identity

One prefatory note. Some privacy advocates insist on huge digital changes from the outset. For example, they insist on abandoning Windows 10 and macOS and switching to a Linux operating system. This is fundamentally correct. You are only as private as your operating system, because systems like Windows and macOS are the all-encompassing programs that house all of the other programs you use. So if you would like to jump into the deep end with the Linux operating system right away, skip to the beginning of Chapter 4 and then come back here. On the other hand, if you prefer the slow-and-steady route to avoid hitting a wall of discouragement, then stick with me and we will work our way up to that point. Make no mistake, though, that our destination is changing your operating system. Also note that the following two chapters pertain to digital privacy as a whole. I have reserved *phone-specific* privacy for its own chapter: Chapter 5.

Find Physical Solutions to Digital Problems

I have a habit of telling new clients that, just as one would not use a chainsaw without any knowledge of it, so too should one not use digital tools if one isn't willing to understand them. It's a harsh thing to say, but I don't back down from the logic. The Internet is a double-edged sword that can just as likely cut off your own leg as hit your target. Even if you are digitally-savvy, it's wise to use the Internet only when you have to. Always ask yourself if an online solution is necessary to your problem. It usually isn't.

For example: need to pay for something? Use cash. Kindle or physical copy of a book? Physical. Paper notebook or word processor? You get the idea. *Oh, but you can pay for your parking with the City Parking App.* Cash at the meter works just fine. Need to talk to someone? Do your best to meet them in person. Want to buy gold and silver bullion? Buy it in a physical store with cash. And if you live in a place where any of this is illegal or difficult, consider it a warning sign about the state of freedom and privacy in your jurisdiction.

Digital purchases and programs open up the door for your data to be exposed to the billions of people who share these networks, many of whom are not exactly friendly. When you trust your credit card to a company, you're trusting that company—along with all of its employees and partners—to protect it, which they don't and can't always do. The more entities you trust outside of yourself, the more likely your information will be compromised and your privacy veil pierced. The hundreds of reported (note: "reported") data leaks in the last few years are a testament to his fact.

Online actions can also be used to profile and track you. Your city app probably lets local law enforcement know where you are and at what time (and perhaps when your two-hour parking might be about to expire). Your Kindle books let Amazon and their admins know what you read, how quickly you read it, which sections you focus on, and possibly your location via Wi-Fi. Mac users have been known to pay more for online purchases than non-Mac users.[62] This is online profiling at work.

As a historical side note, your particular reading materials could get you arrested, fired from your job, publicly denigrated, and in some cases killed. Some of this is still the case today even in supposed bastions of free speech and expression like the United States. If you don't believe me, I encourage you to look up the *obscenity exception* to free expression, which still exists and which, by the way, made it illegal to own a copy of one of the great works of literature (James Joyce's *Ulysses*) for twelve years following its publication. Or consider reading about the American *Sedition Act of 1918* or the *House Un-American*

---

[62]   https://www.wsj.com/articles/SB10001424052702304458604577488822667325882

Activities Committee of the Cold War era. In case you were unaware, full free speech and free expression have never existed in the US, or anywhere else in the world, either as a matter of law or a matter of culture.

All of this data can accumulate over your life and come back to bite you at any point in the future. Imagine a future, for example, where insurance companies and governments check your reading material, your food purchases, and the speed of your driving before they will offer you service or issue you a passport. This is already taking shape with a new informal credit score system that will be able to take all of your information—from purchases to driving speed as calculated by your phone GPS—to tell companies whether they should grant you a loan or a job.[63] The IMF (International Monetary Fund) has called for a credit score based on a person's internet history,[64] and on whether that person purchases broccoli or pizza, if such buying decisions can be linked to one's likelihood to pay back loans. I'm not joking.[65]

Moving forward in an accelerated post-COVID-lockdown environment, you can expect online purchases to become more regulated, more surveyed, and more restricted. You can expect more government tracking, more crackdowns on pre-paid gift cards, and possibly more value-added taxes (VAT) to offset gaping tax deficits across the globe. There's talk of central bank digital currencies (CBDCs), which is a real possibility.[66] [67] (See episode 3 of my podcast on CBDCs). In short, you'll want to be sure to know how to buy in person with cash or by bartering. I save my full thoughts on private shopping for Chapter 6, but I'll offer a few ideas to get you started:

Digital Solution	Physical Alternative
Kindle book with credit card	Physical book at local bookstore with cash

---

[63] https://www.washingtonpost.com/opinions/2020/07/31/data-isnt-just-being-collected-your-phone-its-being-used-score-you/
[64] https://blogs.imf.org/2020/12/17/what-is-really-new-in-fintech/
[65] https://www.imf.org/en/news/articles/2018/11/13/sp111418-winds-of-change-the-case-for-new-digital-currency
[66] https://www.msn.com/en-us/money/markets/lagarde-says-her-e2-80-98hunch-e2-80-99-is-that-ecb-will-adopt-digital-currency/ar-BB1aXnU2
[67] https://finance.yahoo.com/news/yellen-signals-interest-backing-digital-164843289.html

Netflix subscription	Borrowed physical disc from a friend; free movies wherever they can be found online (use a VPN)
Treadmill from Amazon	Treadmill from Craigslist ad (cash)
Credit card purchase on Steam	Physical Steam gift card bought with cash from a shop
Utilities paid online	Utilities paid for months in advance with cash option (yes, it's an option)[68]
Phone service with Giant Telecom Company	Prepaid monthly service (cash) via SIM card. Many quality options exist today that piggyback off of major company's towers.
Bitcoin account on Kraken or Coinbase	Actual Bitcoin with cash: from an ATM; a friend; or an acquaintance at a crypto meetup; peer-to-peer exchange
Tinder dating app	Hiking trip with people your age (Meetup.com, for example, using fake info)
Fight with boyfriend/girlfriend on Facebook messenger	Commitment to have such discussions in person at the first sign of escalation; fight on secure messaging app
PlayStation game downloaded at midnight of release date	Tradition to pick up a physical copy on launch day
Animal Crossing virtual farm	Farming outside, in real life
Checking insurance quotes online	Visit to insurance broker in person (same with all meetings)

You might think me old-fashioned and perhaps even neo-Luddite for suggesting such alternatives to your ethereal digital lifestyle. After all, the

---

[68] If you're already registered with your utilities company under your own name, then paying privately doesn't help you much. See "Everything Else" for the basic thrust of private utilities.

promise of the digital age is that you can do things more conveniently, so why shouldn't you? But not all promises are good, and frankly, you're not a more advanced human for having digital shortcuts: sometimes you're quite the opposite. Humans were made to interact, flirt, and be entertained in the real world and much of the "progress" in human behavior is actually regress. Your privacy regresses above all.

Three Rules of Computer Use

Before you can use the Internet you'll have to have a device capable of accessing it. Whichever device and set of programs you choose to connect to the Internet, you'll want to make sure you observe, practice, and internalize the following rules. These should never be broken:

1. **Keep your computer programs updated, especially your operating system.** If you see an update on your computer or phone, run it immediately. Updates are released when a company discovers a vulnerability and wants to patch it. Make it a daily task to check the corner of your screen for updates, and restart your system right away if you see the suggestion to do so. If you don't know where your update options are on your device, take time to find them right now. Realize that some devices become so old that they no longer receive updates. Apple is known for cutting off older devices from new updates, and Microsoft did this to Windows 7 users in January 2020.[69]

2. **Don't click anything, open any file, type into any text box, install any program, visit any website, or insert any storage drive if you aren't certain what it is and where it came from.** When in doubt: research. A two-minute Internet search can often be the difference between doing something stupid or not. Don't assume every program and website is safe. Nor is it ever acceptable to type anything into text boxes that you encounter via emails (more on this later). Start treating the online world like you would walking down a city street; be wary and distrusting until you prove otherwise.

3. **Keep your programs and accounts to a minimum; delete them when you suspect they are of no more use.** Every new program is a new

---

[69] Programs update differently depending on your operating system. Take time to figure out how yours works and consider using a program that automatically updates them for you. The program MacUpdater is one such option if you don't trust yourself to keep up.

vulnerability. It's wise to sit down every few weeks on your device (phone, computer, tablet) and see what programs aren't serving you any longer. Get rid of them. Privacy demands minimalism.

These three rules will also protect you from most malware, which has diminished in past decades. It used to be that antivirus programs were essential services, but now malware creators have moved on to the greener pastures of online extortion, and phishing attacks—most of which happen via email and online account hacking. This also means that your default antivirus, such as Windows Defender on Windows 10, should be good enough for your needs. Macs (sometimes) and Linux systems (most times) tend *not* to require antivirus software. No anti-malware program is bulletproof. *It's much more important to practice safe online behavior such as what I just described than to download a third-party antivirus program which reports back to corporate headquarters regularly and that has immense access to your computer.*

How to Use the Internet

Most people own computers to browse the Internet. Your web browser—Google Chrome, Safari, Firefox—mediates your relationship with the Internet, and you need to give some consideration to which of them you use. If you don't know what browser you use, pause reading and go find out. Never blindly use something without knowing what it is.

The Mozilla Firefox browser is a solid choice for privacy right now. For mobile devices I recommend their app Firefox Focus. This may change in the future, but it has kept this title for the last many years.[70] The Firefox browser comes from a fairly transparent organization—the Mozilla Corporation—that is outspoken about privacy. Firefox is open-source (it's code is publicly available to view) and it holds up to security audits. You can also customize it to make it even better (keep reading). Stop using Safari and Chrome and start using Firefox, but always be on the lookout for the next best thing. Since your browser is likely the most important program for your privacy and security, you would do well to stay informed about its history, its company, and all news pertaining to it.

---

[70] On August 11, 2020 Mozilla Corporation announced layoffs and restructuring of their company (https://blog.mozilla.org/blog/2020/08/11/changing-world-changing-mozilla/). Things are fine, but always keep an ear to the ground for the news about the companies you rely on.

I'll get into the fine-tuning of Firefox in a minute, but I want to start with an overview that you can apply to any browser you work with. In case you didn't know, websites track you as you move around them. One traditional way of collecting information about you is through cookies. An *Internet cookie* is basically a bit of text that sticks with you during a browsing session. Let's say you put an item into your shopping cart on Amazon and then you click "proceed to checkout," which technically takes you to a new page. If you didn't have cookies enabled, Amazon might not remember what was in your shopping cart by the time you reach the checkout screen.

Cookies are not inherently evil; in fact, they're essential to Internet usage and behave similar to memory. Without memory you would go from one second to the next as a blank slate; personal identity requires you to build from one experience to the next. Unfortunately in recent years cookies have begun to be used in more sinister ways. They are now commonly used to share your browsing history between websites. Let's say you added that pair of women's running shoes into your Amazon cart. Now when you visit Nike's website, they might see this cookie and have an idea of what you're interesting in buying. They might serve you an ad for a similar shoe. They might also store and hold on to this information and build a profile around your browser's *fingerprint,* or distinct identity.[71] Being advertised to is hardly the end of the world, but there are larger consequences at stake here.

For example, let's say you're logged into Gmail and you decide to take a break from work to watch a video on YouTube. You may notice that you're now logged into YouTube under that Gmail account. These are cookies at work. Now whatever video you watched will be linked to your Gmail account. I don't think I have to be too explicit here. Just imagine any two websites you visit knowing it's you who visited them. Or imagine every website you've ever visited knowing that the other has been visited. Things can escalate quickly as your online fingerprint becomes more distinct and more expansive. This accumulation of data can cause embarrassment, higher prices, and basically more information sucked up into the giant Big Data cyclone.

Controlling your cookies and Internet history is one major way of taking control of your privacy online. What follows is a series of suggestions that involves changing your cookie/history settings, but also changing your behavior. Please read the following steps carefully and reread them:

---

[71]   See Chapter 8 for more explanation of online fingerprinting

1. Transition to Firefox as your default browser and embrace a no-cookie and no-history lifestyle. Let's be clear about the consequences. This means your browser won't remember your logged-in accounts, and so you'll have to log in each time you restart the browser. A password manager (explained shortly) will help you do this more quickly. It doesn't have to be as frustrating as you think. I rely on the Internet for my life and business and deal with this method just fine. Indeed, I prefer it. It reminds me that accounts should only be accessed when I am fully aware of what I'm doing.

2. To set your browser to forget cookies and history, do the following. On Firefox, click the three horizontal lines on the top right. Select "Preferences" and then "Privacy & Security." Select "Delete cookies and site data when Firefox is closed." Also select "Strict" under "Browser Privacy." While you're at it, scroll down a bit further to "History" and select "Use custom settings for history" and then select the option "Clear history when Firefox closes." Now if you close your Firefox browser and open a new one all memory of your previous browsing session will be gone.

3. Note that these settings could be different in the future or in different browsers. Remember the concept and the vocabulary more than the specific instructions. Your browsers from now on *do not remember cookies or history*.

4. Because your cookies and history erase only after closing your browser, you'll have to make sure you close it regularly, or you will have defeated the purpose. Don't get bogged down with twenty tabs that you keep up for days at a time. Regularly close your browser (at least once an hour) and pull up another one, thus deleting all the cookies that you have been storing and resetting the scene. If you're a tab warrior who keeps dozens up at a time, it's time to change your behavior or surrender your possibility of privacy.

5. If you're overwhelmed by the above suggestions, you can approach a no-cookie lifestyle more gradually. Start by cordoning off the most nasty tracking websites—Gmail, Facebook, and Amazon—on their own browser. For example, you can keep Google Chrome downloaded and use it for one of these websites. For everything else you use your Firefox browser.

6. You can do something similar to point number 5 within Firefox itself. Download "Firefox Containers" which you can find by

searching for it at https://addons.mozilla.org/ or searching for "Firefox add-ons" and then install it from there. Basically, Firefox Containers can make a new tab its own browser within your browser, thus separating it from the activity of your other tabs. So let's say you logged into Gmail on your browser. If you were to pull up a new tab to visit YouTube, you would automatically be logged in to your Gmail account. But if you instead open a new tab with a Firefox Container, you will *not* be logged in to YouTube because it will be an isolated environment without the taint of those cookies. You would be surprised how handy this simple add-on can be for preserving your privacy across websites. I didn't recommend it initially because it is easy to forget you've used a tab already and you can expose cookies unknowingly. Betting against your forgetfulness is not wise.

7. To use a Firefox Container, after downloading it, select the new icon on the top right of your Firefox browser. Choose which container you would like to open. You can add containers and tweak settings here as well.

Can't I have privacy without clearing my cookies and history after each session?

Not really. Retaining privacy while browsing online demands that you constantly break the fingerprint that is created for you. It demands that you refrain from logging in to accounts in the same session. You can't be a private person and access this convenience. There's no budging here.

On a final note, I want to reinforce that even with a locked down browser you can hemorrhage your privacy by making stupid decisions: giving out your information to whoever asks for it; downloading suspicious files and programs, etc. Erasing cookies will not make up for fundamental mistakes such as these. We will discuss how to further erase your online fingerprint in upcoming chapters, but I want to make sure you have time to digest this method first.

Additional Tweaks to Firefox

While you're downloading add-ons such as *Firefox Containers*, you may as well grab a couple more.

- Start with *Ublock Origin*. Download it and you're fine with the default settings as a beginner. This add-on blocks a lot of spam and advertisements, which themselves can expose you to additional fingerprinting.
- Next, search for *HTTPS Everywhere;* download and install it. This add-on forces all websites to use the HTTPS protocol, which is safer than the alternative.

Now that you have a fairly locked down browser to use, let's finish with a few basic principals of Internet use:

1. Use a privacy-friendly search engine such as DuckDuckGo or Startpage (which replicates Google results). Make it your default. On Firefox this is "Settings" [three bars], "Preferences," "Search," "Default Search Engine," "DuckDuckGo" or "Startpage."
2. Avoid logging in to accounts as much as possible. You can still use YouTube, Twitter, and most other sites without logging in.
3. Find web services that respect your privacy. Fortunately, a new generations of services is cropping up for people like us. Websites like https://privacytools.io offer lists of such services, and you can easily find them yourself by searching. It's worth supporting these startups over their big brothers.
4. Never volunteer to give companies your usage statistics "to improve their services" or however they phrase it. Often these check boxes are embedded in installation programs, so keep a keen eye out.
5. While analyzing your installation packages, make sure the program doesn't install any extra items (bloatware), which in the past were a common tactic with free programs.
6. Take time to learn new things about the online world and how it works. People who live in fear or without curiosity in the status quo will be victims either now or later.

VPNs

We're not quite ready to surf the Internet yet. You may have heard the acronym VPN, which stands for Virtual Private Network, on your favorite podcast or YouTube channel. There's a lot of deception in these advertisements, so let's clear something up. A VPN is a program that can hide your real IP address from your service provider and from the websites you visit. That's about all. Let's break down what that means.

Your IP address is the distinct identifying number that your device is assigned when you connect to any Internet network. You can check it at any time. Search for "what is my IP" and various websites will tell you. Any time you connect to the Internet via your Internet Service Provider—Comcast, Sky, or the Starbucks Wi-Fi down the road—that network assigns your device an IP address. Now any website you visit and anything you download can be tied back to your computer. A court order could reveal to the jury every website you've visited. It also means that when you visit reddit.com, Reddit will see your real IP address, which can tell them your ISP provider and your location (to within a few miles) and allow them to start building a profile on you. Or let's say you use a Gmail account under your real name. Google can see your IP address and basically know where you live. For physical privacy reasons alone you should hide your IP address.

A VPN service overrides your real IP address with its own, which you share with the other VPN customers. This is a double layer of protection. The VPN also creates an encrypted funnel between your computer and the VPN company's server. This means that the details your Internet Service Provider once saw about your Internet traffic are now an encrypted blob of gibberish, and for the websites you visit it will be an IP address shared by thousands of other customers. Such traffic is now technically able to be viewed by your VPN company, but you will have chosen a reputable VPN with a zero-knowledge or "no logging" policy, meaning that they see nothing and have nothing to give to those who come knocking. Let's be clear though that a VPN simply defers your IP address to another entity, and you have to trust that VPN company. A VPN is quite useful because it means that you can use an Internet connection without the service provider seeing what you're doing and the websites you visit from collecting IP information about you.

VPNs have some other minor benefits. They will offer some protection if a malicious actor is also using your Wi-Fi connection (such as in a public place like a coffee shop or an airport). Most VPN services will also offer a number of server locations around the world, meaning you can look as if you are in a different country, or a different region within that country. This is particularly handy if a website is blocking your region.

But that's about where the usefulness of VPNs ends. Like all other digital tools, it is not a magic wand. Nor is it a magic shield around you. If you download a nasty file with malware using your VPN, it will not protect you. If you post a photo of your house on Facebook and expose yourself to the world, your VPN will not protect you. If you give away your name and phone number to a text box on some shady website or email, your VPN will not protect you. A VPN will only hide your IP address from the Internet Service Provider and the sites you visit. Got it?

Still, you should use a VPN any time you connect to the Internet. That includes your phone. All reputable VPNs allow you to connect to multiple devices and have both desktop programs and phone apps. When you start up the default VPN program, you'll log in, and then select which server you would like to connect to. These are physical locations that the VPN company runs. While it can often benefit you to pretend to be somewhere very far away, by default you should consider selecting the "automatic" option. This will connect you to the fastest server—likely the closest one to you geographically. Keep in mind that you are connecting through a digital tunnel to a location at a distance. In other words, your Internet speed is going to be slightly slowed, but hopefully only by a small percentage. It's a sacrifice you make for anonymous Internet browsing.

So which VPN service should you choose? Like most privacy products, you should look for a service (company) with the following features:

- Zero-knowledge
- Open-source code
- No logging policy
- History of third-party audits (which test the VPN service's claims)
- Clear subscription model (don't use free services unless you want to be the product)
- Can pay with cryptocurrencies, cash, or gift cards
- Privacy-friendly jurisdictions. I'm not as convinced that this matters so much, since if the other elements are in place (no logging), jurisdiction shouldn't matter.

Picking the right VPN company is crucial. Their service sees all of your activity, just like your ISP would. I hesitate recommending specific companies for fear you won't do your own necessary research. But I will say that you can start by researching Mullvad, ProtonVPN, ExpressVPN, and IVPN. Like all services, these companies sometimes change policies and owners, and you should make sure to occasionally research them to see that they're not reneging on their promises. Don't be afraid to email customer service and ask if they have all the features I just mentioned. Indeed, for your most important software (VPN, operating system, browser, password manager, encryption client) you should perform research every few months to see what they've been up to. And check out my podcast interview with IVPN for an excellent background on how these things work.

I'll say one more thing about VPNs and save the more advanced aspects for a later chapter (Chapter 8). Because websites now see an odd IP address—one that is shared with others—you might come across to some of them as suspicious. More popular VPNs get this more often because they have been flagged numerous times. You'll likely have to perform more CAPTCHAs and your accounts will be suspicious of you and send you a text message or email to verify it is you. At times you'll encounter websites that block you entirely. Your online purchases might sometimes not go through. But also know that websites and accounts are getting used to VPNs, and they can be trained to detect that you usually come from odd IP addresses. So I don't want you to be too fearful—just aware of the occasional problem now and then (I discuss more techniques in Chapter 8). Please resist giving in. You should be insulted when you encounter these hurdles using a VPN, because it is blatant evidence that they are tracking you and judging you based on what they perceive to be your "identity." Gone are the days when surfing the Internet privately was the default, but VPNs are popular and we are a growing demographic. They'll have to give in soon.

Email

If you're like me, one of the first things you do in the morning is check your e-mail. And, if you're like me, you also wonder who else has read your e-mail.

- Kevin Mitnick, Cybersecurity Expert

You may recall just a few years ago when antivirus programs were essential. Today virus creation is hardly profitable, and instead emails are the primary attack vector for malicious actors. Indeed, most computer attacks for the average user occur through email. Such attacks tend to work like this:

1. Someone acquires your name, your email address, and the organizations you are a part of, usually through a data breach (from your bank, or a tech company, or any of the hundreds of companies whose data you have given and which is now floating around in the Dark Web).
2. They send you an email that replicates your bank's letterhead, addressing you by name.
3. They use persuasive language such as "Your account has been compromised. Log in here to change your password."
4. You fall for the trick and give them your log-in information, etc.
5. They immediately take the stolen information, log in to your account, and do their dirty work.

The only sure way to prevent this is to be disciplined. You might even consider giving up email altogether (or as much as you can), as some security experts have done, and rely solely on secure instant messengers: Signal, Wire, Session. You might be surprised how little you actually need email.

First things first:

- Stop giving out your email address. Period. Your email should be given out only to the most essential people and services in your life.
- Go through your main email account and check the damage. If you're one of these people bombarded with dozens or hundreds of email "offers" per day—in other words, you've not exactly been chaste with your address—then you might even consider deleting the account and starting over. I'm not joking.
- But if you think you're still in control, start unsubscribing from all of these subscriptions.
- Instead of scrolling down to the bottom and selecting "unsubscribe" (which paradoxically let's the company know you've read their mail and might lead to more spam), try to let your email provider eradicate these messages for you: select their option to "add to spam," "unsubscribe," or "block emails from this domain," etc. Just be careful not to block anything important.
- If you're overwhelmed, aim to delete a few emails and unsubscribe from a few unneeded services every time you check your email. Slow and steady progress will clear out your inbox.

- Promise yourself not to give away your email address so casually in the future.

I still use email, mostly for business purposes, but I almost never give out my main email address. Let me explain. I first and foremost take great care before giving any email address to any organization. If I sense they're looking for a one-time activation, and I know I won't ever need to access the email address again, I search for "email generator" or "temporary email" and use this ephemeral account to furnish my activation code. For slightly more important services, such as one-off online purchases (where I might want my receipt and order number), I'll give an email address from a provider such as 33mail, SimpleLogin, or a similar *alias email service*. Let me explain how that works.

Basically when you sign up for 33mail (using your real email address), you can generate unlimited sub-email addresses that you can control and shut off with the click of a button. The disposable email will funnel back to your real email address. I know this is confusing, so let's take an example:

1. I create a 33mail account with a username; for example: "FlyingTuna."
2. Now whenever I need to give out an email address, I create a new one on the fly. If paying a parking ticket, I might put "parktic@Flying Tuna.33mail.com" where "parktic" is my descriptor. The moment I press submit, this email address is instantly created by 33mail (I can create as many addresses as I want).
3. I will receive email from this institution now to my real email address, but through the proxy of "flyingtuna.33mail.com." This makes sure the parking department doesn't know my real email address, while at the same time the email arrives to me. Pretty neat, right?

Just don't forget that 33mail still has their own record of these emails. And since 33mail is aging, it occasionally gets blocked by websites, especially ones that have sophisticated recognition tools. This is a cat-and-mouse game, so instead of recommending a particular alias email service, I give you the concept and tell you to try experimenting. Another great option is SimpleLogin. Most of these alias services are free with paid options. Don't use alias email address for important accounts, as these services are not as stable as more traditional email services—their funding could dry up. Alias email accounts are good for:

- Newsletters (such as the Watchman Privacy Newsletter)

- One-time online shopping orders
- Brick-and-mortar shop requests
- Test emails

Now let's talk about your main email account. My current recommendation is ProtonMail. I migrated from Gmail to ProtonMail and haven't looked back for a second. ProtonMail is free (like Gmail), but has a clear profit model (unlike Gmail). It is open-source (unlike Gmail), which means we can see what is happening under the hood, and so far things have been good. Most important, ProtonMail is a zero-knowledge service (unlike Gmail), which means that ProtonMail has no access to your account. ProtonMail is also based in Switzerland so they benefit mildly from Swiss privacy laws and from being outside of the "Fourteen Eyes" intelligence-sharing nations.[72] With a paid ProtonMail account (which supports the service) you can have multiple addresses that all funnel in to your single inbox. It has most of the bells and whistles of a standard Gmail account. Another option is Tutanota, and I'm sure more private email services will be cropping up in upcoming months and years.

Services such as ProtonMail allow you to use multiple addresses within the same account (if you use their paid model). In other words, they let you create multiple ____@protonmail.com addresses that all come to the same account. This is another opportunity to diversify your emailing. You might have an address that you only use for financial accounts. You might then have an address that you only use for friends and family. I recommend separating your email addresses for various things in your life (especially business and personal). Don't use a single email address for everything.

Here's the hierarchy of email services:

1. For emails that you will truly only use once, just search for "email generator" and use one of those. Don't use these for anything sensitive or important.
2. For emails that are slightly more important, such as one-time purchases, which you might want a record for, use a forwarding service such as 33mail or SimpleLogin
3. For important emails from financial institutions, friends, and any account online, you're best off using an established email service.

---

[72] See "Everything Else" for more on this data-sharing cabal

ProtonMail is my recommendation here. You can set up a ProtonMail account today for free.

In terms of emailing behavior, you would do well to note the following. Emailing is an old infrastructure that was not designed for privacy: nor can it supply much of it today. This is partly because most people use different email services and encryption usually requires the same service for both sender and receiver. If you send an email from your ProtonMail account to another ProtonMail account, then this message will be encrypted and visible only between the sender and receiver. However, if you send that same email from your ProtonMail address to a friend's Gmail address, it will have left the ProtonMail ecosystem and been exposed to Gmail. Private communication is best reserved for private messengers such as Signal, Wire, Element, Session.

Your emailing behavior is just as important as the service you select. Here are some rules to follow while emailing:

1. Don't click on emails if the sender looks suspicious. When in doubt, delete. Remember, just because the email says "Amazon" or has the Amazon logo does not mean its from Amazon. It's just as likely a fake. Get in the habit of reading the sending email address and use that as the real judgment about who the sender is.

2. Don't click on links in emails if you are not 100% sure where they will take you. If you're not expecting that email, and sometimes even if you are, its best not to click on links at all. You can usually hover over the link to get a preview of where it is taking you.

3. Don't type in personal information of any kind in emails: log-in information, financial information—any kind of information. Treat emails as static images and rarely interact with what is in them.

4. Never download attachments unless you're expecting them from a close friend.

5. Don't treat any email message as official communication. If HSBC financial services sends you an email that you have a problem with your account, pull up another tab and log into your account directly from their website. Or call them. Find out the truth from the source, not from your email.

6. Be skeptical of fear-mongering language: "Your account has been accessed by a third-party." "Your State ID number has been stolen."

"You owe the IRS $5000 in back taxes." Be especially wary if the message asks you to give out any information.

7. Don't put a signature in your emails—especially if it gives your phone number or other important information. And never leave an out-of-office or vacation reply. If I was a thief I would love to know that kind of information.

I can't emphasize this enough: emails are not to be interacted with aside from reading. My most common client is someone who has accounts comprised and money taken out. They can't figure out why this happens, but it's pretty obvious to me. Almost every time it's because they have given away the keys to their kingdom by responding to a phishing email.

As a final note about email, you would do well to remember that any service that you use online is not yours. ProtonMail and even Gmail can shut down at any time or kick you out and leave you without access to your past, present, and future emails—as unlikely as that would be. People who want to own their messages either run their own email service through their own home server (complex and beyond the scope of this book), buy a domain and use a domain email address (much easier), or at least back up emails regularly. Backing up emails involves downloading files of your emails so you have a copy even if your service kicked the bucket. Most email services have this option, but some hide them behind paywalls or have special instructions for how they can be downloaded. For ProtonMail, you must have a paid account and follow their instructions at https://protonmail.com/bridge.

Passwords and Two-Factor Authentication

As more of our lives migrate to various websites it becomes crucial to protect this information with strong passwords that remain in our private possession. As humans it is mentally impossible to create, much less memorize, strong and random passwords. This means sometimes we have to rely on something outside of our selves. You could organize your complex passwords in a text document, but if your computer was compromised you could be in serious trouble if someone copied this file. That's why most serious privacy advocates, myself included, recommend a *password manager*. A password manager stores and protects your passwords behind its own master password, and helps you to create long and truly random passwords.

Wait, isn't using a privacy manager just trusting another company/program to not get hacked, and this time the damage could be access to all of my account passwords?

This is good thinking and quite true. I have three responses:
1. I prefer managers that are open-source and offline (local) only. Offline systems are much (much) less likely to be hacked.
2. You could select an online password manager from a reputable company that promises zero-knowledge, which means even if the company got hacked they would have no information about your accounts: kind of like robbing a bank to find nothing in the vault.
3. If you have terrible passwords right now (reused passwords, passwords of few characters, not truly random passwords) and you know you won't change this behavior, then you're already at great risk. A password manager—even a casual online one—will probably decrease your risk.

Most password managers work in a similar way. You start by creating a single master password—you only have to remember one—which you should write down and store in a safe place. You'll need this any time you log in to the manager. Now you're ready to start generating passwords.

I easily recommend (September 2022) KeepassXC. This is a free and open-source software that stores data on the hardware of your computer and not online (on the "cloud"). Keep in mind that its offline functionality (it can't easily migrate between computers) might require some planning if you change devices a lot, or rely on your phone to log in to accounts.[73] KeepassXC is available for Windows, Mac, and Linux, and operates essentially the same on all platforms. You install the program, create an account, and begin organizing by folders your various log-ins. Like all privacy changes, make gradual progress a habit: change a few passwords each time you think about it.

---

[73] I simply copy my password database file onto a USB drive and transfer it between my physical computers. Transferring to a phone, however, would be more tricky.

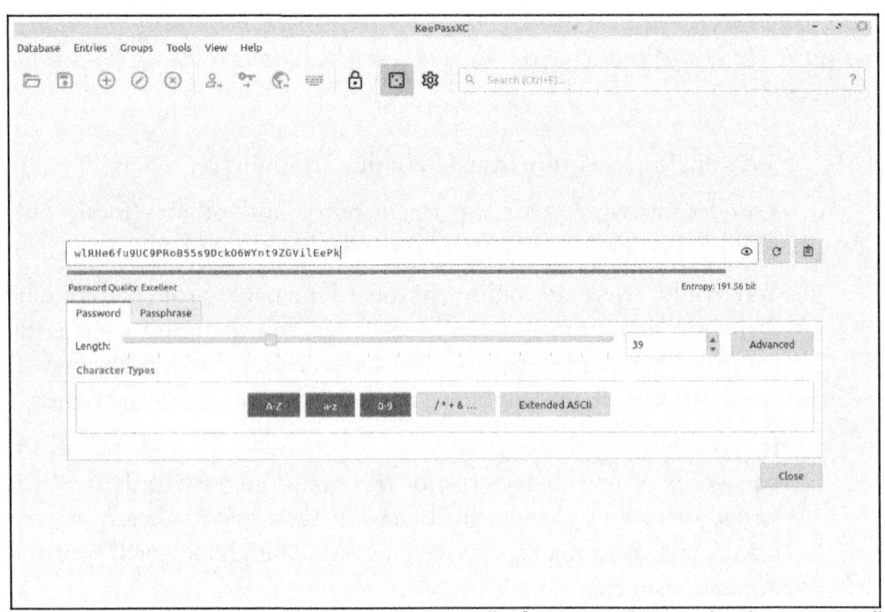

Figure 1: A password manager helps to organize and protect all information tied to your digital accounts; it will also include a random password generator such as you see here.

As you go through your old accounts and consolidate them into one database make sure to delete all those you don't need. Old accounts are vulnerabilities. This process can even be therapeutic, as all movements towards minimalism are. Now, let's be clear: websites back up their servers. Well-financed websites back up their servers often, and social media accounts are rumored to maintain "ghost accounts" of people who have left their service. This means that whatever you have uploaded to the Internet probably will exist in some form for as long as those servers exist. But you can offset some of this risk by deleting what is available on current servers. Delete old accounts today.

A few quick notes about password creation:

1. Don't rush password creation because getting locked out of accounts is not fun. With zero-knowledge services such as ProtonMail, if you forget your password you can never access the account again. It's gone forever.

2. As a general rule select the longest password that the service will allow with as many funky characters as it will allow.

3. But take caution here. Sometimes a website will only allow a certain amount of characters and they won't necessarily tell you. You might not see that your 128 character code has been cut off. More than once I've copied long passwords into a "new password" text box only to realize later on that it only accepted the first seventy characters or so. These days I make sure to compare the final two characters on the website to the final two in the password generator. Or I opt for passwords that are more reasonable in length and don't max out for the sake of maxing out.

4. If you ever need to create a password and don't have a manager nearby, then make one using a complete sentence. Choose something meaningful to you, such as a favorite quotation: "Themassofmenleadlivesofquietdesperation2." Change some of the letters to numbers (3 for E; 4 for A) and you're in even better shape. Find a place to add an uncommon symbol (^ ~ { >) and even a space and you'll be doing even better.

5. Password managers such as KeepassXC will create a file on your computer that is an encrypted version of your passwords. Make sure to back that file up regularly (once a month, at least) onto a separate storage device such as a USB drive. Keep it in a fire-proof safe along with other important files and documents that you back up from your main computer. If this file gets lost, you will not have access to the passwords of all your accounts.

6. Since you're now using a password manager, use its random generator to create a random username. Why be "BobSpaghetti" when you could be "DuUhqznAoqOudHnxL"? This makes your account more difficult to crack and track. One of the first techniques a private investigator will use to track you down online is to type in a known username and see what other services you use it on. Staying random makes that route unfeasible. Just make sure you stick to alphabetic characters and keep it on the shorter side. Some websites get confused when you get fancy with your username. For that reason I've gotten in the habit of using KeepassXC's "passphrase" generator, which can get me a nice username like: "despise goofy unfocused drainpipe

explode conjoined shallow." Still very secure (spaces are an excellent password enhancer, by the way) and its usually more often accepted in the username slot.

7. While you're at it, make your "security questions" random characters or phrases as well. So-called security questions are essentially a secret way to have your account hijacked. Former prospective US vice president Sarah Palin had her Gmail account taken over by someone who guessed her question "Where did you meet your spouse" by watching a few hours of her videos.[74]

8. Every now and then when you log in to an account, change the password.

The problem with KeepassXC is that because it is offline it can't easily be transferred to other devices that you may use. You could always just copy the password file onto the other computer and install KeepassXC to use it, but this isn't so simple if your other device is a phone. I encourage you to have a single computer to perform your important log-ins, but if that's not an option, then this is where Bitwarden comes in.

Bitwarden is similar to KeepassXC, but it runs on the cloud, which means you can sync accounts easily between devices. While I'm skeptical of cloud software, Bitwarden is zero knowledge, open source, etc., and is not as likely to let you down as other managers. Download the Bitwarden program or app on all the devices you need and it will sync your passwords for you automatically.

Just as important as solid passwords is *two-factor authentication*. This is the next generation of password protection. Basically it means that in addition to your password you have to furnish a second proof of ownership of your account in order to log in. You've likely encountered plenty of these, whether its having a text message sent to your phone or an eight digit number sent to your email address. *What we're looking for is two-factor authentication by default for every log in.*

Unfortunately there's no standard option for better 2FA, but I will cover two options. The first is a YubiKey, which perhaps you have heard about. This is a physical device the size of a USB thumb drive that you purchase (around $50 or its equivalent) and keep around with you on your key chain, for example. The basic procedure involves inserting this device in your computer as proof

---

[74] https://en.wikipedia.org/wiki/Sarah_Palin_email_hack

that it is you signing in to your account. You'll have to go to the settings of that service first and make sure to set up YubiKey support, of course. If you're interested in trying a YubiKey, I would first encourage you to check which websites support its use. While support is growing, many major websites do not, including banks and other financial institutions such as PayPal.

There are positives and negatives to using YubiKey as a security device. Frankly, I don't enjoy using these kinds of devices. I fear losing physical objects (even though you can leave the mini YubiKey in your computer at all times) but more importantly the websites I would want to lock down do not support it. The confusingly numerous options for YubiKeys and their sloppy marketing make things even worse for my clients, who can't parse some of these details. I'm also investigating, like other privacy researchers, the extent to which all accounts using a YubiKey could be combined into a rather revealing fingerprint of your activity. I'll let you know in future editions of this book, or via my newsletter, what is discovered. YubiKey (and other "hardware tokens") are an interesting idea, but I'm more inclined to let them develop at the moment. Many people, however, think otherwise and make frequent use of these devices.

The other option for two-factor authentication is a software solution. Just as you use a program for your password management, so too can you have a dedicated program for handling your 2FA. One such app that I will discuss is *Authy*. There are others you can use, such as Google Authenticator, but in the interest of avoiding Google I will not recommend it. Basically, Authy is a program whose sole purpose is to generate codes for you such as the kind you would use to log in to Facebook and other accounts. Like YubiKey, you can't use Authy everywhere, but support from websites is on the rise. Authy is better than a phone number because a phone number can be hijacked fairly easily. Skilled hackers can in five minutes have access to your phone by calling the phone company, impersonating you, and asking for a replicate SIM card to be sent to them. Then they could get into all manner of your online accounts by selecting the "forgot password, send SMS" option. A YubiKey or an authenticator app is better than the alternative.

Note: Authy is not open-source. Many recommend the app Aegis Authenticator, so feel free to explore the field if it interests you.

Here's how to set up and use Authy:

1. Install the Authy app on your phone and create an account using a phone number.
2. Pick a website that you would like to connect with Authy.
3. Now you'll go both to that website and also your Authy app to set up that connection. Search through the log-in settings of the website to find 2FA options. Note that where it says "Google Authenticator" you can also use Authy.
4. To make the connection you'll probably have to snap a QR code on the screen. Simply follow the instructions.
5. Consider changing the log-in options on that website to *only* accept Authy. If you don't do this, then a hacker might simply choose the easiest way to get into your account, such as your regular phone number or email. You're only as strongest as your weakest link—that's the whole point here.
6. Now whenever you log in to that website you'll be prompted to check your Authy app (which you can have on your phone or desktop) for a code to use.

Password protection is flawed, to say the least. The two-factor authentication methods I just suggested offer security, but in terms of privacy they require you to rely on a third-party, and it's quite possible for Authy and YubiKey to form their own fingerprint of you since they are in their own way centralized services. But all other solutions so far have proved to be either lacking or Orwellian. Some security professionals are now trying to solve the problem but advocating biometrics (facial recognition, fingerprints, etc.) as an option, but as privacy-conscious people we do not give up anything pertaining to our body. The best solution for password problems moving forward is to use more offline software as opposed to online software, and overall to have fewer accounts and online data in existence.

Protect Your Identity

Identity theft is a fitting way to conclude this chapter on the basics of online and digital privacy. Identity theft involves theft of a person's information to the extent that the thief can open a financial account in that person's name. Everything we've learned in this chapter is designed to protect you against identity theft, so I've provided the following checklist to see how well you've been listening:

1. Remove all programs, accounts, and information that is no longer needed (also shred and burn physical items, don't leave car registration in car, etc.).
2. Lock all information remaining after this purge behind secure passwords (via a password manager), as well as two-factor authentication.
3. Practice good digital hygiene such as not interacting with emails, not downloading suspicious files and programs, etc.
4. Avoid public Wi-Fi and use a VPN whenever connected to the internet.
5. Don't ever give out your personal information online or via phone (or by any method) unless you are 100% sure that the person you are talking to is legitimate and that they absolutely must have that piece of information at that moment. When in doubt, step away and come back later.
6. Freeze credit reports and keep them frozen until needed; check them at least once per year, if not two or three times.
7. Limit the amount of information about you in the online world; have fewer financial accounts and accounts in general; be a minimalist.

See the "Everything Else" appendix for more on identity theft.

Chapter 4
Online and Digital Privacy (Intermediate)

It was, simply put, the closest thing to science fiction I've ever seen in science fact: an interface that allows you to type in pretty much anyone's address, telephone number, or IP address, and then basically go through the recent history of their online activity. In some cases you could even play back recordings of their online sessions, so that the screen you'd be looking at was their screen, whatever was on their desktop. You could read their emails, their browser history, their search history, their social media postings, everything. You could set up notifications that would pop up when some person or some device you were interested in became active on the Internet for the day. And you could look through the packets of Internet data to see a person's search queries appear letter by letter, since so many sites transmitted each character as it was typed. It was like watching an autocomplete, as letters and words flashed across the screen. But the intelligence behind that typing wasn't artificial but human: this was a humancomplete.

- Edward Snowden from *Permanent Record*

If you have any interest in getting out of the system that Snowden describes above, you'll have to go well beyond the basics. This chapter is going to demand a bit more from you and it will begin with a serious suggestion to drastically alter to your digital landscape. But I want to give you some encouragement from the start. As part of my work I consult with many older people who feel as though technology is out to purposefully confuse them. I assure you this is not the case—quite the opposite. New digital technologies are almost always designed to make things easier; indeed, more than any other systems we have—our languages, our legal systems—digital technologies were designed from the bottom up to be comprehensible and logical. When encountering new programs you might be uncomfortable, yes, but take heart knowing that all of this is within your grasp to understand. Get rid of your pride and start asking the most basic questions about why you don't understand something. Then look up the answers and practice. Embrace the uncomfortable regularly—that's the only way to improvement.

Linux

We need to discuss Linux. While it is not a simple topic—perhaps not even "intermediate"—it is extremely important for our pursuit of digital privacy. *Linux* describes a number of free alternative operating systems to the ultra-popular Microsoft Windows and Apple macOS. Most PCs run Windows 10 and all Mac computers run macOS by default. An *operating system* is the broader computer program that allows you to view and use all of your other programs. When you stare at your laptop or desktop screen you are looking at the visual interface of the operating system; it also does quite a bit in the background. The consequences should be clear: you are only as private as your operating system.

There is no single Linux operating system but many different kinds, or distributions (distros). Some examples include Linux Ubuntu, Linux Debian, and Arch Linux. There are literally thousands more, since the computer code is available to any talented individual or group to make their own version. But for our purposes we will focus on a popular one: Linux Mint.

Why is Linux superior to Windows and macOS? Linux operating systems are made with open-source code by skilled enthusiasts who often have privacy as a core value of their work. *Open source* is important for privacy because it means that the code is publicly available to be scrutinized. Proprietary code such as the kind used in Windows 10 and macOS is hidden from public view, which we are starting to learn is not the kind of system you want to trust with your life's information: especially with something as all-knowing as your operating system. Linux is open source so you know—or you can trust that the broad community of experts knows—what exactly is going on under the hood.[75] Today there is a greater movement toward open-source applications for any services that involves data management. For now just know that Linux operating systems tend also to be highly secure and consequently nearly virus-free. They are secure both as a matter of their design, and because they represent a small portion of the computer market, and thus are not worth developing specific malware for.

---

[75] Let's be clear: you probably don't know how to decipher code, and just because it is available to be scrutinized does not mean it is scrutinized. Still, open-source is a better bet.

I've said that Windows and Apple are not private. Let's substantiate this briefly. It is quite possible that Microsoft sees literally everything you do on Windows 10. One infamous test found that Windows 10 made 5,500 connections to various IP addresses during a single session.[76] That is to say, your Windows machine seems to send data back to the mothership quite often. You may also have noticed in your Windows 10 privacy settings that the best you can do in many cases is switch to "basic" data gathering and not "none." I'll say no more about Windows 10. As for earlier versions of Windows, they no longer receive updates and thus are sitting ducks for malware; they are not recommended. Windows 11 is even worse.

As for macOS, it would seem to be more secure than Microsoft. I say "seem" because it is also proprietary or closed-source. Apple has taken a strong stance on privacy and security, but they accomplish this via a walled garden. So long as you use their approved applications (often you don't have an alternative) they promise you some measure of privacy. They believe they can handle your privacy, which is a contradiction in terms. That top-down centralized approach misses the decentralized essence of privacy. See my podcast episode "Apple Cannot Give Your Privacy." Thus, while many agree that casual privacy seekers are at home on macOS, I would encourage you while pursuing privacy to simply take it back fully into your hands. This is why I recommend for best peace-of-mind you should start using Linux and not look back.

Which Linux distro to use? I recommend *Linux Mint* because it is easy to install, has plenty of tutorials online, and is probably the most easy Linux distro to adapt to coming from Windows and Mac.[77] Seasoned computer experts might recommend using a more "hardcore" version of Linux such as Linux Debian. If you're up for that challenge, by all means go for it. Debian is fantastic for privacy. But considering that even the creator of Linux, Linus Torvalds, admitted that he has never booted up Debian[78]—precisely because of its installation complexity—I think that for beginners you should probably start with Linux Mint.

You have two options when installing Linux Mint. You can run it alongside Windows or macOS (called dual-booting). Or you can overwrite Windows

---

[76] https://thehackernews.com/2016/02/microsoft-windows10-privacy.html
[77] In 2016 Mint's website was breached and its operating system downloads compromised. The change was quickly reversed, the company has since updated its security, and if one takes proper precautions like I will suggest in the upcoming pages, it is not even an issue.
[78] https://www.youtube.com/watch?v=qHGTsINSBis

and macOS altogether and install Linux Mint instead. I'll show you how to do both. Just note that if you choose to overwrite, you'll obviously want to organize your current files and back them up so they'll still exist when you delete Windows or macOS. In what follows I do my best to offer a textual overview of the process to change your operating system to Linux Mint.

1. Determine which of your computers will receive Linux Mint. You have two options when installing. You can override your previous operating system (deleting everything on it), or you can install Linux Mint alongside it. The latter option is called "dual booting," and it is what we will be doing so that you can easily switch back to Windows or macOS if you're having trouble with Linux.

2. Back up any important files on your computer to an external drive. It's good practice to prepare for any mistakes on your end and you should back up your computer data regularly anyway.

3. Download the digital file of Linux Mint from its official website: https://linuxmint.com/download.php. Select 64-bit "Cinnamon" as the style option in the download links (very old computers might use 32-bit, but it's unlikely you have one that old).

4. Now ideally we want to verify our file that we just downloaded. This is optional. Verification means that we do a few things to prove that the file we downloaded has not been hijacked between Linux Mint's servers and our own computer. This is a fairly unlikely scenario, but it's good practice to start doing this whenever you can. Verification is complex for a beginning user, and will differ on macOS and Windows. I encourage you to study the "Don't forget to verify your ISO" instructions on the download page where you got the file.

5. Install and run a program such as Rufus (https://rufus.ie) or Etcher (https://www.balena.io/etcher/) on your current operating system. Run either program, select the file of Linux Mint that you downloaded in Step 3, and choose the default settings. You will need an empty USB drive (at least 4 GB) to perform this task.

6. Once Rufus or Etcher has completed, turn off your computer. Keep the USB with Linux Mint on it plugged in.

7. Enter your computer's BIOS screen by doing the following. Turn on your computer and be prepared to read your screen. For PC users we are trying to get into the BIOS screen. Also known as the UEFI screen. Your computer *might* give you quick instructions a few

seconds after you turn it on about which button you should press to access the BIOS. For example it might ask you to press F2 or Delete. If your computer does not tell you, try the common buttons: F2, F12, and delete. You can also look up your model number and BIOS in a search engine to find the right key or set of keys.

8. If you use a Mac computer, you'll do something else entirely. Before you turn on your computer press and hold the Option button. Now turn the computer on while still holding the Option button.

9. For PC users, you're looking for something like *boot order*. When you find it, change the order to favor the USB first and save these settings. This will ensure your computer loads the operating system on your USB and not from your hard drive, which it would normally do.

10. Exit the BIOS screen and restart your computer if necessary. If you've done the steps correctly you should start up the Linux Mint operating system. Feel free to test it out for a bit. When you're ready, you can select the "Install Linux Mint" icon on the desktop.

11. Work through the installation. For "Install multimedia codecs" select yes.

12. For the option "Erase disc and install Linux Mint," pause for a moment. Selecting "yes" will erase your previous operating system and everything on it. Instead (for the sake of this dual-booting example), select the "Install alongside [Windows]" option. You will then get a chance to allocate space on your hard drive for Linux. Choose somewhere in the middle or use your own judgment. Then continue.

13. When it asks for your name, give something generic (Jane) and also select "Encrypt my home folder." Choose a password.

14. Once installation completes, you will now have a Linux computer at your disposal.

If you're having trouble, please check an online tutorial. I hope to have my own in the near future, and I will let you know via my newsletter on watchmanprivacy.com or via The Watchman Privacy Podcast.

While Linux Mint will look similar to the operating systems you're used to, we should mention some subtle and serious changes that you will have to deal with. Just like reorganizing your house and everything in it, you won't find things where you are used to finding them. It will be frustrating until you adapt. Installing programs is different—and many of your familiar programs won't work on Linux—and you may at times be forced to type in code in order to accomplish tasks. You'll need to learn new programs such as LibreOffice as a replacement for the Microsoft Office Suite and they won't have all of the same functionality or convenience. Other programs such as your favorite video editor or Adobe products are unlikely to be an option. In other words, you must be prepared for some adjustments. Here are a few things you might find different:

1) *Different programs.* Many Mac and Windows programs work only in those ecosystems. Microsoft Word is not easily accessible on Linux. Nor is PhotoShop. But Linux has solid alternatives to both of these services: LibreOffice and GIMP.

2) Installing programs. With Mac and Windows it's straightforward. With Linux it's not always a matter of going to a website, clicking "download," and running a handy installer. The best way for beginners to install a program is to go to its website and look for instructions for Linux Mint. You often won't see Linux Mint but you will see Ubuntu or Debian. Linux Mint is an offshoot of Ubuntu and Debian. Since Ubuntu is the more recent branch, if you ever see an option for both Debian and Ubuntu, select the Ubuntu option. I know, it's already getting complicated. You're just going to have to remember this. For example, if you go to the Skype website (not a recommended program) you should notice that it detects the operating system: "Get Skype for Linux DEB". What is Deb? Deb is short for Debian, which is a branch of Linux. Linux Mint is part of the Debian branch and so we can use this version. You won't always get a convenient installer specifically for Linux Mint, so you'll just have to remember this. Also note that Mint has its own software "store" called "Software Manager" which you can find by clicking the bottom left Mint "start" button. In a pinch, go there and download the software you want.

3) Drivers. Being a free operating system Linux misses out on some important drivers—the software that makes your hardware components run to utmost efficiency. This means that you probably won't want to play PC games on Linux Mint. It means that your Wi-Fi might not be as strong as it otherwise would be. Linux is not designed necessarily for gamers or video editors, though it certainly is possible to do both (and getting better constantly).

Surely with all that inconvenience it is not worth the hassle.

It's possible you might come to that conclusion. When I first got into Linux I was by no means a confident computer user. But I plunged in and learned as I went along. There were some bumps, but over the course of a few months I became confident. Basic functions like browsing the Internet require no learning—and frankly, that's what we use our computer for 90% of the time. All of the computer programs you need have counterparts on Linux, many of these programs being free and open source as well. The bright side of all of this is that you might be forced to become more of a minimalist and you will gain computer literacy. Ultimately you are going to have to show some patience, trust in your ability to adapt, and remember why you are doing this.

Keep in mind that, as with all things, Linux doesn't override your need to make wise decisions. If you install a Skype app and talk away to your friends, Skype will do all of its normal surveillance; Linux will not help you here. If you practice bad online hygiene using Linux you won't be any less prone to privacy invasion. And while Linux might protect you from installed malware directed against your computer, you still must make the prudent decisions described in previous chapters.

Acquire Things Secretly Online

Any time money and the Internet are combined, you lose your privacy rather quickly. Websites with payment widgets are beholden to all kinds of security features, logging of information, and regulations. It's at moments like these that you should consider getting free stuff online that won't leave a glaring trail back to you. What am I talking about? To speak plainly, I'm talking about torrents and free archives online. Bear with me for a moment as we sort out the ethics. I also encourage you to listen to my podcast episode, "How and Why to Torrent."

First let me make a few obligatory comments. The things I discuss in this section, especially torrents, may be illegal in your jurisdiction. I am not encouraging you to break the law. Make yourself aware of the laws to which you're beholden so that you can make an informed decision. However, in many countries torrenting is not only legal, but common practice, since countries like Russia and India (and many others) do not have the same marketplaces and access to goods as Westerners. For such countries, and frankly for the world, torrenting has been a major contributor to human progress.

Many people are misinformed about torrenting. Torrenting involves sharing files from person-to-person (around the world even) through a program called a torrent client. Torrenting a file or even downloading it from a website is not theft—your government may disagree, but I'm speaking morally here. You have simply done what we all do when we're not willing to pay for something: you borrowed it from someone else. I'm confident that some of you reading this book right now acquired it without paying for it. I don't begrudge you that, and I don't think it is bad. Did you steal from me? Hold on: let me check my pockets—nope. You did not steal anything from me. What's the difference between borrowing a book from your friend or from someone sending it to you from the next country over via a peer-sharing service? I'm sure many of your have borrowed your friend's Netflix password because you weren't willing to pay for your own license. There is no moral difference between these acts.[79]

Ethics aside, torrenting can be a remarkable privacy strategy. Assuming you're covered with a VPN that condones torrenting, downloading something online will not leave nearly as much of a trace as purchasing it online or in person. Do not torrent without a VPN, as this will send flags to your ISP, and if torrenting is illegal in your area, might get you a legal warning. Assuming you use a VPN, you have succeeded at acquiring a good with minimal trail. I am not encouraging you to break the law.

Also, I would be remiss if I didn't note that torrenting puts you at the mercy of downloading files from unknown sources. Remember that you are downloading a file from some stranger's computer. Your Linux operating system should provide some protection, but always select reputable torrenting sites and torrents with good up votes. When in doubt, avoid until you do more research.

The process of torrenting involves the following:
1. Download a torrent client such as qBittorrent, which is highly reputable.

---

[79] I recommend reading or watching Stephan Kinsella (*Against Intellectual Property*) for a cogent examination of the uncritically accepted concept of "intellectual property."

2. Visit torrent sites, which I won't list here, to find things you want to download.

3. Click on the torrent link on that website to load the torrent into qBittorent and it will bring it up in the program.

4. Select the location to which you want to download it—such as your desktop—and run it. Depending on how many people are uploading (seeding) that file the download might take a few minutes or a few hours (or possibly days to weeks).

5. A healthy torrent should take no longer than a few hours. Remember that torrents only exist when people upload ("seed") files, so make sure to repay the favor by not deleting your torrent file and leaving it to upload—even if just for a few hours.

I'm talking about torrents when few other people are willing to do so because they are very important. In today's climate, there are simply some books that I would not want to be caught buying, or which are not available to purchase in cash. You can support these companies and business in other more private ways when you have the chance. Which reminds me: if you've torrented this book, consider purchasing a copy for yourself or a friend. I talk about buying privately on Amazon in Chapter 6.

Torrents work by sharing files among "peers" so that no central database exists. There are, however, centralized database websites that offer certain files for free. Consider the following:

- Ample databases of downloadable books can be found across the Internet. I won't list the sites here. There are very few books that I cannot find.

- Live televised sports are sometimes streamed on YouTube by some daring person sharing a screen. They can be found widely on other websites.

- If you're ever blocked by an age gate on YouTube demanding you to log in—something that is increasingly done for political reasons—find a workaround. In the past, you could use a service called "NSFW YouTube" to add a few lines to the URL and view it through their site. YouTube recently started cracking down on them; instead remember the concept and find your own route.

- You can also check YouTube alternatives such as BitChute, LBRY, DTube, which tend not to use age gates.
- You can get around paywalls in various ways. The Firefox add-on *Bypass Paywalls* gives you access to hundreds of major news websites, as does the website https://12ft.io. The *Sci Hub* project boasts more than 80 million academic articles for free. The first obscure article I ever put in there came up immediately.
- The services I mention here may come and go, but the principal remains the same. Any time you think you've hit a wall, you should just do a bit of research to see how to get around it.

Suffice it to say, if you were an Edward Snowden fugitive-type with little hope of ever getting a bank account again, you could access most of the world's stuff strictly from your browser. Just remember, even if a no-logging VPN is used to hide any trace of ever downloading such material, that doesn't make this behavior legal. Make yourself aware of the laws in your area. I am not encouraging you to break the law.

Some of you may have dismissed this section, though I hope you've given my moral argument serious consideration. If any book were to be torrented and its creator lose out on revenue, it would be my book and my potential revenue. But it is vital that file-sharing online remain alive. To put it frankly: it's one of the last bastions of free thought still left in the world. In places like Russia and India where authoritarian governments restrict access to the global market, torrenting is crucial. It is simply the norm. Torrenting gives power back to people across the globe.

In 2019 after the Christchurch shooting the New Zealand government made it illegal (i.e. they were willing to kill you) to possess a copy of the shooter's manifesto: punishable by ten years in prison.[80] While I have little interest in reading such things, whenever something gets banned, it certainly piques my interest. Government censorship is evil—no exceptions—and as private companies also begin their own version of book burning and whitewashing,[81] it becomes increasingly important for all of us to have offline hard copies of the books, films, and other pieces of knowledge that we find meaningful.

---

[80] https://www.businessinsider.com.au/new-zealand-bans-christchurch-shooter-manifesto-livestream-2019-3

[81] As one small example: https://www.wsj.com/articles/dr-seuss-books-deemed-offensive-will-be-delisted-from-ebay-11614884201

So be curious on the Internet, and never assume you've hit a dead-end just because a paywall hits you in the face. We will miss the uncensored Internet in upcoming years.

Avoid "Always Online" Services and Rental Culture

I remember as a kid ambling into a store, buying a computer program with cash, cramming the disk into my computer, and installing it. It would remain in my possession and full ownership for as long as the disk existed. I owned it, I could sell it, I could make copies of it (sometimes), and I could loan it out to someone. As ownership starts to erode in favor of rental culture, this is becoming much more difficult, and dangerous for our privacy.

"Always online" products or *cloud software* should be avoided as much as possible because they are highly integrated to databases and nothing you do on them can be considered private. There are some exceptions—such as zero knowledge services—but you'll likely notice these by their overt emphasis on privacy.

I'm a firm believer that gaining knowledge and awareness is almost always the first step to take. Start by taking note of the always-online and "software as a service" trends around you. For example, Adobe no longer sells physical copies of their popular Photoshop software. Your only option for Photoshop is to pay for monthly or yearly license to *rent* their service. A renter is one who can be barged in at any time, one whose service can be dropped at any time, and one whose data may not be owned by the user. Everything you do on your cloud service of Photoshop is monitored by Adobe—it might even be their property. Meanwhile, Microsoft monitors their Skype and Office 365 services, censoring words and banning accounts that use "hate speech."[82] The *Forbes* article I've referenced diligently notes that Microsoft's policing of hate speech and "illegal" activity might necessitate them banning pro-democracy or pro-women's rights language in several countries. Then again, Microsoft isn't exactly know for its thoughtfulness.

Also notice the powerful rhetoric of always-online products. *The utter convenience. Stop paying hundreds of dollars for products—pay one small price per month. You don't have to buy your own hardware. We'll make sure you*

---

[82] https://www.forbes.com/sites/kalevleetaru/2019/07/26/censorship-comes-for-the-desktop-how-microsoft-has-infused-values-into-windows-and-office

have the latest updates to tax laws. The latest, greatest product updated every five seconds.

I prefer my own interpretation:

Become a renter for life. Forget you've subscribed and let us soak up the forgotten monthly subscription. Pay the full price three times over in years' time. Share your information with the world. Give your ownership away. "You'll own nothing. And you'll be happy."[83]

Now for a solution. After becoming aware of this trend, perform an audit of the services you rely on. Some of them will have no good alternatives and others will. As a general rule the *free software movement* will likely have a reasonable alternative. This is where FOSShub.com can come in handy. These people still believe in ownership. Here are a few ideas to replace your current always-online services:

Software as a service	Ownership
Photoshop	GIMP
Windows 10	Linux Mint
Dropbox and Google Drive	External hard drive or SSD
Steam PC download	Gog.com
Kindle Unlimited	Library; physical books; free books online
Google Stadia, Xbox Game Pass, GeForce Now	Physical disk game
Microsoft Office 365	LibreOffice

Ownership grants serious privacy benefits—you can use it without being connected to the Internet—and it also ensures the world is headed in the right direction. Renting is always cheap in the short-term. But historically speaking (and projecting into the future) you'll see that the death of ownership is likewise the death of financial freedom and independence, to say nothing of privacy.

---

[83] This latter quotation comes from a disturbing 2020 video from the World Economic Forum: https://twitter.com/wef/status/799632174043561984 [Tweet has been deleted]

File Encryption

Those who believe in ownership will start accumulating files on their computer and while these offline files are fairly protected, they are still vulnerable to physical theft and the occasional advanced malware. Especially if you travel, if you live with multiple people, or you have a corporate or government job where you are at risk of theft, protecting the files on your computer is paramount. This is where encryption comes in and I'll show you in this section how to set it up. Before we do that, though, you'll want to get your digital life in order.

A private person keeps careful control of their files. They keep them in view, keep them to a minimum, and protect them in encrypted files. Start with the following:

1. Spend time to organize your files carefully so that you have in a single purview every digital file in your ownership.
2. To organize your files, make use of folders. There's no reason to have a scattershot of files spread across your desktop, on random hard drives, and in various sections of your computer. Search your Pictures folder and your Documents folder and move everything into your own new folder with its own sub-folders.
3. While you organize over the course of days or weeks, delete files you don't need and especially target the large files. To determine which files are large, you can right click and select "properties." Videos, photos, and large PDFs with colorful images tend to be the largest files you possess.
4. Whittle down your entire collection of files to a few folders that sit on your desktop.
5. Promise yourself not to lose control again.

When I started getting serious about this I went through my entire computer and reduced 100 gigabytes to around 5 gigabytes. This allowed me to rid myself of extraneous things but also to consolidate all files in a manageable size. Small size is important because it allows you to transfer the files quickly and to put them in encrypted containers with ease.

Encryption is a good thing but one that requires some patience and some responsibility. What is encryption? You can think of it as a password system that assigns a set of keys that only you and the receiver have. During the two World Wars Germany relied on its own form of encryption, the Enigma Machine, which allowed them to send messages among themselves that had to be decoded on the other end. It's the same concept today. When we say "encrypt your phone" or "encrypt your computer," what we mean is to create a password that will scramble the data within the device and only unscramble it once the code has been input again.

Encryption can also be done at the file level, so that you can create a folder on your computer that requires a special password to access. As a privacy-conscious person this will be your best method. Finally, you can encrypt an entire disk: such as the hard drive you use on your home computer or laptop (which we won't discuss here—it's usually done at the operating system level).[84] But let's go step by step to set up an encrypted folder.

Here's how to get started with disk encryption for a folder.
1. Download the free program VeraCrypt.
2. Start up the program.
3. Select "Create an encrypted file container."
4. Select "Standard VeraCrypt volume."
5. Choose a location to put your encrypted file (such as the desktop) and give it a name.
6. Press next. AES encryption is fine.
7. Select the size of your file.
8. Create a password.
9. Press next. "FAT" is fine. (For individual files larger than 4 GB you'll have to select another option—it can get complicated if using Linux)
10. Move your mouse around as instructed.
11. Press "exit."

Now you have a file that is protected by encryption. Any time you want to open it you will do the following:
1. Start up VeraCrypt.
2. Pick a slot (such as Slot 1).
3. Press "Select File" and select your file.
4. Press "Mount."

---

[84] If you followed my Linux Mint installation instructions in Chapter 4 then you have already set up an encrypted hard drive.

5. Type in your encryption password and possibly also your computer password (if prompted).
6. You may now make changes to the folder you have created, including adding or deleting files inside of it.
7. Select "dismount" when you are finished with the folder.

I encourage you to practice this multiple times before putting any sensitive data exclusively in one of these containers.

Now you have a way to lock down to a profound degree various files in your possession. This is a powerful tool, but I understand it is also initially a lot of work. Massage it into your routine slowly. For highly concerned people, nothing is saved outside of the VeraCrypt file. That's asking a lot, but once you get into certain habits anything can become easy.

Speaking of habits, it's a good idea to back up all files on your computer once a week. First, put them into a VeraCrypt folder. Then, back up that folder on a storage device of your choosing. You might, for example, put this encrypted folder on a keychain USB drive and take it along with you: insurance against a disaster, and all your life's files, encrypted, fitting between your fingers. Set a time every week (Friday evening?) to perform this backup procedure.

Tor

TOR (The Onion Router) is a private series of networks that works in some ways similar to a VPN, but with a few added benefits and a few drawbacks. The Tor Project produces the Tor browser, which is a handy tool in your privacy arsenal. You can download the browser from torproject.org.

The Tor browser has a number of advantages compared to using a regular VPN:

- It is free and requires no information from you.
- It works in a decentralized manner, which means you don't have to trust a single entity or company.
- The traffic is encrypted in multiple layers compared to a VPN and has fewer (if different) vulnerabilities (such as the VPN company when using a VPN).

- You can copy it to a USB drive and easily transport the entire program to another device.

If you really don't want anyone to know what you're searching, then the Tor browser is a great choice. Keep in mind that it is slower than your regular browser because it routes through multiple servers instead of one—and the servers are maintained by individual concerned citizens (don't worry though, each Tor node has incomplete information of the surrounding nodes). I don't want to underestimate this: *Tor can be really slow* and is not meant for downloading or torrenting (don't ever torrent with Tor as it can slow down the network and compromise the person running the node).

Arguably the greatest perk of Tor is that it allows you to access an entirely different plane of the Internet: the Dark Web. You may have heard about the Dark Web from the story of Silk Road, an underground marketplace that was tracked by the feds and shut down. As with any free market that is driven outside of the scope of normal functioning, Silk Road and the Dark Web have been branded as nasty places for nasty people. I trust if you've read this far you can see through the propaganda. Like any tool, Tor and the Dark Web can facilitate good and evil.

We won't get deep into the things you can do on the Dark Web or with Tor, but I'll give you a few tips to get you started:

1. You must use the Tor browser to access the Dark Web and many websites have their own URL for the Dark Web. Dark Web search engines are where you should start, and these can change often.
2. Avoid maximizing the Tor browser screen, especially if you have a unique resolution on your computer. Keep it at the default size. Websites can detect your resolution size as a way to fingerprint you. (See fingerprinting in Chapter 8).
3. Don't log in to your regular accounts or try to buy anything from regular online shops—you're likely to be flagged much more than when using a VPN. Basically, the Tor browser has its own obvious fingerprint.
4. Use the Tor browser to research and take part in forums that you wouldn't generally want to be seen in. It's a great place for exploration without judgment.

5. Use Tor to get around school or state-sponsored censorship of particular websites.

Chapter 5
Phone Privacy

All media works us over completely.

- Marshall McLuhan
The Medium is the Massage

(NOTE: I recognize that this is an extreme chapter. But my initial response to phone privacy was, "don't have a phone." Phones by their very nature eradicate privacy. This chapter attempts to solve that problem and it is difficult.)

It's time to stop calling "smart phones" *phones* since their oral function is of minor importance. Let's be honest and accurate: smart phones are the machine half of our new cyborg selves. These all-but-implanted computers send and receive our messages, handle our finances, give us direction(s), entertain us, think for us, and supplement our devolving memories and visual imaginations. With the advent of 5G-compatible phones and other always-connected devices, we move toward being worked over completely by the medium of the "phone." Elon Musk is speeding this future along with *Neuralink*, which promises to sew a computer directly to the brain and cut out the clumsy business of user input and slow bandwidth altogether. Human testing began in 2020.

Mobile phones—"smart" and "dumb"—are different from your laptop and desktop computer in three crucial ways, and this is of supreme importance for understanding phone privacy. They include:

1. Geo-location. Unlike their regular computer counterparts phones contains specialized computer chips that push out an electro-magnetic signal to the nearest cell tower. This is essential to their

functioning and to our concerns. This chip allows a phone to perform text, talk, and internet ("data") functions wherever it is in the world. In other words, when your phone is working as it's supposed to, it is also pinpointing your location on the planet to within a few meters. This data is available to your mobile service provider, its employees, those who would hack this provider or intercept these signals, and government/policing agencies.

2. Operating systems. Smart phones have different and inferior operating systems to traditional computers, partly because they are much newer and don't yet have a well-established tradition. They are also designed to allow for apps to share among themselves, and since apps are right next-door to your phone's highly-integrated microphone, camera, and GPS-functionality, this poses considerable risk to your privacy. In short, phone operating systems prefer ease of access and not security and privacy.

3. Outdated messaging. Many mobile phones by default use SMS text messaging and standard phone calls—you know, those basic programs pre-loaded on your new phone. Until you install a private Internet-based messenger such as Wire or Signal, your messaging will be vulnerable.

Let's be clear about something. It is impossible to my knowledge to use a mobile phone and not reveal part of your identity, by which I mean your location. It's not a question of buying a private phone; right now no such thing exists. It's not a matter of choosing between Android and Apple, or changing your phones settings, or downloading privacy apps, or buying "dumb" phones with cash.

None of these methods will help you solve the geo-location problem inherent to phones.

Your location is tightly interwoven into your personal identity. Imagine a drug dealer who buys a new burner phone every hour. He must still connect to cell towers for those phones to work and these towers capture his location. It now just takes one or two more data (such as the insecure conversations being listened in to), to determine his fuller identity. And if he makes these calls from a similar place (or places), then this pattern itself is the identity.

I see complete phone privacy as protecting your geo-location. For that reason I have broken this chapter into two parts. Part 1 covers basic phone hygiene. This won't solve the fundamental problem of geo-location data, but it will help you lock down your phone in every other way. Part 2 will explain how to use a phone while hiding your location: the more hardcore method.

Part 1: The Basic Approach to Phone Privacy

Here are the basic principals for private phone use, which will be covered in more detail in the next few pages:

1. Separate your phone from your name.
2. Save most activities for your real computer.
3. Only use secure messaging apps.
4. Keep your applications to a minimum.
5. Avoid applications and features that demand personal information.
6. Use a VPN on your phone, even when using data.
7. Keep your phone cameras covered—especially your front-facing camera—and be wary of its microphone.
8. Don't give out your real phone number.

Let's start with what your phone reveals about you. All purchased phones have serial numbers embedded within them called IMEI numbers. Once you put a SIM card in, you'll also have an IMSI number attached to that card. These numbers are indelibly tied to your phone or SIM card and broadcast to towers any time your phone connects to one. They are also connected to whoever purchased the phone, so you must be sure to do the following to avoid establishing this trace:

1. Buy a new phone,[85] with cash, and do not attach personal information to it during the transaction.
2. Buy a SIM card, with cash, and do not attach personal information to it during the transaction. This is not easy in all countries, though places such as the UK, Ireland, and the US have prepaid phone services in abundance.

---

[85] Buying a used phone will carry with it the baggage of the previous user. This could help to obscure its identity, sure, but it could just as easily hurt you depending on how questionable the previous user's actions were.

3. Do not give your real information (name, address) if required to create an Apple ID or Google account to use your new phone. Make up an email address (ProtonMail) specifically for this action.
4. Do not turn it on until you have considered the geo-location implications in this chapter.

Okay, so you have a private phone ready to go, but your privacy will diminish very quickly depending on how you use it. Let's take a step back and be honest about our phone behavior. Are we phone-addicts? Phones have been designed more than any device to be psychologically exploitative, with even the fake loading screens and bright unread message icons helping to pump a generous hit of endorphins into our brains. Most of us don't need our phone at all times. What is so vital that it can't wait until you at least reach your computer? For the last couple of years I've traveled around regularly without a phone partly to test my reliance on it—it turns out I don't really need it and you probably don't either. Your phone is a device for travel; it is not a device for regular computing. Save that for your more secure laptop or home computer.

Your laptop, for one, has a better operating system, especially if you've installed Linux Mint like I suggested. You know from Chapter 4 that an operating system is the larger program that houses your other programs. It's the gatekeeper. You may have noticed when you start up a phone app for the first time it needs "permission for X, Y, and Z." This is because smart phones love to share information between apps. Nor is this entirely by mistake. Smart phones are designed to dumb down users, to make everything convenient and interconnected. Your social media app might take a peak at your contacts, and vice versa. Your menstruation app might connect with Facebook with or without your permission. Social media apps are particularly bad about this. If you can, save your social media for your laptop. Do the same for financial apps, and all apps that you can manage.

Keep your phone lean. The more applications, the greater the odds that they are sharing information or reporting it back to headquarters. Staying lean is a self-reinforcing act, since the leaner your phone, the less likely you are to use it. Just ask any of the wise people who have removed their emailing app from their phones for productivity reasons. It's a good idea to go through your phone monthly and see what you're not using anymore, or what you think you could do without. And if you don't know how to uninstall programs—in other words, you've been wielding a chainsaw without reading the instructions—stop using your phone until you have figured out these basics.

Seek the minimal at all times. You would be surprised how many apps are unnecessary or that can be replaced by simply using your Firefox Focus browser (my recommended phone browser):
- YouTube
- Weather apps (which insist on knowing your location)
- Any kind of news app (world, sports, finance)
- Twitter
- Reddit
- Internet speed test
- Restaurant recommendations
- Google Maps
- Twitch

The list goes on. Sure, dedicated apps might have some special functionality, but: it's a trap. Particular apps to avoid are those which track you, such as fitness apps. If you are so serious about fitness that you literally have to record every step you take, then I would advocate getting a separate device for this kind of thing. Or do without one like every athlete before you. Keep in mind that Fitbit and its competitors also record data,[86] so you'll want to be very careful not to tell them too much about you. While you're having a look at your health options on your phone make sure to switch off any default functionality. On iPhones, for example, this involves going to Settings > Health and making sure everything there is disabled.

The applications you *should* keep on your phone are your secure messaging apps. We've discussed several times in this book the importance of texting and calling on zero knowledge, open-source messaging apps: Wire, Session, Signal, etc. The problem is that you can only send to people who also have the app. Convince the person you're speaking with to start using one of these. In many

---

[86] And Google owns Fitbit:
https://www.forbes.com/sites/kateoflahertyuk/2021/01/17/google-confirms-fitbit-deal-is-it-time-to-quit-your-smartwatch

cases I tell the people in my life that I will not respond to messages outside of these apps. I have had great success with this tone.

The other essential app on your phone should be your VPN, which you should use as often as you can. Most VPN services will allow you to use their service on multiple devices. Use the VPN on your phone when you are on data ("roaming") as well as any time you're on Wi-Fi. A phone VPN will eat up a bit of your roaming data—maybe 5 percent if not more—so make sure to calculate for that.

Don't forget a pass code for your phone. For the longest time I refused to put a pin number on my phone because I thought it a waste of precious minutes of my day. I still think the amount of time we spend putting in pass codes on phone is enough cumulative time to have discovered a cancer cure by now. Regardless, I decided to create one because the risk is just too great. You should do likewise, especially if you travel. If you don't currently have a pass code, go into your settings and create one of 8 or more numbers or swipes. I don't recommend using a fingerprint for obvious reasons, but also because biometrics can be taken from you (for example, by judges and police) while what's in your head cannot.

Finally, remember that your phone has a microphone and camera that allow you to look into another person's world, which means they can also look into yours. There have been countless cases of phone cameras being exploited by malicious actors or even popular applications—don't forget that Siri on the iPhone and its equivalent on Android are always listening by design.

You have a few options to remove this listening and viewing capability:

- Cover your camera with a piece of electrical tape when not in use. This might include your front or your back camera, but whatever you feel comfortable with.
- You could surgically remove your microphone and listening chip and plug in a headset instead every time you use it. The headset should have an attached microphone to replace the one you have removed.
- You could keep a cut-off microphone plugged in when not in use. This tricks the phone into stopping its listening capabilities. One brand on Amazon is Mic-Lock.
- You could keep your phone away from you in your house, and otherwise make sure it is behind something soundproof when you're

having conversation. Even stuffing it into the couch cushion can help a bit.

Notice I don't suggest downloading any apps that promise to shut off the microphone. I'm not fond of giving an app permission to use the microphone, and I have doubts that they do what they say they're doing. Even reputable apps can update and change their functionality overnight. The best thing you can do is simply be aware of where your phone is when you are talking.

Finally, it should go without saying that you shouldn't be giving your phone number out. I don't even know my phone number, though I do know the burner phone numbers attached to my MySudo account (explained in the next pages). So what do you do when someone asks for a phone number? Consider the following:

- For new friends, give them a Wire messenger handle instead of a phone number.
- For organizations who obviously don't need your phone number (online stores, etc.) try putting in all zeroes. The question then becomes: "who doesn't need it?" Does your doctor? Plan these things out in advance.
- Learn by memory a good, more convincing, fake phone number to give out. One of the favorites of the privacy community is a story-reading phone number: 720-865-8500. You might also remember the number of a major museum or something of this kind. Just please: don't use a random number—that's very inconsiderate to the person who will get spam.

Interlude: Buying a Phone

I get a lot of questions about which phone someone should buy, and my default response is to explain that it doesn't really matter as much as you think. Let's start with the basics. Many people assume that dumb phones— old-fashioned models that have limited features—are inherently more private than smart phones. Sure, dumb phones don't have the social media apps and other revealing features, but they do connect to satellite towers the same as smart phones: thus revealing the user's location at all times. Most dumb phones that I'm aware of also rely on standard text messaging (SMS) and satellite phone calls, which as we've already discussed are visible to service providers and others who might intercept them. In other words, the adventurous allure of dumb phones outweighs their actual usefulness. On the contrary, the benefit of smart phones is that they can use secure messaging apps whose content cannot be deciphered by anyone. But here's the fundamental point to remember: any time you use ANY phone—dumb phone or smart phone or Linux phone or GrapheneOS phone or whatever—it connects to a satellite or a tower, and thus reveals your location.

That's not to say that some phones aren't better than others. For starters, any phone that can use private messengers is superior. That excludes many dumb phones, but also recent batches of experimental "privacy phones." Chief among these are Linux phones such as the PinePhone and the Librem 5. While I applaud the creation of Linux phones, these phones have two problems. First, they do not solve the reliance on the same cellular towers, and thus they are as vulnerable to geo-location as any other phone (the same problems apply to alternative privacy operating systems such as GrapheneOS and LineageOS). Second, these phones don't currently allow you to use popular messaging apps such as Signal and Wire. That means you can't use them to talk to most of the people in your life, who by now I hope you have convinced to join these messengers. In effect, this makes these Linux phones useless for the only thing I want a phone for: talking to my circle. I hope these companies can solve their numerous hardware issues (another story altogether) and allow private messaging onto their systems, but for now I cannot recommend them above any other phone.

The next question I get is Apple versus Android. And once again, it matters less which phone you use as how you use it. My suggestions have been to make your phone life minimal, and you can get all the essential applications—private messenger, browser, offline maps—with either of these brands. Android is a more open environment than iOS. This is its strength and weakness. While you do have the opportunity to download more kinds of apps, not all of these apps are curated, and your risk of getting malware is higher on Android. Android phones are also more diverse, and don't always get security updates as consistently as Apple phones do. As a basic rule, if you plan to use more than the basic apps I've suggested, you're better off with an iPhone. Just make sure not to give real information to any phone upon starting it up for the first time. This includes when creating your mandatory Apple ID.

When it comes to the actual act of buying, remember to pay cash for a phone and don't give out information along the way. Yes, that means your current phone, if purchased with information connected to you, can never fully be private. When buying a new one, Amazon and other online retailers are out. While you could buy one with a gift card paid in cash and deliver the phone to someplace that isn't your own (such as an Amazon locker), these days Amazon is highly suspicious of new accounts using gift cards, especially for high-price items. You could easily be locked out of the account and lose your pricey gift card as well. Physical stores are best. Furthermore, always buy "unlocked" phones that are not tied to any carrier. This allows you to pay for service through month-to-month providers that don't require your personal details. Not only are leased phones bad financial practice, but they also gives the company who "sells" them a foothold into your life, and leave the indelible mark of your identity on that particular phone.

Part 2: The Serious Method

Are you ready for the bitter pill? Nothing you can do can stop your phone from broadcasting your location to the far reaches of the world. This section will show you how to escape the geo-location exposure of your phone, which is its greatest privacy obstacle. As we established earlier in this book, your location is choice information and you should guard it preciously. Reread Chapter 1 if you have doubts about this. Then consider the story of Zachary McCoy.

Zachary was notified by Google one day that they had given his data to law enforcement. *What?* It turns out—after McCoy burned through his savings and family money to hire a lawyer and investigate—that he had unknowingly rode his bike near a crime scene multiple times while using a biking app. Police had immediately set up a "geofence warrant" in the area and forced Google to reveal anyone who had crossed it. McCoy, who had a Google app on his phone (as most of us do), became a suspicious person. Such policing strategies are becoming more common: requests from state and federal law enforcement authorities in the United States by one study have increased "more than 1,500 percent from 2017 to 2018, and by 500 percent from 2018 to 2019."[87] For McCoy and many others, location data is the difference between having financial and physical freedom, or not.

---

[87] https://www.nbcnews.com/news/us-news/google-tracked-his-bike-ride-past-burglarized-home-made-him-n1151761

For those of us fortunate to never have been at risk of physical harm, our location seems a trivial thing and something we are okay to give up for the convenience of mobile phones. But I would urge you to think more deeply about the matter. Geo-tracing, the tracking of people based usually on their phones, is highly desired by any number of private organizations and governments.

Consider the following examples:
- Verizon Wireless in the US offers a service called Verizon Insights, which sells the historical data of people in particular areas (a Trump rally, for example) to companies who want to target them with ads. It's not difficult to imagine how this could go wrong. I have no doubt that most other telecom companies have a similar service.
- Police widely use phone tracking to determine who has been at protests.
- Other private organizations track phone data, such as an advocacy group that tracked messages from an anti-lockdown protest in the United States during the COVID-19 hysteria.[88] The result was a predictable flurry of media articles demonizing the behavior. Keep in mind that many people believe anti-lockdown people to be the equivalent of bio-terrorists.
- Car insurance apps increasingly use location to judge the behavior of their clients and to adjust rates accordingly.
- Cars increasingly have built-in GPS units.[89]
- Various studies have found that you will be charged more on some online stores depending on your zip code.[90] [91]

---

[88] https://www.theguardian.com/us-news/2020/may/18/lockdown-protests-spread-coronavirus-cellphone-data
[89] In one infamous press conference, a Ford executive said that "We know everyone who breaks the law, we know when you're doing it. We have GPS in your car, so we know what you're doing." That was way back in 2014 and things are much worse today. https://www.businessinsider.com/ford-exec-gps-2014-1?op=1
[90] https://www.wsj.com/articles/SB10001424127887323777204578189391813881534
[91] https://www.washingtonpost.com/posteverything/wp/2014/11/03/if-you-use-a-mac-or-an-android-e-commerce-sites-may-be-charging-you-more/

- Governments have broad access to this information. So definitive is metadata[92] that Michael Hayden of the NSA and CIA once admitted that "We kill people based on metadata."[93]

These are just examples in peacetime. Much more has taken place during our "war" with the "invisible enemy" of COVID. Lockdown geo-tracing has become a premium item. A mandatory app in Poland notified police "if users fail to respond within 20 minutes."[94] South Koreans, whose phones are closely attached to their state ID, received text messages revealing who they walked near on any given day. These location-revealing messages exposed spouses having affairs, ruined friendships, and even caused one man (a glitch) to risk losing his job and family when he appeared in a shady part of town. Another Korean man with the virus threatened a restaurant he visited to make his illness public unless they paid him off.[95] Meanwhile, in Taiwan, the government created a mobile fence around people based on their phone that they were told not to leave.[96] The stories have only become worse as the government lockdowns have continued.

So what can be done about your phone's location data? First it's important to realize that your phone transmits your location in multiple ways. The first way is the regular electromagnetic signal that it transmits to nearby cellular towers. The second way is a built-in GPS unit that works with location-based apps: anything from Google Maps to weather apps (which record and sell user data[97]). There are some basic things you can do to mitigate some of the effects of tracing:

- Turn off GPS and location services when you don't need them. Airplane mode usually accomplishes this.
- Don't approve GPS functionality for new apps; investigate already-installed apps to remove their GPS approvals.
- Avoid apps that rely on GPS.

---

[92] Metadata is data about data. In other words, not your phone's actual message content but the fact that you called your sister at 1:30 a.m. for two hours after you called Planned Parenthood earlier in the day (you're having an abortion).
[93] https://www.rt.com/usa/158460-cia-director-metadata-kill-people/
[94] https://news.yahoo.com/selfie-app-keep-track-quarantined-poles-204858799.html
[95] https://www.theguardian.com/world/2020/mar/06/more-scary-than-coronavirus-south-koreas-health-alerts-expose-private-lives
[96] https://www.reuters.com/article/us-health-coronavirus-taiwan-surveillanc-idUSKBN2170SK
[97] https://www.theguardian.com/technology/2019/jan/04/weather-channel-app-lawsuit-location-data-selling

- Keep Bluetooth off as well, since it's also been known to track your location, including the aisles you go down in stores.[98]
- Consider a Faraday bag, such as the kind made by Silent Pocket. These bags are named after English scientist Michael Faraday, who made a number of discovers in the realm of electromagnetism. They essentially block all signals to and from your phone. It's a pretty extreme kind of thing. It is, for example, one of the only reliable ways to prevent electrical equipment damage during an EMP (electromagnetic pulse). For our purposes, a reliable Faraday bag insures that our phone is sending absolutely *nothing* out into the ether.

However, these are imperfect solutions. At some point you'll need to use your phone's data, and turning it on might very well update all the previous locations you have been. As for signal-blocking bags, you can't use your phone when it's sealed in a container that blocks its functionality, and the moment you remove the phone from the bag, you are spewing out your data like a broken faucet. Even the newly popular GrapheneOS operating system on Pixel phones (which have used for a while now), while excellently stripping out all Google analytics, still must connect to cell towers to function. There's only one method to my mind that can solve this problem.

The MySudo-iPod Touch Solution

The privacy community[99] has developed this technique. I don't claim ownership of it, though I have had success in using it, and desire to share it with you with my own touches. As a heads-up, it involves spending some money, and the application needed here (MySudo) is not available in every country. You can, however, replicate the idea using your own Internet-based services, which are becoming more plentiful as we move toward data abundance.

The iPod Touch, as it happens, is one of the best privacy "phones" you can imagine. Bear with me for a moment. Here's the basic approach:

- You purchase an iPod Touch and an iPhone privately (cash, no personal information).

---

[98] https://www.nytimes.com/interactive/2019/06/14/opinion/bluetooth-wireless-tracking-privacy.html
[99] Most prominently Michael Bazzell and Justin Carroll

- You purchase a subscription to the MySudo app with an Apple gift card, which allows you to have multiple VoiP numbers (Internet phone numbers). This means you can send and receive phone calls and text messages using a legitimate phone number, but solely through the Internet or data.
- You connect your iPod Touch and iPhone so that they can both use the same MySudo account
- You use your iPod Touch at home, since it has none of the chips that phones have, and is thus devoid of GPS and NFC signal capabilities.
- You keep your iPhone in a Faraday bag and only take it out when you are some distance from your home. It is your travel phone. You never take it out otherwise—at risk of messing up the entire strategy.

This system accomplishes most of what we want. It allows us to use phones to their full potential without revealing home location. We can use a regular phone number to make calls to other regular phone numbers from home. We can't do this with Signal, Wire, or Session, since the receiver must also have the app. *Unfortunately there is no simple way to protect your geo-location info while using your phone out and about.* All that we have done here is give ourselves the ability to use a "phone" (iPod Touch) that can call regular phone numbers from our home without the tracking.

If you follow this process, make sure to do the following:
- Test your Faraday bag to make sure it is unshakably reliable.
- When connecting your iPhone and iPod Touch, do it miles from home. The MySudo apps will ask for a QR code to share. You could print it off—or take a photo of it with another phone—so that your devices don't have to be in the same vicinity.
- Consider buying headphones to use with your Touch, which understandably skimps on some of the quality hardware of other Apple devices (such as the speaker).

This is not the easiest system to follow, and unfortunately involves dropping some cash to purchase the devices and the subscriptions.

Please note that MySudo is not without issues. Since it relies on data it can be less stable when far from towers. It also is incapable of receiving "short codes" as of August 2022, which are one kind of verification message that services send to you during account registration or for suspicious log-ins. In late 2020 PayPal changed to short code overnight, locking out many MySudo users who only had that way of getting into their account. I still use MySudo, but I take extra caution with company's that have reputations like PayPal, and I make sure to have alternative two-factor log-in options such as Authy for all websites.

Though we're moving quickly toward internet calling and away from the concept of a phone number, there are still surprisingly few easy options for regular calling from your desktop computer. You could use a Skype phone number or Google Voice number. These aren't my favorite companies by any means but they get the job done when you need to make that call to someone who doesn't share your encrypted apps. MySudo, as a privacy-focused company with all the things we want, should be your first choice. My point is that your basic movement should be toward using Internet-based text and talk service. A clever person could, for example, use MySudo or even Google Voice with a laptop or iPod Touch and simply stop near a Wi-Fi spot anytime he needs to check messages or make calls. Most of us hop from one Wi-Fi spot to the next already. Think about how you can set up your own system that doesn't rely on phones.

In summary let me reiterate that phones are not vessels for any kind of privacy. All phones have young operating systems that allow promiscuous integration between apps and geo-location. Most phones have cameras, microphones, and biometric sensors aplenty. Most damning, phones are all too often connected to our personal location and cannot function without broadcasting this location to nearby towers—and anyone who is listening. The phone surveillance debacle is exactly what happens when we let technology become our master. Take back your digital privacy by performing more of your essential functions on a locked-down Linux PC.

[Note: Updated in late 2022. If you refuse to take the serious method, at the very least make use of a Pixel phone converted to GrapheneOS. While this does not eliminate the geo-location problem we have discussed, it does give you a fully-functioning phone that strips out all Google elements. So long as you buy the Pixel phone with cash, and a SIM card with cash, and immediately convert it to GrapheneOS, you will have a pretty good phone. See online tutorials for GraphoneOS]

Interlude
A Brief History of the Death of Privacy

Now that they're located, I can trace their movements anywhere on Earth, and can watch their actions in detail if I want to. That's far better than locking them up.

- Childhood's End

Modernity and particularly the twentieth century is the story of many things —some dreadful—and intertwined through all of them is the death of privacy. Privacy is not dead, but has slowly and continuously been dying. What do I mean by privacy? We need not over-complicate it. I mean the social climate that supports a person's ability to be left alone if that is what they wish.

The defining feature of the last hundred or two hundred years has been centralization, which arrived in many forms: urbanization, industrialization, central policing, the nation state, the welfare state. Looking back it all seems so inevitable. Yet paradoxically, it was decentralization that launched modernity.

Some accounts of the origin of modernity list Martin Luther as its chief prophet, or Descartes, and with good reason. Both men made the individual the locus of authority. Luther upended the centralized Catholic establishment, insisting that unmediated individuals alone could find their salvation through God. Descartes likewise put emphasis on subjective experience, showing logically in his *Meditations* that all knowledge is filtered through our mind, our thinking ability the only thing certain to exist.

Ideas have consequences. The philosophical decentralization of Luther, Descartes, and their compatriots played out in the birth pangs of the modern nation state. Pleased to have gained power from Rome's loss, now "protestant" regions of Europe formed their own clearly-defined areas, solidifying their borders, laws, and customs. *Cuius regio, eius religio* ("whose realm, his religion") was born. This double-edged statement of self-assertion and state coercion is the defining statement of modernity. Its dueling central- and decentralization played out across the next centuries and made its way, for our concerns, to the nineteenth and twentieth centuries.

Urbanization
‾‾‾‾‾‾‾‾‾‾‾

The Industrial Revolution began in Britain and turned London into the largest city in world history. In 1800 around 90% of Britons lived in rural areas and 10% in urban. By 1900 these numbers had reversed. This astonishing migration remains the trend for developing nations: today one in eight people lives in the largest 33 cities on earth.[100]

The funneling of people into cities puts a great strain on society. With urbanization comes differing levels of success and the formation of mobs or "classes"—Karl Marx wrote his manifesto in the heart of London at this time. Mixing different groups and animosities demanded stronger policing and surveillance. In 1829 London formed a central police—the first of its kind—to handle a new class of deviants: anarchists, socialists, and various cult-like groups, who blossomed in the stimulating hyper-connected city life. Police began to patrol the streets to crack down on illegal activities. There was much to find. The police and people mutually reinforced each other's existence.

Urbanity and privacy do not happy bedfellows make. In the slums of London and Dublin dozens shared single rooms and the intimates of life were communal more often than preferred. Such horrific conditions were documented by no less than George Orwell in his *Road to Wigan Pier*. These people, who had chosen to give up farm for city, lost self-reliance in the process (it's estimated that 20% of British kids don't know where milk comes from) and impatiently looked to their new gods for help. These politicians pushed through regulations that halted industry and slowed for a century the

---

[100] https://www.un.org/development/desa/en/news/population/2018-revision-of-world-urbanization-prospects.html

process by which slums would turn into single-roomed apartments. Crowded spaces do not make good sanctuaries for privacy.

The Nation State

Through nineteenth-century imperialism European countries penetrated previously untouched civilizations, crudely carving chunks of Africa in the image of their own nation states. Even today these artificial lines house contradictory cultures and are rife with chaos. But the European spreading of language, technology, and travel would create a new concept: global immigration.

As swells of new migrants left hopeless places for dreams of wealth, governments begin enforcing identification papers and sovereign borders, both a rarity to this point in time. The 1914 Emergency Powers Act of Britain required Britons to own passports in order to travel. A passport holder become a different creature, a *citizen*, branded with the mark of chattel and now property of a "state." And now unable to leave without permission. Twentieth-century citizenship was more a return to feudal serfdom than akin to its noble Greek city-state origins.

Technology is a double-edged sword. The steam engine and railroad systems opened up the world to people, but also shrank the available landmass in which to hide, giving a new breed of bureaucratic governments logistical tools to control the masses. The First and Second World Wars evinced just how quickly an army could travel and conquer unlikely regions of the globe. No people would escape the grasp of the nation state. The first always-connected system was formed.

The Warfare/Welfare State

The welfare state was a serious development in human history. Make no mistake: this wasn't an act of kindness by governments. Each time the government convinced people to give it money—the threat of violence always in the periphery—it grew in power and self-esteem. Governments soon demanded ID cards of all kinds as a way to track these people and ensure they could not escape their dues. The welfare recipients were dutiful employees of Government, Inc., and in exchange for their pittances they were expected to provide all manner of detail about their lives to "prove" their identities. But so thankful and convinced were these people by the project of nationalism and statism that they willingly walked into meat grinders in Europe during the First World War.

A good crisis must never go to waste. Though European governments found hardly enough money for a year of war, they chose to leave the gold standard, creating money and debt out of thin air, in order to fund three more years of sending young men to the sausage machines of France. Such "monetary" theories were already in the air. In 1905 Georg Friedrick Knapp put forth so-called modern monetary theory: its message that "money is a creature of law" and not a mere measure of produced value. The Federal Reserve in the US was created in 1913 to print American dollars according to its whim. With direct control over money supply the welfare state was ensured, passports and other identification issued, nationalities solidified, taxes levied and surveillance established to track down a new category of enemies: evaders. In later decades the language would be revised: "enemy of the state" and "unpatriotic" now suffice for daily discourse. Laws such as the 1917 US Espionage Act remained in place to quell free speech and discourage disobedience to this new order.

Today your tax dollars fund your own surveillance. For Americans the NSA Utah Data [Surveillance] Center runs on $40 million of taxpayer money per year—just for electricity.[101] The average American works until August for the government to pay for such pleasantries. Some believe that privacy is simply a matter of passing more laws. Do they mean laws like the PATRIOT Act? Like the state laws in the US that are being written with the "help" of Big Tech?[102] I'm sure that enlarging government with new powers and money will protect our privacy. There can be no question of that.

Science and Art: The Era of Knowing

Art and entertainment both recorded this new privacy-draining reality but also contributed to it. Realist and Modernist art, which thrived at the turn of the twentieth century, took great pleasure in erasing private spaces. Emile Zola, staunch proponent of naturalism—an aesthetic philosophy that sought to capture everyday life—imagined art as bridging the gap between public and

---

[101] https://archive.sltrib.com/article.php?id=56304956&itype=CMSID
[102] https://themarkup.org/privacy/2021/04/15/big-tech-is-pushing-states-to-pass-privacy-laws-and-yes-you-should-be-suspicious

private. Art in the eyes of Zola and William Dean Howells and the numerous apologists of this creed saw the home, and the bedroom, and the private activities of daily life as the territory for art.

Modernists went further. James Joyce offered not third-person description but pure subjectivity through his stream-of-consciousness technique in books such as *Ulysses*. Every mundane and nasty detail—not meant for public discourse, as the book-banners would argue—that comes to the protagonist's mind is recorded. This was thought to be freeing for the individual, though it had the effect of stimulating and normalizing new ideas of surveillance and exposure. So persuasive was the Realist creed that it became the untranscendable standpoint of most art today, taught in MFA programs, expected of most fiction, and neurotically pursued: *Red Dead Redemption 2* had a dedicated artist for its realistic blades of grass.

Other intellectuals helped to speed along privacy's end. The new field of psychology performed its own mind-reading as it tried to understand the patterns of human thinking. This was led by Sigmund Freud and his influential *Psychopathology of Everyday Life* (1901). In the book Freud the character wanders around encountering people whose mental motivations he guesses based on the evidence at hand. Its structure is similar to the Sherlock Holmes stories, which began a decade earlier, and which had begun to popularize the detective tale. Holmes' deep desire, "to lift off the buildings and reveal their inhabitants," would represent many of the intellectual impulses of the new century. Sociology, anthropology, and the new post-Darwinian sciences (genetics, biometrics, etc.) were eager to pierce the vale of man to discover what he was thinking, why he was behaving as such, and what he might plausibly do next. Its social manifestation was central planning.

Francis Galton was the epitome of the Victorian scientist. Omnivorous in his interests, relentless in his experimentation, and penetrating in his analysis, Galton's gaze turned in nearly all directions. In his early adulthood he traveled widely, including the Victorian-obsession of Africa, where he would map out the cartography of Namibia and for which he would earn a fellowship with the Royal Society and produce a book, *The Art of Travel*, which is still sold to this day. Such thirst for knowledge led him to the laboratory where he put to use his agile mind in scientific and mathematical endeavors. Through his tireless experiments he would become the first major proponent of questionnaires, fingerprinting analysis, forensics, biometrics, and behavior studies. He would also make impressive advances in statistics, genetics, and even meteorology. He coined the term "nature versus nurture" and "eugenics" and such were his insights that Charles Darwin addresses him numerous times in his 1871 sequel *The Descent of Man*. Galton's desire for quantitative measure was so extreme that it even led him to empirical studies on the power of prayer and the proper way to cut round cakes so as to preserve moistness. Nothing in the physical realm escaped his grasp. He was the father of what we in 2021 is called "Big Data." The rise of science has coincided with a stripping away of privacy as a social value.

The Advertising Industry

In his extreme essay "The Culture Industry" Theodore Adorno suggests that popular culture and its advertising has so completely hijacked the human psyche and enveloped its world that it can think of little else. Others have made similar observations; Marshall McLuhan suggests that media are a mesmerizing extension of the human nervous system and involved in a sinister distortion of reality. In the twentieth century the private sector advanced just as steadily as the public (governmental) sector, worming its way into every house on every package and every TV screen and radio broadcast. The twentieth century is the story of large corporations tapping in to psychology to develop their advertising.

One of the less appreciated reasons for the expansion of capital in the twentieth-century was its appeal to the new field of psychology to direct its previously amateur advertising. It is only fitting that the father of advertising and public relations, Edward Bernays, was the nephew of Sigmund Freud. Freud had already taught the West that he had discovered a hidden container within the human mind and roughly mapped out its motives with the help of the likewise burgeoning behavior theory and Darwinism. In surprisingly revealing texts such as *Propaganda* (1928) Bernays explains the careful psychological manipulation that has taken place in the professional advertising industry from its inception.

Today few people have original thoughts; their sentences string together phrases heard on Netflix, their ideas replicate pundits and podcast hosts. The average person in the developed world looks at screens for twelve hours a day, mesmerized by pixels designed (in content but also in form) to exploit their psyche. Privacy assumes an autonomous region of the individual, a part of our identity that is not subject to external penetration and that is distinctly "myself." But most of us today don't even have that.

<u>Privacy in the New Dark Ages</u>

The science fiction of the past is becoming the present. Elon Musk's Neuralink, which began testing in 2020, promises to embed computers into human brains with the idea of connecting them to the Internet and, consequently (and ironically), to each other. The so-called Internet of Things is the new direction of technology, enabled by faster satellite networks such as 5G, which abandons the bottleneck of cabled physical connections. Planned economies and government intrusion show no signs of giving up; if anything they are growing more insistent as "smart cities" are under development.[103]

In short, centralization is beginning to rule. The original Internet (Web 1.0) promised anonymity and openness. Today a handful of websites dominate Internet traffic and dictate what others can and cannot express. Many websites refuse to serve people who hide their IP address. A handful of financial companies determine who can have the privilege of paying for goods and services. Federal and worldwide organizations gain power as local ones lose theirs. Privacy is decentralization. Anything that happens beyond the local is exposure. As decentralization dies so too does privacy with it.

---

[103] https://en.wikipedia.org/wiki/Smart_city

Chapter 6
Financial Privacy

Obligatory note: This chapter is not legal or financial advice. Nothing in this book is advice of any kind. You should consider consulting a qualified professional who understands your specific needs before doing anything in life.

Money is an incredibly important dimension of our lives and is consistently under threat whenever it is exposed. From petty thieves and malware extortionists to fellow voters, police cabals,[104] and sue-happy pedestrians, modern humanity shows no end to its appetite for other people's assets. Opinions range widely about what financial privacy is and these opinions often split along lines of age and wealth. My chief aim in this chapter is to give a holistic sense of each of these dimensions of financial secrecy, which encompasses everything from which currency you use, where you choose to bank, what financial applications you use, to even what clothing you put on in the morning. Every decision you make has the power to expose your financial status. Hiding your wealth from whoever you can is one of the most important things you can do in life.

Financial privacy involves protecting any asset that you have by hiding the thing itself or your ownership of it. These assets might be tangible (your money, your vehicle, your business) or intangible (your identity, your online business, your digital data). Thanks to moral decay and increasing poverty in Western countries, your enemies to financial privacy are expanding every day. Thieves are ever-growing in number, and in the digital era have many more angles of attack. Sophisticated extortionists hijack computer cameras to snap nude photos and threaten publication if no payment is made. Public

---

[104] https://reason.com/2014/09/12/how-cops-got-a-license-to-steal-your-mon (original story has been deleted from *Forbes*...)

"intellectuals" publish books with titles like *In Defense of Looting* to tepid approval. Equally immoral are the masses of sue-happy "fellow citizens" eager to soak up whatever money they can from you: from "tripping" on your iced walkway to taking you to court for refusing to bake a wedding cake.[105] This is especially the case in the litigious United States, which is so legally backward that a burglar sometimes has grounds to sue if they're injured while ransacking your house.[106] [107] Financial privacy, by hiding and separating your assets, can protect you from many of these assaults on your wealth.

What is Your Wealth and Do You Own It?

I like to begin with the deepest fundamentals and I look at history as a man might seek out genetic testing for heritable disease. Modern financial assets are surprisingly complex. You have tangible and intangible assets; assets based on government decree (fiat) and assets that have intrinsic value. If you tell your financial advisor that you want to buy gold he'll give you a dozen options: physical gold, gold bullion in a safe offshore, gold money, gold stocks, mining stocks, options, etc., etc. Wealth is no longer an issue of simply owning physical things in the here-and-now.

On the contrary wealth historically was stored not in banks but by holding tangible assets: real estate, gold and silver, art, furniture, and other objects. This meant it was private so long as one protected one's house from invaders. Today, conversely, most of us trust our currency to banking institutions and only have theoretical control over it. Acquire even a small income and you're likely to put that currency into one of these banks. Indeed, the banking system as it exists today, a product of the early modern period, has become such a central institution to developed economies that using money outside of the system is a highly suspicious act. Try paying for something substantial with an envelope full of £50 notes in Manchester or $100 bills in Boston and see if you don't get a few stares, or a nice chat with the police. Countries such as France and Italy have made it outright illegal to make cash purchases over a certain and fairly small amount (more on this later).[108] The point is that today we are expected—indeed, required—to trust our money to banking institutions and their digital transactions if we want to remain above suspicion.

---

[105] https://www.foxnews.com/us/colorado-christian-cakeshop-sued-discrimination
[106] https://www.rodriguezlaw.net/can-burglar-sue-injury/
[107] https://www.homevestors.com/blog/crazy-stories-homeowners-sued/
[108] https://www.stripes.com/news/italy-transactions-exceeding-1-000-euros-must-be-electronic-1.165892

The cruel irony is that today's banks don't even keep the money we entrust to their vaults. This behavior, called *fractional-reserve banking*, means that most banks hold only a tiny percentage of the money you give them and, consequently, that these banks can only pay you if they happen to have money available when you visit.[109] If an economic downturn hits and people make a run on the banks, almost no one will get their money: now or later. And you can forget FDIC insurance. That's right: not only will you be put on an explicit or implicit blacklist for paying with physical currency too often or in large amounts, but by putting your currency like a dutiful subject in a bank you renounce your ownership of it.

The privacy consequences flow from these facts. Governments have enjoyed the centralization of money as a means to survey their citizens. Most banks today have to perform endless KYC (know your customer) checks on you before you can use their service. This makes bank transactions highly transparent. It's not difficult for a bank employee, a hacker, a private investigator (who perhaps knows a bank employee), as well as government and its policing agencies to have a rather detailed road map of your financial life. Nor is stashing cash offshore any longer an option. Thanks to insulting international regulations such as FATCA and CRA,[110] if you open a bank in another country—a decent privacy option in past decades—that bank must reveal its existence to your home country or risk being coerced in various ways. Banking privacy is dead.

I bring up the fundamental problem with banking today to show you the scope of the problem. As we discuss financial privacy in this chapter just remember this deeply rooted problem within our system. Financial privacy today is more about thinking either beyond the system, or remaining within it and thinking about smaller ways to protect privacy and security when faced with adversaries.

---

[109] Some banks, especially in Germany or Singapore, have better service, better interest rates, more international flexibility, and hold a larger reserve of your money (see *Global Finance's* "World's Safest Banks" list).

[110] Short for "fat cat," the Foreign Account Tax Compliance Act in the United States; CRA is the Common Report Standard which functions similarly for other countries who have agreed to its terms (note: many have).

First Keep a Low Profile

Mark Skousen's Complete Guide to Financial Privacy (1982) was essential reading in its day. Unfortunately, thanks to recent banking regulations and the broader digitization of financial industries, many of his privacy techniques are no longer applicable. But Skousen is correct in the fundamentals of financial privacy, and this anecdote from his book sums up the first and most importance lesson:

> Two millionaires were partners in a commodity investment firm in Chicago. One lived in a huge estate on the South Shore, drove a Rolls-Royce and had a summer cottage in California. He was audited [by the IRS] every year. The other millionaire lived in a nice middle-class neighborhood, drove a mid-sized Chevrolet, and put his money in 'out-of-the-way' investments. He has yet to be audited.[iii]

I'm certain that the second person was also more protected from petty thieves, scammers, lawsuit-seekers, and private investigators. Whether you're a wealthy person with a serious target on your back—especially during an era of "eat the rich"—or a twenty-something graduate student living month-to-month who simply can't afford to be sued, you need to start thinking carefully about what you present to the world.

Keeping a low profile as a means to protect your finances can be simple. It might involve not wearing your fancy watch and Sunspel polo shirt in a dangerous neighborhood; or buying a five dollar bag of ice-melting salt for your sidewalk to protect against a multi-thousand dollar lawsuit; or driving a run-down Ford instead of a Mercedes Benz. It might mean that you don't share photos of your stacks of gold on Facebook for the world and your tax agency to see. It's tempting to flaunt your wealth, but doing so enhances your risk. Consider the following ways to keep a low financial profile:

- Invest your money on the interior or chassis of your car instead of the exterior.
- Remove decals on pricier vehicles: "Lexus," "Mercedes," etc. You could even replace them with decals from a cheaper brand.
- Dress to fit your surroundings. In more low-key areas avoid expensive logos on clothing, business attire, shiny watches, etc.

[iii] Page 176

- If you like to wear watches, avoid metallic ones, which attract much more attention than leather or fabric straps.
- Deter quota-driven cops by making a habit of driving the speed limit and use tools to detect them in advance (Waze, scanners, etc.).
- Donate to local police departments and put an "I Support the Police" sticker on your back windshield. "Blue Lives Matters" stickers should do similar work.
- Consider public transportation or ride-sharing instead of taking your own car out.
- Avoid posting anything online. If you do, make sure it doesn't reveal your house, wealth, or lifestyle in any way.
- Avoid talking about your finances to your kids, friends, or anyone else. Never admit what kinds of things you own.
- Be careful criticizing governments or tax agencies publicly. As for me, I love the governments and tax agencies of the world.

The billionaire Howard Hughes, one of the richest men of his era, refused to live casually, which ultimately cost him his peace of mind and, it seems to me, his life. He stubbornly chose the best hotels wherever he went and spent far too long in media-saturated cities such as Las Vegas. People *knew* when Howard Hughes was staying somewhere. The irony is that Hughes craved privacy. With his wealth and resources he could easily have purchased a private island where no one would have bothered him. You will get the attention you deserve.[112]

Use Cash, While You Can...

As we discussed in Chapter One, cash is a privacy-lover's financial tool. Money that you *possess*, as opposed to credit cards which you *process*, allows you to pay for things in the here and now, and to do so privately. When you buy products on credit, or online, you're making a promise to that company that they will get paid. Since they don't see the cash in front of them, they need some kind of guarantee, and this means a promise from VISA or some other *fintech* solution, which of course is backed by your KYC, credit history and all the information tied to it. As I explained in Chapter 3, your digital payments

---

[112] See *Howard Hughes: The Hidden Years* by James Phelan for the story of the world's most reclusive man—who spent hundreds of millions on his privacy.

reveal *when*, *where*, and in many cases *what* you purchased. It's not difficult to get a clear picture of what someone is all about based solely on their credit card trail. Do your best to get off of a credit card cycle, begin building a stockpile of cash through prudent living, and start using cash for as many purchases as possible.

Properly executed cash transactions—i.e. those without personal info attached to them—can in themselves be private, but they also create additional privacy opportunities. A stockpile of cash means the next time you go to buy a vehicle you can look for a private sale instead of going to a new car dealer, where they will demand every piece of information from you short of extracting your DNA.[113] Cash has other benefits. Studies show that people who use cash spend less than their credit card peers. Paying with cash also means you can get discounts; try asking your local store owner directly. These owners appreciate cash—they lose at least 3% every time you swipe your card for their service—and they might appreciate private cash for their own reasons. Philosophically speaking, having cash in hand brings you closer to what money really is. One article on the topic argues that this is precisely why Germans refuse to give up cash.[114] Since around 92% of the world's wealth exists only as numbers on a computer screen,[115] being more in touch with something closer to physical money gives you a greater appreciation for the process of earning and spending it. Just don't forget that government currency units are themselves just an image of what money really is.

Unfortunately cash is headed toward extinction in many parts of the world and this poses great risk to your present and future privacy. This sad reality first sank in with me when I committed to using cash a few years ago while traveling in the US. I noticed that merchants would scrutinize even the smallest of my bills and often looked inconvenienced by my insistence on using it. On one occasion, which I have yet to replicate, the clerk at a clothing store even pulled out a machine and ran each of my $20 bills through it! When I asked what she was doing she mumbled something about "counterfeit bills." Another person at a Target in the United States stared at my $20 bill as if it was the first time he had ever seen one. I've begun to ask clerks about cash

---

[113] Listen to *The Privacy, Security, & OSINT* Show - Episode 135 for a humorous and stressful example of how difficult it is to purchase a new car without giving too much information (in the US).
[114] https://www.bbc.com/worklife/article/20200520-will-coronavirus-change-germans-love-of-cash
[115] https://economictimes.indiatimes.com/tech-life/12-weird-but-true-facts-about-technology/changing-fonts-can-save-printer-ink/slideshow/51419400.cms

and note their similar response: "Yeah, not many people use cash these days." As can be expected, during and after the COVID-1984 years, cash will be villainised for transmitting that "invisible enemy," as Donald Trump called it.[116] While no one has rejected my cash yet, I've encountered shops that limit cash purchases to a single inconvenient cashier till, and all shops seem to have signs demanding correct change. In some cases refusing a cash purchase is illegal, so you might play that card if you're ever rejected.

The 2020-2021 fear pandemic aside, nations vary widely when it comes to their cultures of cash, and you would do well to take note of this. Of course there are many un-banked nations in Africa, the Middle East, and South America where cash is still the norm—though local cash is sometimes worthless or unavailable (Euro and Dollar preferred). Furthermore, just as these regions skipped computers for smart phones, so too will they move from cash to digital currency seemingly overnight. The financially sound nations of Germany, Austria, and Hong Kong still rely heavily on cash, though reality can change quickly, as you can see in Hong Kong. Other countries have rejected cash, such as Sweden, Singapore, and increasingly the UK. After the Charlie Hebdo attacks in Paris many European Union countries restricted cash in various ways. Italy and France limited physical cash transactions to as little as 1000 euro,[117] although no one can feasibly monitor Emil and Pierre if they have a friendly transaction in the privacy of their homes. I encourage you in your travels to take out cash and test it on the locals to see how far you can get. People traveling in China recently have noted that cash is almost entirely rejected in its cities, and everyone—including the homeless—bank using the mobile app WeChat and soon will all be on a central bank digital yuan.[118] [119]

Assuming your country still accepts cash, you would do well to keep some on hand. During the Euro crisis in Greece, the government shut down all ATMs, forcing Greeks to barter with whatever they had.[120] The Mediterranean island nation of Cyprus had their own financial crisis, which shut down banking and even led to politicians stealing half of the money anyone had over 100,000

---

[116] https://www.theguardian.com/world/video/2020/mar/23/invisible-enemy-trump-says-he-is-wartime-president-in-coronavirus-battle-video

[117] https://www.french-property.com/news/money_france/cash_payments_limits

[118] There's a great book called *AI Superpowers* by Kai-Fu Lee that describes this trend, which I highly recommend.

[119] https://www.reuters.com/world/china/china-expand-digital-yuan-experiments-central-bank-vice-governor-2021-04-18/

[120] https://www.express.co.uk/news/world/587493/Banks-ATMs-Greece-crisis

euros.[121] Scary stuff. More recently, during the COVID government lockdowns, many banks and ATMs have been shut down or have minimized their cash reserves. Calls for federal digital currencies have already been launched,[122] and the currency-printing presses of the world are conveniently having trouble introducing more coins into circulation despite working at record rates.

Just don't keep all of your currency in physical cash. You won't be able to send it very quickly and you'll lose the opportunity to invest in anything that requires an online transaction. Furthermore, cash under your mattress will always be victim to the whims of politicians: it's value will slowly erode through inflation, or might be revoked altogether. In November of 2016 the authoritarian prime minister of India, Narendra Modi, abolished the 500 and 1000 rupee notes for reasons of [terrorism, crime, you name it.]. With these notes now "mere paper," as he said, chaotic crowds rushed to turn them into the new approved rupee notes within the allotted time.[123] As you can imagine, some Indians even died as a result of this shock to the financial system,[124] and I'm sure that people who turned in large bundles of cash on these days were put down on suspicion lists. Different but equally troubling events occur in the USSA where police practice "civil forfeiture," otherwise known as theft. If you're caught with an envelope of cash in your car in the US—let's say you were driving to buy a used vehicle from a Craigslist ad—then they can take it from you. It becomes your job to go through the legal process of proving that it is yours and obtained lawfully. Police extortion of course is already expected in many of the "undeveloped" nations of the world. So while cash can be good to hold, it requires some precautions. Make sure to keep any ATM receipts and consider digitizing them.

There's also the question of storing cash. Higher denominations store easier, while smaller denominations are less suspicious and less likely to be taken out of circulation. Have a balance of small and large. You might still be able to find 500 euro bills, which can store a lot of money in very little space, but these recently stopped production to combat money laundering and terrorism and

---

[121] https://www.businessinsider.com/r-amid-fears-of-greek-controls-cyprus-shows-restrictions-are-bearable-2015-6

[122] https://www.msn.com/en-us/money/markets/lagarde-says-her-e2-80-98hunch-e2-80-99-is-that-ecb-will-adopt-digital-currency/ar-BB1aXnU2

[123] https://www.indiatoday.in/india/story/live-pm-narendra-modi-addresses-nation-350943-2016-11-08

[124] https://www.latimes.com/world/la-fg-india-currency-20161115-story.html

all the usual excuses. In better news, the Swiss still make a 1000 franc note which, though under pressure for the same reasons, still exists. The Swiss franc is as stable a currency as they come—a point not to be overlooked when collecting government currency units—and you could do a lot worse than collecting a few of these. Assuming you've already picked up a few ounces of gold.

Let's discuss your acquisition of cash. While cash may be private, it still has to come from somewhere. Remember the flow of information? Think for a second about the flow of cash. If you take money from your ATM, then your bank and other surveying parties know that you have some of it in your pocket.[125] This might not be a big deal, but it could bring you unwanted attention and, in the event of a lawsuit, you could be expected to make that cash available since its existence is documented by its serial number.

Instead of an ATM, use the following methods to get cash more privately:

- Pay for something at a store with your debit card and get cash back. As far as the bank is concerned, you simply spent a lot of money at a shop.
- Pay for something for a friend with a card and have them reimburse you with cash.
- Take out cash with a credit card ("cash withdrawal") which should be documented as a credit card transaction. Not all credit cards allow this, but for those that do you should also be able to take out larger amounts than with your debit card.
- Use any opportunity to collect more cash from friends, Craigslist, your renters, etc.

Be sure when living a cash lifestyle to be aware of the reporting that goes on behind the scenes. In the United States, any cash transaction over $10,000 (including ones that add up to this amount over a period of days or weeks) are expected to be reported to authorities.[126]

---

[125] Some theorize that they even record the cash serial number and connect it with a store you shopped at. It's not exactly an easy trail to establish, but could theoretically be used to get a broad sense of your whereabouts. One solution is to exchange your bills for different bills at a local store.

[126] https://www.irs.gov/businesses/small-businesses-self-employed/form-8300-and-reporting-cash-payments-of-over-10000

You can also only take so much money out of an ATM. In many cases this is a mere few hundred dollars or so (following the crisis in Cypress the Cypriot people could only take out 100 euros per day[127]). Expect these withdrawal limits to shrink in the crisis moments when you need cash most. You might be able to solve such problems by having multiple checking accounts, by calling your bank to ask them to raise it as high as it will go, or by making use of credit card cash withdrawals. You could always visit a local branch of your bank, but they'll likely view you suspiciously if you ask to take out your own money. It's best to get the cash you think you might need now and accumulate it slowly. Considering the abysmal interest rates of savings accounts in places like the US, you may as well hold onto the physical cash yourself.

Living a cash lifestyle has drawbacks for which you must plan. Walking around with a fat wallet is asking to be robbed. Plan accordingly:

- Put in your wallet just enough for the day or week and hide the rest somewhere safe.
- Use a money belt, or a money clip in your sock when transporting cash. Be creative and commit to a routine.
- Thanks to worldwide inflation (money printing by central banks) you may soon have to lug *a lot* of cash in your wallet;[128] for this reason you should invest in a wallet designed to hold lots of cash.
- Hide your money at home in boring locations: in between book pages (a great way to send cash via mail, by the way), in junk mail envelopes, etc.

As a final note on cash, as a privacy-conscious person you should commit to paying in cash for everything you can, and to inform yourself of the war on cash and where it is going (start by following The Watchman Privacy Newsletter). The key to getting money in the bank is to first get off of your credit card cycle. If you're barely getting by each month you should examine your life to see what's going on: (1) Do you live in a city that is unnecessary for your life and three times more expensive than a smaller town? (2) Are you spending too much either on essentials (housing utilities) or non-essentials (3) Do you need to develop skills—via books, YouTube, and the Internet, etc—to get a higher-paying job? Taking full reign of your financial life is a prerequisite

---

[127] https://www.rt.com/business/cyprus-bailout-withdrawal-banks-756
[128] An extreme example is Zimbabwe, which peaked out at printing 100 trillion dollar notes. They're serious collectors' items these days.

to anything else, and if this is your problem then privacy is the least of your concerns. Get disciplined, start saving a minimum of 10% of your monthly income (bump that up higher when you can), live with parents and friends if necessary, check in to counseling, and get your life on track today. Then get some cash in your hands.

Private Online Shopping

Okay, okay, but forget cash, I just want to buy a few liters of Poo-Pourri from Amazon without someone knowing about it.

Fair enough. The problem is that any online transaction inevitably has a trail. This is simply how the Internet works. Consider the flow of information for an Amazon purchase. You use your credit or debit card that has your name and address and you input it into Amazon's text box and press submit. That means Amazon knows that information, as does the bank that issued your card and the card processor (VISA, for example). Additionally, thousands of Amazon employees can access this information (if you doubt me, ask an Amazon chat representative any question about your orders) as can thousands of employees at your bank or card processing company. All of whom can be socially manipulated by hackers, by the way. Furthermore, the transaction is attached to your Amazon account permanently, so any *future* Amazon/VISA/Bank employee/hacker/etc. will see it as well. And, lest we forget, governments can gain access to this transaction, and lawyers would love to take a peak if they are granted a warrant in order to better "judge your character by the things you purchase." There are a lot of people that could have access to your online purchases and a lot of ways they can be used to harm you.

For a one-time private purchase online, use a gift card. Let's take Amazon as an example.

**Note: this process has been revised since Amazon in early 2021 started ramping up scrutiny of account creation. It is nor more laborious, but still might be worth it for you. I personally lost a high-denomination gift card to this new scrutiny as Amazon locked my account and refused to reopen it even after I sent proof. The new system is not to be trifled with and demands that you condition a new account to fit their level of suspicious. Here are the new more rigorous steps to take:

- Create a new Amazon account and don't use any real details. Do this in a public Wi-Fi spot without at VPN and with at least a ProtonMail account—not an alias email account.
- Go to a physical store and buy an Amazon gift card with cash. Don't go big to start. It's best to start with a small amount.
- If you can, wear a hat and mask that hides you from the cameras.
- Now buy a cheap item on Amazon with the gift card and send it to an Amazon pick-up location nearby (not all items are eligible, including third-party items).
- Go pick it up and hide your face from the camera.
- Now your account should be "trained" to buy other items.
- You could also just ask a friend to buy the item for you and pay them with cash. Don't forget the simple solutions.

The gift card method can be used by most companies that issue gift cards. Just keep in mind that websites are increasingly scrutinizing. Sophisticated algorithms determine your level of risk and might flat out reject your purchase or account creation if you don't win this game. You can lower your risk by using public Wi-Fi with no VPN, by making sure the billing and shipping addresses are in close proximity, and by making your fake info as "real-looking" as possible. Begin with small purchases—use the company's gift card if possible—and pay for some of their services (Amazon Prime, Amazon Video). This will make them happy.

Oh, but I don't want to give up my Amazon account. It's like a history of my life that I would be giving up!

Exactly, a history of your life that tells *way* too much about you. I remember sifting through a friend's Amazon account that he used for a decade. You could tell a lot about him based on this history. Start a new account now and consider changing your account regularly from now on, particularly when you move. Reserve a section of your password manager for old Amazon account log-ins in case you need to review your history later on.

Maybe this is a bit too inconvenient for you and your regular *Poo-Pourri* buying spurts. It certainly is more work than having Amazon deliver to your house with one action from your phone. Let's move to another option then: *digital burner debit cards.*

We are fortunate that many new types of financial institutions are cropping up to assist with privacy, even if internet-based operations will always be traceable in some way. One option is digital burner debit cards, which I suspect will gain popularity in the upcoming years. What is a digital burner debit card? Basically it's a legitimate and disposable debit card that you create online and that you fund with a connected checking account. For example, let's take the US-based Privacy.com:

- You sign up for an account and give them your information (name, address, date of birth, phone number) for KYC reasons—the same as with any banking institution.

- Once you are verified on Privacy.com (I don't recommend taking a selfie with your ID if they can't verify your account—though they have become more unyielding in 2022) you can start creating and using digital cards.[129]

- Once inside your new account, simply press "create new card" and the website automatically generates a usable card number (VISA, Mastercard, etc), expiration date, and confirmation code: all the stuff you would expect from a physical card.

- You can now use that card with any name and address you want and it should be accepted immediately—assuming the shop doesn't flag the transaction, which happens occasionally, and which can be exacerbated by the variables I previously mentioned.

- Now when you buy your toilet paper on Amazon and they ask for payment, you can give them this card number, use a fake name and billing address (try to be convincing), and Privacy.com will process this transaction on the spot.

- As an added benefit for services like this, you can pause, delete, or set limits to cards to protect against companies pulling more money from your account without your permission.

Let's be clear about what a service like Privacy.com does for you. Privacy.com knows that you just bought a thing from kinkytoys.net. Your bank, however, does not know. Nor does kinkytoys.net, assuming you gave a false name. Burner cards are simply a way of hiding from some, but not all, your third-

---

[129] Customer service tends to involve reasonable people, so if you're asked to give ID explain your case and that you are a follower of various privacy shows. They might let you continue.

parties. As such, they are by no means a silver bullet, and you should treat them with the same skepticism you would treat any institution.

Oh, and you can also sometimes use Privacy.com cards for purchases in person as well. Generate a few cards in advance and store those numbers in your phone or print them out and put them in your wallet. If you find someone who will accept card numbers as opposed to physical cards, give it a try. One common tactic is to say that you forgot your card, but then pull out your phone and say that you have your card number on it. Plenty of shops will work with you under those conditions and type in the number manually.

Privacy.com has limitations. Most significantly, it is only available for US persons right now. These cards also cause confusion for merchants at times. A friend recently told me she placed an order from a popular clothing company that sent her a full receipt. Only a week later did she call them and discover that the transaction would not go through—apparently their systems do not accept these cards, and they didn't have the courtesy to let her know. I know many who have cards rejected now and then, but they also have generally high success rates in most places, including airlines and hotels.

[Update in late 2022]

Privacy.com has become more scrutinizing of accounts. They still have flexibility, so if you can provide them with proof of identity without giving a selfie, that is always preferred. Financial institutions will always require some amount of ID. I have come to rely more (while traveling in the US) on prepaid debit cards, including for online purchases.

Alternatives to Privacy.com exist and will no doubt be cropping up more regularly:

- PayPal behaves somewhat similarly, though I'm reluctant to recommend it wholeheartedly given its reputation of terrible customer service (I've had experience with it myself). With a Paypal account you can make purchases from websites where the website—and your bank—only see a PayPal transaction. PayPal will of course know everything, but it could be better than nothing in a pinch.
- Revolut and TransferWise are two new fintech options that are globally-focused and worth looking into. We'll discuss more options in future Watchman podcast episodes and newsletters.

- Prepaid debit cards, paid in cash from a shop like Dollar General, regularly work well. You will have to pay around $6 for this one-use card: though you can purchase amounts up to $500 at a time.
- You can also use cards on your MySudo app, if you're using it based on my recommendation from Chapter 5.
- Finally, you can in some cases make online purchases using cryptocurrencies such as Bitcoin. We'll talk in a moment about the potential of cryptocurrencies, but know that it is increasingly an option.

Be on the lookout for creative payment opportunities. Some VPNs allow you to pay for your yearly subscription with random gift cards, for example. And increasingly (at least with VPNs) you can send cash through the mail, as unbelievable as that sounds in today's climate. As more of our purchases happen online, websites are looking to attract customers—privacy focused ones included—in whatever ways they can.

Gold, Precious Metals, Collectibles

In this section I use the term gold to stand in for all precious metals—although gold has its own favorable attributes that make it particularly desirable. It's worth your time to explore this topic on your own.

Gold has been valued by humans and used in financial transactions for millennia.[130] This trend shows no signs of stopping. Unlike dollars or euros or pounds gold has value quite distinct from government approval. While governments can ban gold or take their currency off the gold standard, gold retains and often increases its value because of its intrinsic value: its beauty, industrial utility, malleability for jewelry, etc.

Gold is your ally in financial privacy for several reasons:
1. It transcends national boundaries. Assuming you can get your gold across the border, you can find a ready buyer in nearly any part of the world. Most countries allow gold to come in while some have

---

[130] Places such as India are known for interest in gold: Indian women own nearly four times as much gold as is in Fort Knox: https://www.npr.org/sections/parallels/2014/04/14/301412384/a-gold-obsession-pays-dividends-for-indian-women

restrictions and others reporting requirements. Reasonably-sized and spread-out gold jewelry can often get around this.

2. Gold carries a lot of value in a small amount. In current prices (2022), a single ounce of gold could buy you a very cheap car or pay for living essentials for a month or two.

3. Gold is not traceable. Even if it did have markings of some kind, it could be melted down and reformed to erase these.

4. Gold tends to increase in price during crises such as the ones we will be encountering in the 2020s. In other words, during the times you would want privacy, gold not only tends to hold but increase in value—sometimes mightily.

5. Gold does not degrade over time. You can store it underground or at the bottom of the ocean and dig it up decades later and it will be the same. Silver and the other noble metals, it should be noted, do degrade.

6. Gold is not always subject to taxation and reporting depending on where you live. For Americans, who are otherwise steeply regulated by the IRS, precious metals held in private foreign vaults do not need to be reported (they can also be purchased with cash and no reporting requirements). Astonishing, I know. This exemption, along with foreign real estate, are two of the only assets that Americans don't have to report.

It is in your interest as a pursuer of privacy to own precious metals as a way to hold and even transport wealth. I am speaking, of course, of physical metals. Owning gold stocks is not the same as owning gold. Nor is trusting your gold to a foreign vault, as beneficial as that can be in other ways. There is no replacement for having physical gold in your possession within arm's reach.

The privacy of gold depends on how it is purchased, and purchasing gold privately is fairly straightforward:

1. Obtain cash in the most innocuous way you can (see earlier in the chapter), and preferably in a different city/state/country than the one in which you will be buying gold.

2. Visit a shop, friend, or gold show and buy gold coins or bars with cash. Do not show any ID or give any personal information.

You'll also want to consider some of the following aspects of gold buying as you make your purchase:

- Choose carefully where to buy your gold. Reputation is all you have to go on since testing is not exactly an option. Buying or bartering from a trusted friend might also be a good option. Just choose someone who would never rat you out.
- Start visiting local shops. You want to find a place that accepts cash without requiring any information from you.
- If you can't find a shop, expand your search. You might search for "coin shows" in your area.
- Be very careful buying from sources that have no reputation. While gold can be tested to see if it is real, this is difficult and not likely to be possible at the time of purchase.[131]
- It doesn't hurt to ask the seller how they verify the authenticity of their gold. You might detect a suspicious tone, get a sense of their character, and even start to build rapport.
- If buying a serious amount of gold, find out the laws surroundings such transactions. In the US, a money order can get around the $10,000 cash reporting requirement.
- Leave your phone at home when going to buy gold. You don't need that GPS record attached to you.
- Be sure to wear your COVID mask when entering any shop to block your face from the camer...from infecting others, of course (you should be able to play that card for the next decade).
- Selling is also an important consideration and might bring about new reporting requirements. I talked to one gold shop owner who said that local laws demand that your ID be scanned. The copy is destroyed months later and never leaves the shop. But that still leaves the printer hard drive, and any law enforcement who presumably can look at these. This is unacceptable.
- Be patient. There's no reason to buy gold until you have found the right place that you trust.

---

[131] With that said, one option is to bring a weighing scale to the sale—anything more or less than an ounce (or a troy ounce depending on the coin) should elicit suspicion.

Some people ask me about buying gold online. It's unlikely to work. The scrutiny of IP address, physical address, and other aspects will be intense. Your best bet if you want to experiment is to be as unsuspecting as possible: public Wi-Fi, no VPN, Windows operating system, Chrome browser, no virtual machine, realistic name, actual physical billing address near your location, shipping address nearby, etc. Still, they'll compare the shipping address to public postal records and if it doesn't match up, they'll cancel in a heartbeat. Your only option at that point is to find a small shop or a church who would be willing to accept a package for you. They'll also likely give you a call to confirm your identity, so give a burner number that you can answer. Smaller orders are more likely to go through.

Then you have the problem of paying privately. If you use a credit card then you've automatically established a connection to yourself, so that's not a good idea. Some online retailers use BitPay to accept Bitcoin (you'll probably only want to choose the most reputable online dealer). If you have clean Bitcoin (discussed in the next section), then you might be able to pull this off. You'll just want to be careful what you use that Bitcoin account for in the future, since now it is attached to a precious metals retailer.

In short, buying gold with cash in person is by far the best way to do it.

Gold is not without its flaws. While it holds a lot of value per ounce, it's not entirely portable. Mileage varies in terms of taking gold on airplanes. In many cases you're expected to report items over a certain valuation, and you can be sure the scanning machines of your airport will detect the metal. Then again, the scanning agent will likely have little interest and simply move you along (more likely during a domestic flight). Gold has also been made illegal in various countries and throughout history, including the United States.

If you must transport gold, you should consider the following:
- Move it by car instead of plane.
- Hire a private shipping service to handle it.
- Move it slowly to your destinations over the course of many trips.
- Always bring proof of ownership with you. (Digital, hidden in an encrypted container. See Chapter 4.)
- Avoid putting it in checked baggage. At least when you walk through the scanners you have a chance to talk to the agents.

- Put the coins in your wallet with your other coins. If you have half-ounce coins these will be as small as most government coins.

Another option to acquire gold might be to buy a gold watch or gold jewelry, which have added value because of the craftsmanship. You'll be just another person walking around with a fancy timepiece. If you're in a bind, also consider diamonds, which might show up even less—if at all—in airport scanning.

In terms of other valuable items that function similarly to gold (as a physical asset on your person) consider the following:

- Diamonds and jewels, though these have value largely as a result of a seriously good marketing campaign as opposed to any serious intrinsic value. Fake diamonds are also becoming almost indistinguishable from real ones, and "home grown" diamonds are becoming common. In short: make sure to keep verification of diamond authenticity.
- A wristwatch by a world-famous watchmaker such as George Daniels might be worth as much as seven figures and might not pique too much interest. It's just a watch, after all.
- Paintings will also do the job and may even increase in value better than some assets.
- Comic books. A nice copy of Action Comics #1 sold for more than three million dollars in 2014 and could easily be slipped into the zip section of a suitcase.[132] The comic book market is robust and by no means a bubble. Make sure to get a CGC rating for rare comics, which is a global standard.
- Antique boxes, furniture, and other items. These can be quite valuable and even smaller in size than you would think.
- Shoes. Believe it or not, shoes such as Jordans are valued in the six figure range these days.[133] This is a very stealthy way to transport wealth. Beware the bubble, though.
- Stamps. The stamp market is surprisingly robust and stamps store a lot of wealth in a tiny package.

---

[132] https://www.cnet.com/news/supermans-action-comics-no-1-sells-for-record-3-2-million-on-ebay
[133] https://stockx.com/news/most-expensive-air-jordans

- Non-fungible tokens (NFTs). Okay, these aren't like gold at all. But they are digital assets purchased with cryptocurrencies that in mid-2022 have a lot of value attached to them. Just pursue at your own risk.

The challenge here is purchasing these items with as little a connection to you as possible. Going to a comic book convention and pulling out a briefcase of cash might not go over so well. Be patient in acquiring assets, think quantity as well as quality, consider whether their value will remain in the long run, keep searching, and try to avoid suspicion as best you can.

Cryptocurrencies

In their frequently prescient book *The Sovereign Individual* (still a great read) authors Davidson and Rees-Mogg predict an untraceable "digital currency" that would escape government regulation and ultimately bankrupt the tax-mongering nation state, replacing it with sovereign individuals who would once again become financial institutions unto themselves. It's an idealistic future and one that doesn't ruminate on the vast growing pains in that violent process. Still, cryptocurrencies present one of the best opportunities for private banking, private purchases, and true ownership (i.e. private property) and you would do well to become familiar with their workings. I have expended a lot of effort on this topic via a paid course which you can find at www.bitcoinprivacycourse.com. I share the basics in the following pages.

Bitcoin is simply computer code that is verified by an army of computers running Bitcoin nodes across the planet. Part of this code includes the blockchain, a public ledger of all the bitcoin in existence. The owners of particular segments of this chain—what we call "bitcoin"—possess the private keys to it, which allow them to give ownership of those bitcoin to someone else or to hold onto it in anticipation of future value increase ("hodling"). The blockchain is updated and verified by "miners"—beefy computers running Bitcoin software—and by individuals running "full nodes" that keep a record of that ledger. The code of Bitcoin has solid economic models like scarcity in place and can hardly be tampered with, leading many advocates to argue that Bitcoin offers the best alternative to the corrupt fiat money system that we currently have.[134] Users like you and me interact with this blockchain by downloading a computer program called a wallet that can store and organize

---

[134] I have interviewed people such as Jimmy Song who explain this in detail.

private keys. From the wallet one can easily transfer one's coins to someone else's wallet for a small fee that goes to the miners. With Bitcoin it is possible to send a large transaction across the world in a matter of hours (or minutes) with the click of a button and without any KYC or "verification." Try doing that with a bank account. Regardless of how you feel about Bitcoin, you have to admit that it is revolutionary and empowering.

What about the privacy of cryptocurrency? Especially given the suffix *crypto* ("hidden"), one would assume digital currencies are private. Not exactly—and not all of them. Let's establish some basic facts:

- First, as Internet-based technologies they will always have some trail that leads back to your online identity. You can distort this by using VPNs, TOR (see Chapter 8), and by making sure whenever you interact with crypto-related resources you do so with the privacy techniques described in this book.

- Second, not all cryptocurrencies are coded the same. Bitcoin's blockchain—the collected transactions of every transaction ever—is public. By contrast, the privacy coin Monero has a blockchain that is hidden.

- Third, depending on how you acquire your Bitcoin, you might erase your initial chance at possessing it privately. If your Bitcoin comes from a Kraken or Coinbase account that has all of your personal information attached to it by means of mandatory KYC, there will always be a record that you owned that Bitcoin. You can either sell it back to the exchange and buy via other methods, or send it to a self-custodial wallet such as Samourai or Sparrow that can remove the deterministic links tying you to that exchange via their CoinJoin Whirlpool software.

- Fourth, your Bitcoin can be revealed moving forward. The only way to keep privacy while using Bitcoin is to make use of the Samourai Wallet or the Sparrow Wallet and the privacy features that they offer, and to practice what is called "coin control," or labeling and keeping track of particular chunks of bitcoin (UTXOs) that make up your wallet. This is complex and beyond the scope of initial discussion.[135]

---

[135] You may start this complex journey here: www.youtube.com/watch?v=vu7h89w5byE

Some privacy advocates will say that one should never use a "surveillance coin" like Bitcoin and instead only use Monero.[136] While the features of Monero certainly maximize privacy, it is nowhere near as popular as Bitcoin. The invisible blockchain of Monero also threatens the transparency that some believe is paramount to the trust that cements Bitcoin's value. Bitcoin's juggernaut status means it is much more decentralized—diversified across the globe and in other ways—and detached from small groups of developers or malicious actors that could alter its underlying code. The practical reality is that Bitcoin is much more used across the world than privacy coins—or any coins, for that matter—and that fact alone means one should learn how to use it and make it private the best one can. You can always swap your Bitcoin for Monero using non-KYC exchanges such as the Exodus Wallet or the website Changenow.io, among others.

There are some additional vulnerabilities to crypto. For one, they rely on electricity and the Internet. If the Internet were to go out—note that 29 countries shut off the Internet in 2020 a total of 155 times,[137] including Russia[138] and Belarus[139]—then you don't have easy Bitcoin transactions. Although satellite options and other alternatives are in development from the clever and adversarial-minded crypto community.[140] As for usability, while some businesses allow crypto purchases, it is a small percentage. You probably can't pay your taxes or rent in crypto, meaning its function as currency is limited. However, as of 2022 more options are cropping up, and dedicated people do live almost entirely on Bitcoin.[141]

The first thing you'll need to do before acquiring Bitcoin privately is to download a wallet. I recommend starting with the Sparrow Wallet on your computer which can be downloaded at www.sparrowwallet.com:

- Start it up and select "Public Server" and "Create New Wallet"
- Give it a name and on the next screen select the option "New or Imported Software Wallet" and press "Apply"

---

[136] See a reasonable debate here: https://stephanlivera.com/episode/363
[137] https://www.accessnow.org/keepiton-report-a-year-in-the-fight/
[138] https://www.foreignaffairs.com/articles/russian-federation/2019-03-29/why-russia-might-shut-internet
[139] https://www.wired.com/story/belarus-internet-outage-election/
[140] https://www.econoalchemist.com/post/receiving-bitcoin-blockchain-data-with-a-blockstream-satellite-node
[141] Here's a great example of how one lives on Bitcoin: https://www.youtube.com/watch?v=FoIvkMKY5S8

- Under "Mnemonic Words" select "12 words" and then "Generate New"
- These twelve words are your "seed phrase" which is the identity of your wallet. Write them down somewhere safe and then re-enter them into Sparrow to confirm.
- You can leave the passphrase blank and select "Import Keystore"

You now have a wallet that can send and receive bitcoin. The current instance of Sparrow Wallet on your desktop is simply a temporary custodian of your bitcoin wealth. Your real BTC identity is tied up in your private keys, which are themselves tied up in your "seed phrase." The seed phrase is everything, which is why some people etch them in steel to ensure longevity.[142] You can use that seed phrase to restore your funds on any wallet that supports the BIP39 protocol (which is most of them) and on any computer you come across. This is a radical concept and something that many people do not understand. Let's say you had a Bitcoin Sparrow Wallet with 0.1 bitcoin. If you ever lost that computer, you could go to another wallet (Sparrow or otherwise) on another computer, restore your seed phrase and have access to that same 0.1 bitcoin. The seed phrase ensures that bitcoin remains a digital technology and can be used to hide and transport your bitcoin wealth across borders in just your head. Before doing so, and before sending and receiving transactions I would encourage you to watch a few videos on the basics. BTC Sessions is a great YouTube channel for such things. And my course covers such topics as well, as does my podcast.

---

[142] https://blog.lopp.net/metal-bitcoin-seed-storage-stress-tests-round-v

How to Acquire Bitcoin Privately

1) Get Paid in BTC

You can simply ask to be paid in BTC, let's say for a service or product you offer on your website or in your physical store. Or as a "tip" or "donation" online. Advertise that you accept and prefer Bitcoin and see what happens. In one evening you could make a helpful YouTube video, provide a Bitcoin wallet address in the description, and ask viewers to send you a donation. Just remember that displaying an address in public is an easy way for people to track down how much money you are collecting in that address. Change this address regularly, as Sparrow and most wallets let you generate unlimited receiving addresses these days. If you intend to run a business on Bitcoin, your should look into how to run a BTCPay server. This service will allow you to create fresh addresses that cannot be traced back to you. Another option for receiving payment or donations is to use a Paynym,[143] but this only works when your donors are sending, and your are receiving, via the (excellent) Android-only Samourai Wallet.

2) Peer-to-Peer Transactions

A second method is to trade with someone who already has bitcoin. Simple, right? But how do you know who has bitcoin and what they want in exchange? Start with family and friends and acquaintances. You would be surprised who in your life has some bitcoin handy. Perhaps your friend of a friend is a miner who wants to offload some of his coin. Avoid bitcoin from exchanges at this point. To find a stranger interested in peer-to-peer (P2P) Bitcoin transactions, try the following:
- Via crypto groups on Meetup.com or via the many Telegram, Discord, and Matrix groups where Bitcoiners and other privacy-seekers dwell. Some starting options include the Samourai Wallet Telegram Group, Citadel.chat, and join.bitcoiner.chat. You'll succeed in these groups (and perhaps develop long-term friends and trading partners) if you go in slowly and with the intent of engaging rather than asking for a quick transaction.
- Crypto events such as conferences, where many crypto-owners can be found.[144]

---

[143] https://bitcoiner.guide/paynym
[144] https://bitcoin-only.com/conferences

- If you don't have any luck with these, you can find strangers online willing to trade bitcoin for cash (in person or via payment services) or even gift cards. The best services/websites are Bisq, Hodl Hodl (European focused) and LocalCryptos. I know dedicated privacy bitcoiners who get most of their private crypto in this way. It takes some time to learn the system, and you should not give up information along the way. The website https://kycnot.me gives a good overview of what KYC is demanded from these services. A good service such as LocalCryptos will serve as an escrow so that the seller keeps their end of the bargain; they will simply arrange the transactions and not require information otherwise. Even if you paid someone on LocalCryptos with Paypal, that simply shows up as a private payment between two individuals: LocalCryptos does not have anything on it. If approached correctly, the peer-to-peer method is quite promising. Just avoid sellers who demand identification (obviously), and spend some time to see how it works before jumping in.

It's really a matter of looking until you find someone willing to trade. Remember that if you develop within a community, which will likely include Bitcoin miners and other people who want to get fiat currency to pay their bills, then you can have a potentially endless stream of Bitcoin at your disposal.

Obviously, if you meet with strangers in person, don't give out personal info and take precautions. A public place with Wi-Fi is a great spot, especially since you can use your computer to confirm that the transaction has gone through (with a VPN, of course). Wait until at least one confirmation goes through, which should take a few minutes. Leave your phone at home or put it in a Faraday bag so there's no GPS trace to you and this transaction. Use your laptop instead.

3) Mine It Yourself

You can actually mine BTC to acquire it and this gets you perfectly clean and private bitcoin. "Mining" is what processes the Bitcoin blockchain—it's what keeps the whole thing going. A small reward of new bitcoin is automatically given to miners for their work. In early 2022 a single Antminer S9 might earn around eighty dollars worth of bitcoin per month while a newer more efficient

Antminer S19 Pro might earn you $700 per month—at ten times the price of buying the machine. This does not include the huge electricity costs, which might wipe out 20-30% of those profits depending on where you live. If the price of Bitcoin goes up, you can expect your mining profits to go up as well.

If you have interest in mining you must buy a dedicated ASIC machine such as one of the Antminers I mentioned above if you want to get anything more than pennies. Given chip shortages, popularity, and manufacturer preference for bulk sales to large mining companies, you have to do some work to pick one up. Avoid eBay and Amazon. Instead try a website like MineFarmBuy.com or UpstreamData.ca. These are trusted by the Bitcoin community. You can also lurk on Telegram groups such as KaboomRacks. These are simply the ways to acquire these things. Try to pay in a private way (many of these companies only accept bitcoin) and have it shipped to at least a PO box separated from your real address. Use a router-level VPN if you don't want your ISP knowing what you're up to. The best guides come from Diverter_NoKYC and Econoalchemist who I have interviewed on my podcast about this topic.[145][146]

As a final note, these machines make tremendous noise and chew through electricity such that, if you live in America, you will likely have to bring in a certified electrician to create a 240 outlet for you, and will have to think carefully about when and where you use them. Various methods exist for cooling and blocking out the noise on these machines. The Ohmm Black Box by Upstream Data is one such remedy for residential mining.

4) Bitcoin ATMs

Yes, there are Bitcoin ATMs, most of which are in the USA. Exchanging cash for Bitcoin is great, but this option has several problems. The first problem is whether you have one nearby. Check coinatmradar.com, bitrawr.com/bitcoin-atms, and Google Maps (using TOR or a VPN). The second problem is whether a particular ATM let's you buy Bitcoin without giving KYC information. Few allow this. I've had success at several ATMs that only wanted a phone number for SMS "verification" and a name. With the name, of course, you can put whatever you want. For the phone number, you can visit an SMS verification website and use that number, though ATMs are

---

[145] https://diverter.hostyourown.tools/mining-for-the-streets/
[146] https://www.econoalchemist.com/post/home-mining-for-non-kyc-bitcoin

catching on to this and either rejecting such numbers or placing daily global limits on these. One popular site is freephonenum.com, but a better option is TextVerified.com, which requires an account and payment (Bitcoin possible), but gives you a number that is solely yours: this makes it much more likely to be accepted. You can visit one of these sites by bringing your laptop and connecting to local Wi-Fi so that you don't need to use your phone and risk its GPS trace. You could always ask someone to do this process for you.

ATMs charges high fees, usually ranging from 5% to 20%. This might be reflected as an actual fee or as an extra high price for Bitcoin on the screen. The high fees help to pay the businesses that run these machines and to help them account for the wild fluctuations in BTC price on any given day. Also note that some Bitcoin ATMs struggle with constant errors. A colleague of mine visited one ATM six days in a row and there was something different wrong each time. These are flawed machines that rely on bad Internet connections. If you're having trouble you might try early mornings and weekends when the network traffic is clearer. ATMs might also have limits on how much they will give out on any given day for all customers combined. These are highly privatized machines that vary widely in terms of fees, mechanics, KYC demands, etc.

Also remember that you're on camera, possibly from the ATM and the store you're in. So wear a big hat and a mask. You can also take a sticky note with you that you put on the ATM camera. Approach from the side. Take it off when you want to swipe your wallet QR code (generated from your Sparrow Wallet), which you should always print off on paper.

Most ATMs will demand KYC verifications, and especially if you select anything higher than the lowest amount to buy. I've noticed in 2022 that it's becoming quite difficult to find ATMs that don't demand ID. For that reason you might want to focus on the other methods in this chapter instead of wasting your time driving great lengths for ATMs.

5) Novel Options

As crypto becomes more popular new opportunities crop up regularly. Here are a few ideas:

- Some Bitcoin stores exist where you can buy and possible sell in Bitcoin. You're also likely to find people who might be up for a good trade.
- Sell an item on Craigslist and advertise "crypto accepted" for purchases
- Visit a crypto community like Bitcoin Beach in El Salvador and do your selling/trading there
- Get someone else to go through KYC for you (such as an ATM) and pay them in cash
- Look for jobs that pay in Bitcoin. Sites like the subReddit Jobs4Bitcoin are fantastic for digital work such as video editing, etc.

Once you start accumulating Bitcoin you'll want to keep a few things in mind. It's best not to make too public of a display about it, otherwise you may tempt thieves and others who would do you harm.

This brings up a final point. How will you store your Bitcoin? Crypto exchanges such as Coinbase, in addition to stripping privacy and easy ownership, are also vulnerable to hacking the same as any financial institution. In fact nearly all of the major crypto exchanges have been hacked.[147] Your software wallet (Sparrow) is much safer in that regard, especially if you use Linux, which is less prone to malware. But if you refuse to use Linux, or want to diversify your risk, you might consider a *hardware wallet*. Allow me to explain:

- A hardware wallet is a physical device that can create a seed phrase and sign crypto transactions without any connection to the Internet. I prefer the Coldcard for Bitcoin.
- This makes them less susceptible to digital attacks as compared to "hot wallets" that are always (or often) online.
- You purchase the device (from the company's website preferably), and initialize it.
- You write down the seed phrase that the device gives you and store it safely.

---

[147] https://www.cryptoglobe.com/latest/2019/12/these-top-exchanges-have-been-hacked-so-far-or-not/

- When you want to transfer bitcoin to your hardware wallet, you set up a transaction between your Coldcard and Sparrow wallet using a MicroSD card. You transfer the partially signed bitcoin transaction (PSBT) on the SD card between your computer and the Coldcard until the transaction has been made. This is an involved process that you should watch various tutorials on before proceeding.
- You now have your bitcoin wealth enmeshed in a seed phrase created by a device that remains disconnected from the Internet.

I find hardware wallets somewhat overrated, since the likelihood of your software wallet being compromised if you are careful of your computer habits is highly unlikely.

Other Private Payment Methods

Some of the best ways to acquire items privately happen outside of the traditional payment methods.

Use the following list to come up with your own ideas:

1. Barter. Don't underestimate the value of your skills compared to what other people want. Barter your skills online and in your local community. You can put up a listing on your local Craigslist or Reddit, for example. Start up a barter system in your neighborhood or among your friends.
2. Money orders and cashier's checks can offer some measure of privacy and tend to be accepted in situations where cash might not be. Favor money orders over the two, but don't buy them with your other post office purchases. They work similar to cash but aren't beholden to the same cash reporting requirements. Leave everything blank that you don't need to fill out.
3. Gift cards. Once again, don't underestimate these handy tools.
4. Prepaid debit cards. These are very useful since they can be swiped like normal cards and work for most things that don't require a running tally (fueling stations, for example). There are limits to how much you can put on them—the VISA gift cards I recommend go up to $500 in the US. Second, they do log your purchases, which can be viewed by anyone who has your card number (Michael Bazzell once

found someone's home address based on their purchase history and a quick phone call to pest control; he already had their card number, having given it to them as a fake gift). Prepaid VISAs have an initial cost to purchase of a few dollars. Buy these cards far from home and don't return to the same place for second purchases. Buy with a wedding card to avoid suspicion, and note that some places require ID to purchase (CVS Pharmacy) while others do not.

Self-Employment aka Earning Money Privately

Your main hope of acquiring money privately is to work for yourself, and it's not as difficult as you think. I assume right now you do something at your job that is useful to your employer. Simply ask her if you could do the same things but as a contract worker. Tell her that she now won't have to pay the massive taxes and regulatory fees associated with being an employee (possibly as much as 30% of the cost of an employee!). Sure you might lose some benefits, but you'll gain serious independence and privacy. Once you do this you will be self-employed. Now go find a few more clients to give yourself a buffer.

The wise thing to do now would be to create a legal entity to provide a barrier between you and your client and so you don't have to work under your own name. For Americans, a single-member LLC is a fantastic vehicle for doing this. You'll have to learn a bit about keeping records, will have a couple more tax obligations (if you think it's rough being an employee, try being a business owner), and you may want to get some legal advice, but it will be a small price to pay for your freedom and privacy. By contracting your work to a company it will now simply be your company dealing with another company. You will send invoices in your company's name which demand payment to a bank account that your company owns. As an employee you had to give out your name, state ID number, address, and all kinds of other precious information. By using a business entity, you need not give out any of that.

Here's a sketch (not legal advice) of how to start an LLC privately in the United States, keeping in mind that American LLCs can also be amazing vehicles for privacy for international people (better, in fact):
1. Choose the structure. A single-member LLC is a great option for many people, and especially privacy-focused people.

2. Select a company to serve as your *registered agent* instead of using your own address. It is mandatory to have a registered agent on file with the state—even if it's you as the agent. By hiring a registered agent you can use their office as your government compliance address. They can also do handy things like perform the incorporation themselves and process your yearly registration, which keeps you off more record books. All of this is not only legal but fairly standard. Northwest Registered Agent is one popular example of a registered agent, though you'll find good local options on a state-by-state basis. A registered agent usually charges around $100 per year for basic services.

3. Select the state for your LLC. In an ideal world you would be incorporated in a state that does not publish the name of the LLC owners, such as Wyoming, Nevada, Delaware, or New Mexico. Just keep in mind that you are expected to register in your state of residence, and if your state of residence ever found out you were not, they might ask you to do so. Regardless of what state an LLC is registered in, you always pay your mandatory state taxes to your state of residence. That's something you never want to mess with.

4. Complete the LLC registration process via your registered agent service, giving the minimum information. They simply need to get in touch with you if something is wrong. You can give them your PO Box for the address and a phone number from MySudo. Many people have success only giving a first initial and a full last name, for additional privacy. I've seen others succeed with first and last initials.

5. Choose a business name that doesn't reveal much about you or your interests. This doesn't have to be the name you use for business (see DBA "Doing Business As"), but it will be the name registered to the state database, which is searchable.

6. Note that the cheapest states in which to incorporate (and most of them) charge around $100 for annual registration. This is in addition to the registered agent fees. Also note that this is a yearly event and some states have additional small fees. Check out the website and YouTube channel LLC University for great information on the topic.

7. Your registered agent will create the LLC and sign it over to you, so that their name appears on the "Initial Filings" documents. Even in the most private states, such as Wyoming, the Initial Filings document

and the Annual Report are public. If you use a registered agent for these procedures then it will only show their information.

8. The registered agent should send you other start-up documents: your Articles of Incorporation and hopefully a generic Operating Agreement. This is the basic documentation for your LLC. A smart Articles of Incorporation will be bare-bones, with all the important stuff occurring in the Operating Agreement. This is because your Operating Agreement remains in your private possession (and can be altered at any time) while the Articles of Incorporation might need to be given out to your bank and other entities, and is often visible in the state's corporation database.

9. Depending on your locale and type of business, you might be expected to meet various other regulations. If you run your business online and do generic work such as consulting, you probably won't have to worry about any of that. That is definitely the best way to go about it. Keep in mind that registering your business with your town or county will subject you to all kinds of public exposure.

Now you have an LLC while only giving out your first initial, last name, and a PO Box. Not bad! Unfortunately you can't really do business without a bank account. (I suppose you could if you only used cash, but that whittles down your clientele and will get you unwanted attention.) The great irony of creating companies is that it is quite easy to create the entity and much more difficult to get the bank account up and running.

For the American LLC above, you should do the following steps to get a bank account:

1. Register for an EIN number with the IRS via their website. Uh-oh. Yeah, it's time to give out some information. This is simply required if you plan to receive and send money with your company. Give them all the information they want. The application is straightforward but you can view a tutorial (LLC University) if you run into uncertainty.

2. Apply for a business bank account. I have had success with Novo, which is an online-only bank targeting small businesses. They don't have any fees, and have overall good service. Novo does not have physical branches, though you can take out cash from ATMs across the US. No problem there. Novo also doesn't give you a checkbook, though they do allow you to send checks to people via their website or app—you can also deposit checks using their app.

3. The bank application will be the most demanding part of this whole LLC process. They'll want a lot of information, including a home address (PO Box) and a phone number (MySudo), which is necessary for two-factor authentication. They might also ask for your legal ID, your Articles of Incorporation, the EIN document that you just got from the IRS, and, most frustrating, your business address. Try to use your registered agent's address. They might also ask what your business does; try to be generic but not too vague.

Now you have a functioning legal entity—though never forget that you do not need a legal entity to run a business (the benefit is some legal protection and, in some cases, privacy by means of separation from your personal life). What will you do? There are all kinds of business opportunities out there. Scores of entrepreneurs have become wealthy by sitting in front of a laptop selling items on Amazon, or creating useful information for people to consume. The most popular concepts involve giving out information on a topic you know a lot about. You create a website, sell a book, earn money from YouTube, sell shirts, and see where that gets you. Other people earn their money by seizing an opportunity and running with it. They buy items on Craigslist, improve them, and sell them for a profit. Some do the same for used books, or by visiting yard sales. There are a million business opportunities out there. I recommend reading *Unscripted* by MJ DeMarco as you start to get into the entrepreneurial life and listen to the podcast *Radical Personal Finance* (start with the early episodes). Good luck!

Offshore Banking?

Financial diversification is a hallmark of good planning and definitely of privacy. While banking abroad has been at the heart of privacy strategies for a long time, that trend has changed with international laws such as FATCA for the United States and CRS for much of the rest of the world. Basically, the banks of the world have obligations to report your accounts to your home country. Financial privacy is dead in the banking world, but that doesn't mean you can't pursue offshore banking for other reasons.

Creating an offshore bank account is perfectly legal and is simply the wisdom of diversification at work. An offshore bank account might be more difficult for a creditor to gain access to. If you were sued for hitting someone's car and injuring them, a private investigator might be hired to find out how much you are worth. Having assets in a different country can either hide it from such investigation, or make it seem difficult to acquire for most lawyers (which it is) and encourage them to back off. Having a bank account abroad is also a great first step to becoming an international nomad (see Chapter 8). I won't say anymore about this topic in this book, since achieving privacy abroad is now a highly complex endeavor that must involve lawyers, planning, and consultation. I encourage you to check out *Nomad Capitalist*, *Escape Artist*, and *The Expat Money Show* to kindle your thinking in this area.

Accounting and Taxation

Hiding money from your tax agency, especially if that is the IRS, is probably illegal and is certainly a recipe for disaster. These agencies have a lot of power to track you down and make you pay. The IRS can cancel American passports if they allege (note: allege) that you owe $53,000 or more of taxes.[148] Americans are also some of the only people in the world taxed on worldwide income. It would behoove you not only to follow the laws of the land but to take care not to criticize them in a public arena. The IRS has been known to track down those who speak out against it.[149] One famous tax protester, Irwin Schiff, actually was banned from selling his book *The Federal Mafia* in the United States—the supposed redoubt of free speech—and he ended up dying strapped to a federal prison bed for standing on principle (and the Constitution) and not paying taxes. Not all tax agencies are so aggressive. In fact some people leave their home country to join a different one that is more lenient and less interested in pursuing them across the world.

Here is some basic advice for achieving some measure of privacy during the taxation process:

- Consider having an accountant do your taxes. This could offer a bit of leniency if something is ever incorrect on the tax form (it's his fault, after all!) and your accountant should defend you in the case of an audit.
- Just make sure your accountant uses encrypted software and stores your information properly. Inquire about this and encourage them to start using it.

---

[148] https://www.irs.gov/businesses/small-businesses-self-employed/revocation-or-denial-of-passport-in-case-of-certain-unpaid-taxes
[149] I encourage you to read the book *Confessions of a Tax Collector* by Richard Yancey.

- Consider hiring an accountant who is also a lawyer, which can grant you attorney-client privilege—which means what you say to each other is granted legal privacy.
- Alternatively, if you think you can handle your taxes by yourself, then do it. Doing your taxes yourself will ensure that no one alive besides your taxing authority knows your financial endeavors—and even they don't know all the specifics.
- Non-reportable assets for the IRS include foreign real estate (in your own name—not in a company's name), and precious metals stored in a private off-shore vault. Also art, cars, and other valuable objects if they are in a private vault in a different country.
- People who make less money tend to get audited much less. It is in your power to make less money one year compared to another.
- Perfectly round numbers on your tax forms ($500 for office supplies) are a sign that you've made something up. You can look into other audit red flags.
- Many people use cloud software to keep track of their finances. Instead I encourage you to use an offline spreadsheet if it is in your power to do so.
- You can print your own cheques from home by buying cheque paper and using special templates for your typing software. In most cases, this is perfectly fine (you might ask your bank), and will ensure you can customize them to your liking. I recommend as little information as necessary (first and last initial, company name instead, etc.).
- In most countries you can have any mark as your signature. Why not make it something that doesn't actually reveal your name? Some people choose scribbles that are indecipherable.

Chapter 7
Traveling Privacy

[Academic asking the TSA why he is on the life-altering "No Fly List"]

"I explained" said Murphy "that I had not marched but had, in September 2006, given a lecture at Princeton, televised and put on the web, highly critical of George Bush for his many violations of the constitution."

"That'll do it," the man said.[150]

You've made some headway toward privacy. But it's one thing to maintain your privacy when you're locked away at home in the comfort of your pajamas and familiar internet router. It's something else entirely to maintain this privacy on The Road. The minute you step outside of your house you don't just leave familiar products and patterns behind, but you also enter a space in which you have "no expectation of privacy," according to United States law and that of many other governments.[151] As is the nature of travel, you'll have to be adaptive.

Here are the rules and ideas we will unpack in this chapter:
- Don't do anything on the road that can't wait until you are home
- Bring your own equipment
- Don't stand out
- Be cautious accessing the Internet
- Use GPS wisely
- Take precautions when driving
- Take precautions when traveling by air

---

[150] https://www.theguardian.com/world/2007/apr/24/usa.comment
[151] https://en.wikipedia.org/wiki/Expectation_of_privacy

- Take precautions when seeking accommodation
- Consider international options and alternative means of travel
- Move to new accommodation carefully and with a plan

Let's begin with the basics. As a rule, don't do anything on the road that can't wait until you get home. This includes managing your finances, sending highly sensitive messages, researching medical conditions on your computer, etc. We've talked about the added protection of a home network in previous chapters, and we know by now that foreign internet connections are hazardous.

If you must have sensitive conversations while traveling or while in public, make sure you're not on the street or around many other people—certainly don't read off credit card numbers or other sensitive numbers while in public areas. When entering passwords on your computer make sure no one and no camera is behind you. Tools can help. A *privacy screen* is a piece of tinted film for computers and phones that prevents others from seeing it from an angle. Password managers (Chapter 3) perform a similar function, hiding your password on screen while allowing you to right click and select "copy password."

Make sure your phone has a pass code if you spend much time outside of your house (or perhaps any time). Search the settings of your phone to create one. Manually select a code longer than four digits: ideally eight or whatever you can stomach. Something is better than nothing. The same goes for your other devices. Give your laptop or tablet a strong password.

Keep your devices fully charged so you don't have to rely on strange chargers. Since USB cables can transfer data in addition to electricity, public USB charging slots can be implanted with malware or share files without your knowledge or permission. Only use a traditional wall plug. You could also purchase a *USB condom* for these public charging stations, which only transmits the electrical charge from the slot. But by far the best option is to buy and travel with a *portable battery pack* such as the kind made by the company Anker. These small rectangular batteries ensure you don't have to rely on strangers during your travels.

On the topic of self-sufficiency, offset your vulnerabilities traveling as best you can. Having a gold coin (easily sell-able within 15 minutes of arriving at most major airports) and some Bitcoin in addition to a good amount of cash can protect you should you run into a disaster situation and need to get out of there. Study alternative routes out of the country, including taking a bus to a different city or country with an airport. Have backup glasses, prescription drugs, and credit cards hidden in different parts of your luggage or person.

Now that your devices are locked down, do the same with your behavior. Some of the basics of personal safety double as privacy advice:

- If you wear flashy clothes or jewelry that display your wealth—or if you stand out as a foreigner or a tourist—you are more likely to be targeted for pick-pocketing, kidnapping, extortion, or by government officials.

- It doesn't take much to stand out in poorer countries or in more casually-dressed places such as the US. Research the customs and take note of what the natives are wearing and try to mimic them.

- Avoid touristy behavior: wearing a backpack, staring at maps, sporting obvious tourist clothing, speaking too loudly, etc.

- Find a secure way to hide your cash on your person and never compromise on this. A metal-free money belt is not a bad option, especially if you regularly go through airport scanners.

Many millionaires and billionaires choose to live a lifestyle like this wherever they go, carrying just enough cash for elementary needs. They wear uninspired clothing, no jewelry, and even take public buses around town. This was a main takeaway from the famous finance book *The Millionaire Next Door:* that some rich people wisely choose to hide their wealth from a world that increasingly dislikes them or sees them as a choice target for theft. You will get the attention you deserve.

Internet While Traveling

As this book has shown, the Internet is a dangerous place even when you are under a familiar Wi-Fi network with familiar equipment. The fundamental problem with the Internet as a traveler is that you have to rely either on your mobile phone data, or trust a strange Wi-Fi connection.

Let's establish some basics:

1. Use your phone's data as a first resort. Use the VPN on your phone as well. You can even beam this connection to your computer. This is called "Personal Hotspot" on iPhones and on other devices might go by "Tethering," or "Hotspot." They can be found in the settings options of your phone. You might encounter some VPN issues using hotspots; in those cases deactivate the VPN on one device and turn it on for the other.

2. Phone data has become cheap enough in recent years that you may as well keep at least a couple of gigabytes of data at your disposal. If you're being overcharged with your service, consider doing some research to find an up-and-comer who is offering a much better deal.

3. Public Wi-Fi is only to be used if you cannot use your phone data.

4. On public Wi-Fi, As soon as you connected to a legitimate network, immediately connect to your VPN. Do not proceed until you confirm your VPN is running. Still, be careful what you do in case your software VPN crashes.

5. For more extended travel, consider bringing along your own router. You can easily attach your home router into your grandmother's modem without harming her current Internet connectivity.

6. Or consider a traveling router such as the GL.iNet GL-AR750S (or its other models), which has its own security and can be augmented with your own VPN service. It can fit in your pocket and be charged by plugging it into your laptop via USB. This powerful mini router can make an insecure connection secure and blast it out to your multiple devices. It can also ensure you don't have that split second of vulnerability in the second or two it takes to connect to your computer VPN.

GPS Navigation
=

One essential piece of tech you'll likely want during your travels is a GPS or satnav application, most likely on your phone. I would first ask you to challenge this assumption, especially for brief trips. A good memory is an incredible asset, despite the cyborg memory-enhancer that we have in our pockets. The next time you visit a new part of town, try to do so by studying an online map on your home browser. Then try to find your way home.

If you must use satellite navigation regularly for your vehicle consider buying a dedicated GPS unit. You know, those clunky Garmin devices that would sit on top of your car windshield? I have little faith in Garmin, or TomTom, or anyone else not to log my data. But as long as you buy the device in cash, don't give any information during sign up, and you make sure never to connect the device to any other piece of tech, you should be alright. These devices for some reason are still somewhat pricey, and they're not necessarily going to have the functionality of your phone app (traffic and police alerts), but they will pay themselves off fairly quickly and are more than enough to get you where you need to go.

Let's be realistic and assume you want GPS on your phone. It should go without saying that the popular GPS apps—Google Maps, Apple Maps, and Waze[152]—are not your friends in privacy. One decent alternative is OsmAnd Maps, which at least is open-source and not owned by a data-collecting company. It also works offline, meaning you can download maps and simply have your phone's GPS guide you while keeping the data signal off (most GPS applications use both GPS and data signal, which are different). Osm is slower than its well-funded competitors, doesn't have the social features, and might take some getting used to. Frankly, I still use Waze and sometimes Apple Maps. I never input my exact destination and certainly never my home address. Instead I wait until I'm a couple miles from home to start it up and select a public location close to my destination. I shut off the app when I get close, put my phone in a faraday bag, and find my way from there.

Driving

You can judge how free you are by how many permissions slips you need in order to do something. Some parts of the world demand at least two permission slips in order to drive: a driver's license and a license plate (car registration). Some places even demand you have insurance. Each of these has ample revealing data about you.

In *The Art of Invisibility* the renowned hacker and master manipulator Kevin Mitnick tells a story of how easy it was to track someone down based solely on their license plate. Angry at being cut off in traffic, Mitnick called the local DMV pretending to be a police officer, gave the license plate number, and learned the person's name and phone number. A few minutes later he called

---

[152] Waze is owned by Google

the man's phone, cursed him out by name, and issued a fake threat to have his license suspended. He also could have determined where the man lived, since an address is mandatory for car registration.

There are three privacy lessons here: one about not offending someone who can harm you, another about the kind of information that you expose by virtue of being a driver, and a third about how social manipulation can get around any perceived security. But before addressing the problem of car registration, make sure you're following the basics of driving privacy:

- Teach yourself never to go too much over the speed limit and to be vigilant in watching for police. If you have road rage, get rid of it.
- Learn where hot spots are, as well as traffic light cameras.
- Check the legality in your area, and then consider getting a *police radar detector*. They might cost a bit, but will save you time and peace of mind many times over. Phone apps such as Waze can show you the police in the area—provided a friendly fellow driver has marked them.
- Remove the idea of driving while drunk or high from even the corner of your mind. Save all of the funny business for when you're locked behind your own doors.
- Consider supporting the police in your area in order to get a sticker saying "I support the police," which you should then display prominently on your back windshield.
- Drive an unremarkable vehicle. If you drive a red Porsche, you have the attention of everyone and anyone, from lawsuit-seekers to thieves (who would love to follow you home) to the police.
- Research the most popular cars in your area and consider getting one. Subdued colors such as white, gray, and black are extremely common and will help you blend in—useful for all manner of scenarios. If you want a car that attracts attention, you will get exactly that. You can always spice up the inside or chassis of your car to make up for the outside plainness.

There is no trick that I'm aware of to hide your personal information and still have the appropriate licenses and registrations to drive. Some countries of course are more lax than others, which is important to remember. In Mexico the *de facto* penalty for driving without a license or registration might be a lot less serious than doing so in Cincinnati or Brisbane. If you want to get your permission slip to drive in places like this you'll have to give some information to the authorities.

While there is no budging with the data on your driver's license (though a postal box address might be acceptable), at least it sits in your wallet and isn't exposed to the world any time you step outside. Your license plate, on the contrary, is available for anyone to see. Police (or friends of police) can check into you without pulling you over. Private license plate readers, which are pervasive today, can tap into public databases to get an idea of who you are. One option to hide some of this information is to register your vehicle using a legal entity such as a trust or a single-member company (LLC, for example). If you live in the US, where this strategy is relatively easy, a private LLC in New Mexico (no annual fee, no tax number needed since it won't be used for business) can become the owner of the vehicle. Now when someone looks up your license plate number they will see the name of a New Mexico LLC and not a real person. A trust can also perform this duty, though the specifics are beyond the current scope of this guide.

Getting pulled over by the police has serious consequences for your privacy. The officer will run a search of your license plate and driver's license. Much of the time the officer has free reign to decide to let you go or to give you a citation—or even arrest you—and there might very well be a permanent record on you. Some countries are worse than others. In Argentina, getting pulled over might not be a big deal; in the USA, where people valorize but also fear the police, things will likely be more severe. And think twice before fighting a citation—you will have to appear in court, which is not great for privacy-conscious people. You are unlikely to receive justice.[153]

It is in your interest to be polite to a police officer at your window and ease their stress as much as possible. Wise people tend to move far off the road to give them enough space from the incoming traffic. Don't act suspicious in any way when the officer approaches (hands on the steering wheel). Prudent people also avoid self-incrimination by remaining as silent as possible, not answering any questions about "why you were pulled over," and not giving permission to search the vehicle ("I would be happy to comply with a warrant, but my lawyer has instructed me never to give permission by default"). You would do well to watch the YouTube video "Don't Talk to the Police."

---

[153] Bruce Gibney's *The Nonsense Factory: The Making and Breaking of the American Legal System* is a good place to start researching this topic.

Some readers might be baffled by the previous paragraph, as well as the other sections on policing and lawsuit-seeking in this book. That's because in your country, the police probably aren't a big issue and you don't live in a litigious culture that pumps out lawyers like it's going out of style. This is an important reminder for us all that ultimately your freedom is limited by the society in which you live, regardless of what "freedoms" exist in one's constitution. As international speculator Lobo Tiggre says: "On paper, the United States is freer than Mexico, but in fact, Mexico has become much freer than the United States, in spite of its legally powerful socialist government. The average Mexican considers tax evasion to be a universal given."[154]

You might even give up driving altogether to greatly enhance your privacy. Driving can be quite freeing, but after you factor in stress, injury, death, registration, getting sued, getting a police record on you, insurance, and maintenance, you might be better off having someone else drive you. Many privacy-conscious people rely on public transportation, taxis, or possibly even ride-sharing apps. Yes, services like Uber gobble up everything about you. They even have an infamous "God Mode" which can see every person's trip at all times.[155] But assuming you can create an account with minimal or obscure information, get dropped off a few blocks from your destination, and immediately ask the driver to work outside of the app next time for cash, it might be worth your while.[156] Arranging a private car, a taxi, or a friend who will accept cash are other decent options. Wealthy people rarely drive themselves, given the legal/financial/privacy risks of doing so. This is a lesson worth taking to heart.

Finally, I would be remiss if I didn't acknowledge that cars today increasingly have digital equipment that tracks driver data as well as cameras built into them. A few years ago a reporter wrote a nasty article about Tesla and the company responded by publishing his erratic driving pattern. Yes, they knew exactly where he was because all Tesla cars are monitored from their headquarters. Electric cars of the Tesla variety are a privacy disaster. Even standard vehicles increasingly have GPS units built into them. I'm an advocate of buying older vehicles and either learning to fix them up or having them fixed up. You don't have to be a gearhead to learn some of the basics; I promise you it can be fun, and it will make you feel strongly self-sufficient.

---

[154] Doug Casey, *Right on the Money*, pg 285.
[155] https://www.revealnews.org/article/uber-said-it-protects-you-from-spying-security-sources-say-otherwise/
[156] Though Uber today has cracked down on the data you must give them; find competitors or pursue similar ride-sharing concepts. Test things out before you need them!

Air Travel

Flying away from your hometown, as with driving, is both freeing and imprisoning. Let's start with the airport. Given all the monitoring that goes on in these places, it makes sense to act as normal as you can. Obviously don't say anything stupid or threatening, and if you're trying to keep a low profile, there's no reason to be seen in the various shops. Go from security to the waiting area and stay put. When stepping into an airport you are in hostile territory and lose your rights and privacy very quickly. Thanks to post 9-11 government overreach, plane travel has become heavily monitored, particularly in the West and especially in the US and Canada. If a TSA agent doesn't like the way you're smiling—or even if they do—they have the authority to kick you out or detain you. Unless you feel like being a hero and treating these people like they deserve, you would do well to trudge along with the rest of the herd and make as little fuss as possible.

Recognize that anywhere along the way to your flight someone with a uniform can ask to look at your phone or laptop. You can refuse, and they can refuse to let you proceed. If you are returning to your country of citizenship, then they can't refuse you and you might just play the waiting game. But to be honest, the best solution to this conundrum is to have nothing on your laptop and phone.

What do you mean?

I mean move all of your important files into an encrypted folder (Chapter 4), upload the folder to a cloud service (via its website), and delete everything else from your computer. When you arrive at your destination, you can log in to your cloud storage service, download your file, decrypt it, and put the files back onto your computer. You might think this is overkill, but imagine a police-type looking through your laptop right now as it currently is, and imagine them making copies of that information. Not very fun.

Let me unpack this process:
1. Days before your flight, organize the files on your computer as suggested in Chapter 4. Tidiness is next to godliness. Only bring what you need.
2. The night before your trip, move the files you need into a VeraCrypt folder (Chapter 4). Don't forget your password manager database.

3. Upload the encrypted folder onto a secure cloud storage such as Proton Drive or SpiderOak One. In a pinch Google Drive or Dropbox can even work because the folder is encrypted and only you have the keys: Google and Dropbox can see nothing.
4. Make sure you remember the password to your folder and your cloud storage. Don't write them down!
5. Clear your laptop of all your files. Or even better, reinstall your operating system to clear everything (in other words, replicate installation of Linux Mint from Chapter 4). It's always good to have a live Linux Mint USB drive handy for these kinds of things.
6. Arrive at the airport and walk through. Even if they open your computer, you have nothing on it.
7. Once you're through airport security, visit your cloud storage, download your file, and populate it onto your clean computer. You might wait until you leave the airport.
8. Repeat when returning home.

Phones are a different challenge altogether to take through airports. They aren't so easy to wipe, and most of us have our contacts deeply embedded into the software, among other challenges. I don't have any tricks like I do for laptops, I'm afraid, but I will suggest the following:

1. Simply don't bring a phone with you on your trip. Is that crazy? You can always pick up a burner when you arrive on the other side.
2. Or if you use your laptop like a phone as I've described in Chapter 5, then you might be able to get by with just the computer.
3. Clean out your phone so that you don't have anything on it and keep it clean. Wipe out all messaging and phone call history—a factory reset might be in order. As for photos, move them from the phone and take them via Signal from now on so they don't save locally on the phone itself. The only other major thing is contact info. I don't have any contacts on my phone. I save phone numbers and such on my computer password manager and memorize the important ones.

It should go without saying that if your computer or phone is ever apprehended, and especially if it is taken behind closed doors, you should get rid of it and buy another as soon as possible. Don't use it. You don't want to risk living with trackers on your computer, and keep in mind that they may be physically inserted into your computer and not just malware.

A few formalities and behaviors can also ensure you get ushered along smoothly at airports:

- Dress nicely during travel; wear a nice watch and otherwise appear professional (shaven, good hair, etc.).
- Have your story straight when you enter a different country. You're planning to visit a few of the sites and maybe talk to a friend. You have the name of the friend and a legitimate address. You also have the names of the places you'll be visiting and the address of a hotel where "you'll be staying." You are completely calm and unremarkable and boring.
- Approach an airport officer of the opposite sex to decrease odds of conflict. Male to male interactions are to be avoided.
- Don't put a tag on your luggage. If you must, at least tuck it into the inner compartment. Don't leave it dangling for the world to see.
- If you have suspicious books—anything critical of government or political in nature; anything religious or pertaining to privacy—either don't bring them through airport or border security, or put a different dust jacket on them.
- Rethink anything that you take with you. Could a funny photo on your phone of your naked son running around as a baby be construed as child pornography? You bet it could. Do you think your "Liberty in North Korea" keychain could be misinterpreted? Best not to test it. Stay vanilla when crossing borders.
- Practice the story of why you're in a country visiting, anticipate questions, and speak it naturally and calmly.

Airports are not fun for most people, but especially privacy-seekers. For that reason I encourage you to seek alternative ways to travel.

Alternative Ways to Travel

RVs and boats can be very rewarding private experiences. With an RV or a caravan you can essentially be a nomad, moving from campsite to hotel to B & B to friend's house with no fixed address. Should you want an address, various mail services cater specifically to this kind of person (search for nomad mail service). There's really no magic to starting this lifestyle. You simply commit to do it and go forth. Fortunately the Internet is full of people who live this lifestyle and share strategies.

You don't have to commit fully to an RV to begin. You could purchase a trailer such as an Airstream, or invest in a large van that you trick out. Indeed, there is all kinds of customization you can make to vehicles that make them livable and great for long travel, such as extended gas tanks that allow you to travel for thousands of miles.

Water crafts offer some serious opportunities for privacy. There's even a concept called seasteading, whereby you set up residence and even communities in the vast reaches of the world's oceans. The billionaire Peter Thiel has waxed eloquently about such endeavors, and real libertarians[157] have actually built sovereign houses off the coast of various countries—see Ocean Builders based in Panama, for example, whom I interviewed on my podcast.

Living on a boat is an acquired taste, but one you shouldn't dismiss without trying. If you have some money to spare (a million or two) then you can get a *very nice* small yacht, perhaps one that is powered by solar power and can travel the world without stopping. If that interests you, then Silent Yacht is your company.

The nomadic lifestyle is preferred by many people for its flexibility and, sometimes, affordability. Since it replaces a house, you save on all of those costs. Most of us can imagine what the RV life is like, but have questions about its feasibility. Let me assure you that you can find ways to receive mail (nomad mail companies), use the Internet (pervasive cell tower coverage and ample Wi-Fi), earn money (online business), and do most things that are necessary to live a full life. The benefits of this life for privacy, whether RV or otherwise, should be obvious. Having no fixed address and a constant

---

[157] Thiel used to believe in small government but now he runs a company, Palantir Technologies (yes: named after the evil crystal ball in *Lord of the Rings*) that aids in the mass governmental spying on of Americans and likely non-Americans.

scramble of GPS coordinates means that you are living the ultimate privacy lifestyle.

International Travel

It's a great blessing of our world that we have the ability to cheaply and quickly visit most places in the world.[158] This freedom is tamped down by an almost-conscious effort to discourage this kind of travel by the powers that be. Traveling anywhere outside of your country in the era of heightened nationalism can have consequences. And don't get me started about COVID-1984.

The first thing to realize is that when you arrive on the other side of your journey, if you're not a resident of that country, then *they do not have to let you in*. So they can ask to search your devices, they can interrogate you, and they can reject your entry for no reason whatsoever. So while you might decide to get perky with your home Gestapo agents, you probably don't want to cause a hassle for the uniforms welcoming you to your vacation destination.

By the way, you don't need to get that stamp on your passport. In fact, ask them *not to stamp* your passport. You don't need that marker of where you've been. And if you really don't want as much of a record of your visitation, considering flying in to a neighboring country and taking a train or bus to your final destination (cash, of course). No revealing flight itinerary there.

For those entering a new country such as the US with the intent to live there, even as a student, be aware that the scrutiny is extraordinary. Today you are expected to give over social media accounts. Saying you don't have one will make you even more suspicious. One Egyptian student from Harvard was refused access after immigration agents searched his accounts for hours and found that one of *his friends* had posted something on social media that could be construed as sympathetic to terrorism.[159] Many have been denied for even smaller infractions. If you're in such a position you should be mindful of how much scrutiny there will be.

---

[158] I wrote this before the government lockdowns surrounding COVID; expect more expensive flights and fewer of them in the many years to come. And, of course, vaccine "passports."
[159] https://www.latimes.com/world-nation/story/2019-08-27/harvard-freshman-deported-lebanese-palestinian-ismail-ajjawi

Hotels and Accommodation

Why would you want to hide your information from a hotel?

- It is your home for the night, and many a wanted/stalked person has been tracked down at a hotel.
- Hotels don't store customer data securely, as the myriad hotel data breaches have made quite clear. [160]
- Hotel desks are usually happy to reveal who is staying at their hotel to most people who call and ask politely (or in the right manipulative way, such as saying that they have a food delivery for [your name]).
- Hotels show where you have physically been, which you might not want revealed for all kinds of reasons (think COVID and geo-location at the moment).
- Thanks to our degraded society, some hotel staffers are beginning to record customers naked and blackmailing them based on the information they gave checking in. I wish this wasn't true, but it is increasingly common. [161]

Hotels today have all kinds of regulations to put up with across the world, and they have to protect themselves by having your card on file in case you destroy something. The easiest thing to do is to avoid hotels. Find a B & B with mom-and-pop owners, reserve it, and show up to pay in cash. Don't give out your real name. If you call a few of these you'll find someone who is willing to do it. Just be sure to pay them with cash as soon as you walk in to make them feel as comfortable as possible. You can make an excuse: your cards aren't working (internationally, locally), you're a victim of identity theft (it's true of all of us technically), etc.

Stay with friend whenever possible and make use of any social media network you have. Indeed, one of the most valuable things you can do as a human is to cultivate friendships and acquaintances in majors areas of the world. Many Facebook groups exist for couch-surfers and house-sharing. Obviously you should do your due diligence and try to not leave a trail on social media, but just know that there are many options these days to avoid hotels.

---

[160] https://itinerarias.com/11-top-recent-hotel-data-breaches-and-privacy-leaks-in-the-us-with-scary-statistics/
[161] https://www.nbcnews.com/news/us-news/woman-says-hilton-employee-secretly-filmed-her-naked-hotel-room-n943431

If you must stay at a hotel, call to see what they need from you. You can expect all of them to demand a card from you—so they can charge you later if they need to—and most of the time they will ask to see identification that matches the card name. To begin with, make use of a burner debit card (Chapter 6) so that you can choose any name and address. Now comes the tricky part. They may or may not want to see an ID that matches this name. If they do ask for your ID, you can say you left it in your car, or don't have it on you, or whatever excuse (you're exhausted!) you think you can come up with. Tell them you'll bring it to them later. Oftentimes a good complaining or persuasive voice can get around soft requirements.

Michael Bazzell in his book *Extreme Privacy* talks about creating his own fake ID, such as a gym membership (non-governmental, which is legal) to match his burner card name. He has a number of other fairly elaborate strategies that might interest you if you check out his section on hotel privacy. Your best bet in the end is to simply keep calling until you find someone who is willing to register you with the information you are willing to give.

A few final ideas about private travel:

- Make trips around town early in the morning, or possibly late at night, when you're less likely to run into people you know.
- To check if a tracking device is on your car, run your hand along the bottom, get on your belly, or use a mirror tied to a stick.
- Tolls are a privacy-person's worst traveling buddy. Try to pay in advance if you can or get a pass that accepts pre-paid service which you can pay via the website. Route yourself around toll roads.
- If your steering wheel were on the opposite side (US-style if you live in the UK), then you might not show up in the driver photos taken by traffic cameras.
- Think twice before driving in a foreign country. You won't know the speed limits, the familiar police traps, or the best turns. You will be at a serious disadvantage. You're more likely to be involved in a collision or pulled over by police. A Polish entrepreneur who lived in Africa for many years discovered that being white meant he would be pulled over and extorted nearly every time he sat in front of the wheel.[162]

---

[162] Marek Zmyslowski, *Chasing Black Unicorns: How Building the Amazon of Africa Put Me on Interpol's Most Wanted List*

- Gait analysis (analysis of your walking pattern) is the new facial recognition. Some advocate putting rocks in a shoe if you're walking past a camera and in dire need of staying off the grid.

Moving, and How to Do it Privately

To conclude this chapter, let's assume you've made the wise decision to leave your current house (which is in your name) and go to a different place that respects your privacy. Consider the following checklist:

1. Prepare well in advance. Privacy is a road with many setbacks.
2. Use moving as an opportunity to get rid of the myriad things in your life. Scan and burn papers, get rid of keepsakes, untouched books—eliminate half of your physical possessions each time you move.
3. Select your new destination with great care. Don't be afraid to change countries. Read "Becoming an International Nomad" in the upcoming Chapter 8. Do your best to visit your new place and scout out the town/city during the day, but also at night.
4. Likewise, favor a town over a city—and as out of town as you can stomach. Avoid homeowner associations, city limits, and cramped neighbors.
5. If you're buying a house, start researching how to purchase it without attaching your name to it. In places such as the US, this will likely involve the use of a trust. Consider help from a lawyer or knowledgeable person.
6. If you can't move out of your house, back up and store any sensitive items; ask the real estate agent if they can use old photos of the house.
7. If renting, start researching who in the area will allow you to rent in the name of an entity, such as an LLC. Serious cash up front will help to smooth this over. College towns are known for having abundant opportunities with people who ask few questions.
8. Consider moving out of your house before putting it up for sale. This way you won't have strangers and real estate agents walking through.
9. Jettison any account that has been tied to the current address or even the region, even if it is in a false name. Never use these again. This might include Amazon or other online shops to which you have an

account. Forget your membership bonuses. Create new accounts and connect them to a new anonymous payment method.

10. Prepare the utilities at your new place. You don't want to take them out in your name. This is most difficult. If renting, find a landlord who will put them in her name. If buying, a legal business entity (LLC) will be your friend, so call the utilities companies and determine what they need from a legal entity in order to get approved.

11. Set up a mailbox in your new area that can double as a local address. UPS shops are a good option in the US.

12. When moved in, make the necessary physical security changes as described in Chapter 2. Make sure your rental agreement includes a clause that the landlord must give 24-hour notice before showing up on the property. Sort out any of the lock issues and upgrades you might want to make from the beginning and get approval—if necessary.

13. Don't subscribe to the same services in your new address. Use this as a time to try new things, or at least don't order in the same quantity and arrangement as before.

Chapter 8
Advanced Privacy

Give yourself a pat on the back. If you've implemented the strategies thus far then you have made considerable progress in your pursuit of privacy. Let's take it up a notch, shall we? Please note that this section will be a bit more scattered since it is not organized according to a theme.

Spreading "Lies" with Disinformation

An advisor once told me the best way to be an introvert is to be an extrovert. In other words, if you want to avoid talking about the things most core to your being—the things most private to you—then instead of remaining silent and eliciting suspicion, you should be outgoing and gregarious, but in a way that diverts attention away from these issues. The introvert at a party who talks about her somewhat superficial recent experiences will be assumed to be normal, even open, and will often deter others from thinking that there is more to her. This is the concept of disinformation in a nutshell.

I thought the purpose of privacy was to hide, to run away, to erase.

Not always. The truth is, a lot of your information is already out in the wild. While you may be committed at this moment to becoming a private person, your past baggage—including registered vehicles, houses, and accounts tied to your real address—are not going anywhere. Sometimes a good disinformation campaign can do wonders to pollute the information that exists about you, and thus helps your real details to get lost in the shuffle.

Here are some examples of basic disinformation:

- If you use social media, say that you live in a city that you don't and play it up by occasionally posting photos of that city, its restaurants and beaches, etc. You can find these elsewhere online.

- Use social media for other fake information: slight alteration of your name, fake photo (perhaps using thispersondoesnotexist.com), and anything else you can think of.

- Using an alias (perhaps similar to the name of the previous occupant of your house), start receiving packages from Amazon and other companies. Take out some magazine and newspaper subscriptions and otherwise apply for free stuff using this name.

- Return to previous forum posts attached to your real name and edit them with false information about you.

- Create a personal website with slightly false information, such as an address far from you. Do the same with Facebook and Twitter using that same false information. Shares some pictures of that area to be convincing.

If you're inclined to go the disinformation route, take every opportunity to muddy the waters about who you are, what you do, and where you live. This is especially important if you currently have your name attached to your address and have no plans to move.

Data Removal Online

You may or may not be aware of this, but there are hundreds if not thousands of "people search" websites that very likely have some very real information about you: your name, address, previous addresses, phone number, family, alternative names, and possibly more. If you doubt me, search for your name online and take a few minutes seeing what you can find. You'll easily pull up some choice information. And I assure you that the paid ones often give you the information that they promise.

So where is this information coming from? Almost all of them are getting it from public sources: voting records (yes, they're public), housing records, social media, personal websites, job websites, news articles, data breaches, and publicly-available government databases. Seeing this information should be a wake up call to how much information you give out.

The methods throughout this book will help you stay out of these databases moving forward, but you also must deal with the data that exists right now. Fortunately, these companies are (usually) receptive to requests to remove data. Michael Bazzell has an excellent workbook for this, which can be found at: https://inteltechniques.com/data/workbook.pdf. There are hundreds of databases, so be patient and consistent. Do a dozen or so each day and don't get overwhelmed. The basic process involves sending an email (not from main email account) to customer service with a request to remove your profile. You might ask for loved ones' data while you're at it. Here are a few things to consider:

- If the website isn't being responsive, consider using language that might get their attention. You can mention the California or EU privacy acts in your statement. You can also mention child privacy laws as well. Even if you're not protected under these laws, simply mentioning them can encourage them to not take the risk.

- If they request information from you, such as ID, reply with a blank photo. These companies like to create fake hurdles that they assume you're not willing to jump over.

- Start up a spreadsheet for your removal journey. Check up on these services in a few weeks to make sure you're out of the system.

- Be persistent. These websites are manned by humans, and if you respectfully send a message regularly over the course of days and weeks, they might remove you so they don't have to deal with you.

Privacy and the Family

Secrets can exist between two people, if one of them is dead.
- Old Saying

Privacy is almost always possible for the sovereign individual, but if you have a ring on your finger or a car seat in your SUV, then that's probably not you. Most of us have spouses, children, relatives, roommates, and countless others whose interests we have to temper with our own. If you're married, then you especially know about this profound level of compromise in your personal life.

It's imperative to get your significant other or family on board with your privacy schemes. Children are a distinct challenge, and here I partly defer to an excellent chapter on the topic from Jeni Rogers' book *200+ Ways to Protect Your Privacy*. You'll have to make privacy a discussion to have with your children regularly as you would other important topics. And just like other important topics, not only will your kids fail to understand and comply, but they will willfully do the opposite. If you make the unwise decision to have your kids schooled outside of your home, you'll quickly realize just how little control you have over their development. Even if your daughter understands the importance of not putting her name into any online text box that asks for it, when she goes to school and her friends are doing it without question, she'll probably do the same.

The obvious solution is to homeschool or do your best to keep your kids away from these systems. Homeschooling has several benefits for privacy:

1. It allows you to exert more influence on your children—on the importance of privacy, for example—as opposed to questionable teachers, ill-behaving kids, and malicious governmental educational schemes.
2. It will ensure you don't have to give out your address and various other data to schools and local governments.
3. It allows you to teach your children real subjects such as philosophy and politics (the cornerstone of understanding the value of privacy), which are forbidden in public schooling.
4. It will allow you to consider a nomad lifestyle, which helps to ensure you can continue this process without interference.

Many nanny states, even in the "freedom-loving" West, have come to consider children as property of the state. If you live in Europe, or other places where home schooling is illegal, you might use this moment to reflect on how profoundly anti-privacy and unfree your country is. Act accordingly.

Regardless of whether you homeschool, you should engage with your children in the following ways to help them understand privacy:
- Teach them never to answer questions from an adult and to have a default response such as "you'll have to ask my parents that."
- Be selective about which of your children's friends (and parents) you invite to your house.

- Avoid babysitters as much as you can. Do everything in your power to get some trusted relatives such as the grandparents to babysit. Pay your oldest child to mind the younger ones. If all this fails, find the most reputable sitter you can imagine. Find one from your church, or a church.
- If you choose a babysitter, install locks on most of your doors so that the babysitter only has access to the kitchen and living room.

You might try to pitch privacy as a fun thing by doing the following:
- Create a single fake name that everyone in your family shares for matters of package delivery, etc. This is simply your singular family name now. You can even start to use it as a kind of pseudonym for anyone in the family when you interact with the outside world (for unimportant things).
- Do something similar with an email address or a phone number. Create one that manages all accounts that pertain to your family as a whole.
- See who can keep a straight face when giving a fake name at Starbucks (explaining, of course, the ethics of lying and why you are not giving your real name).
- Have clever discussions about how you would do various things without giving out real information. This will get their young gears turning.

As many privacy enthusiasts have discovered, lecturing your family or significant other about privacy will not get you very far, and will sometimes frustrate them. Indeed, I've noticed that many of us in the privacy community can come off as religious zealots demanding that everyone convert to our religion. Imagine having your boyfriend or girlfriend harass you three or four times a day for not being a Scientologist. You'd probably get frustrated pretty quickly.

Here are some ideas for broaching the conversation with others:
- Lead by example. Instead of lecturing, just go about your privacy life. When they ask you what's going on, explain that it is for privacy reasons, and that it is important for X reason. Make sure to have solid and multiple reasons.

- Be sincere but do not judge.
- Avoid an apocalyptic tone. Unless it's entirely true, saying "they're watching us" is never a good idea.
- Take some things into your own hands. It's unlikely your spouse will object if you change the address to your financial accounts to a PO box that you have created.
- Set some non-negotiables to assert how important this is to you. Using a real name for delivery of items should never be allowed, as should giving away the family's home address.
- Use a house-wide VPN. It's beyond the scope of this book to flesh this out, but you can buy a router that can handle a software such as PfSense, and connect your VPN service through it. This will ensure that every piece of Internet traffic in your house is filtered through a VPN.
- Teach your family how to use your various tools and strategies.

Your family wants to please you and is no doubt willing to go a serious way in your direction toward privacy. You just need to give them time. Don't coerce them and have an optimist's mindset of opening their eyes to solutions rather than problems. Stay well-informed of privacy news.

In conclusion, let's discuss a few strategies for roommates:

- Cordon off your own internet by buying and using your own router. Don't let roommates use it, and considering hiding its name (the SSID) so that they are not tempted.
- Be generally flexible so that you can put your foot down about certain things: no listening devices such as Amazon Alexas being one.
- Put a lock on your room. Get permission before you move in, if you deem it necessary.
- Soundproof your room. Don't bother with the cheap stuff—it doesn't block sound nearly as much as the premium foam.
- Visit friends and significant others at their house and do as little as possible in the communal areas.
- Keep passwords on all your devices and don't leave them sitting around.

VPN: Advanced Use

I said in Chapter 3 that we would return to VPNs, so let's get you up to speed. I hope by now you have purchased a subscription to a reputable, zero-knowledge, open-source VPN. Using the default settings are fine, but now that you're comfortable with it let's discuss how we can make it even better.

For starters, fire up your VPN application and consider the following tweaks:

- Killswitch. This shuts off the flow of Internet to your computer if the VPN stops for any reason. VPN software isn't 100% reliable, and this helps to fix that. If you're torrenting with a VPN, this is absolutely required.

- You might also desire to switch on options such as "connect at launch" or "connect with system start-up" if you find yourself forgetting to start your VPN manually.

- Your server location matters! It matters in terms of speed (closer proximity is usually faster) and it matters in terms of reputation (some servers might be flagged on websites while others are not). I have financial accounts that prefer to see the same particular server locations when I log in. Start playing around with the server locations to see what works best for you, and if you find that you are blocked by too many websites, you might consider trying a different VPN altogether. Stay curious and don't become rigid.

- There are other ways to use VPNs besides the standard application. As I mentioned in the previous section, you can purchase a router that allows VPN installation at the router level. This has advantages in terms of reliability and in terms of covering your entire house in one swoop. You can also look into connecting to your VPN through a third-party protocol such as OpenVPN. I won't go into the details here, but OpenVPN protocol offers a couple of advantages, usually in terms of flexibility but also in terms of reliability. Look into these methods if you're feeling up to a small challenge.

VPNs are mandatory for any kind of torrenting, but even if they block your Internet Service Provider from seeing exactly what you're viewing and downloading, your provider will still see that you're downloading a lot of it gigabytes. Uploading can be especially indicative of torrenting—though there is no proof by that fact alone. It makes sense to ration your downloading and do a consistent amount per day as opposed to huge chunks followed by barren seasons. This, by the way, is a good lesson for all utilities. If you use five times the normal amount of electricity in your area, you might generate suspicion from your power company. You might even get a visit from the police, who are looking for cannabis growing and other activity for which they can punish you.

To conclude VPNs in this book, let's think long-term. What is the legal status of these invaluable tools of privacy? For now they are legal in most countries, and because of this a huge range of VPNs have flooded the marketplace. Part of me fears that there will inevitably be a crackdown. There are already websites that refuse to deal with people using a VPN. I'm aware of several major bank websites and shopping sites that simply will not load (these all have lost my service, obviously). The best solution is to keep using VPNs religiously, and to get everyone you know to use them. Pass along your subscription if you have some devices to spare. If we do this, websites will be forced to become more accepting. For now, you'll simply have to put up with some of the inconvenience, and take the initiative of removing certain websites from your life who refuse to accept VPNs. It doesn't hurt to send a message (email or Twitter [not tied to you]) to these companies explaining your concern and decision to boycott.

VPNs help us recapture part of the original vision of the anonymous Internet. Let's keep that going as best we can.

Temporary Operating Systems (TAILS)

If you've read Chapter 4 then you should know something about operating systems. The problem with downloading and installing an operating system to your hard drive is that, well, it is etched onto your hard drive. Even with full-disk encryption in place, an investigator—perhaps a state actor—with serious resources and a lot of time might be able to get in. More likely, you might be compelled to give up your password under physical or legal threat. There are scenarios in which you might want literally no evidence of what you are doing on the computer or have the ability to wipe your computer in two seconds. That's where temporary operating systems come in.

Do you remember in Chapter 3 when we put Linux Mint onto a USB drive? A temporary or "amnesic" operating system such as Tails lives only on a USB drive and loads to the RAM of your computer instead of the hard drive. The moment you remove the USB drive or shut down the system normally, all trace of your activity is erased. While it's not exactly conducive to productivity, a temporary operating system can be great if you are interested in privacy and security above all else and are willing to put up with some inconvenience. Or you just want to be locked down for some particular research that you're doing.

The Linux distribution Tails is great for our purposes. In addition to its ephemeral qualities, all online activity on Tails is protected by TOR—not just the browser, which it also has by default. Provided you also follow the digital behavior we have discussed in this book, when using Tails your data is not going anywhere.

You install Tails in the same way you installed Linux Mint in Chapter 4. You can find the files and instructions for Tails at https://tails.boum.org/.

Once you have your live USB drive and start it up with your computer, you'll be faced with a list of options before arriving at the desktop. Don't worry: unlike Linux Mint you cannot install Tails on top of your current operating system. If you want to create a password (not always necessary since everything is wiped when you finish your session) you may do so in the extra settings; otherwise press "Start Tails."

Inside Tails you'll have a similar functionality to Linux Mint. As previously mentioned, all your traffic is filtered through the TOR network, which means Internet use will be on the slower side. Any work that you do on Tails will have to be saved to an external device or it will be wiped out when you shut down. There are ways to create more persistence in Tails. You can go to "System Tools" and "Configure Persistent Volume" to create such a system, but in my opinion it defeats some of the purpose—if not all of it.

When would you use Tails? If you are in dire need of privacy and cannot risk any exposure. Activists, for example, or people living in a tyrannical regime. Even if you don't fit those descriptions, it's good to be familiar with Tails. If you want to try to use it daily, good on you. I probably won't be joining you —yet.

Online Fingerprinting

Visit a web browser on your main computer and go to deviceinfo.me. Pause for a moment and digest that.

Pretty crazy, right? In past chapters we've discussed how websites and online services can put together pieces of your identity by using cookies, which are bits of code that remember which websites you've visited. But cookies are only one kind of fingerprinting, and websites are becoming much more sophisticated in how they keep track of you. What is fingerprinting? You wouldn't be surprised to know that it has a fairly sordid history: read the "Interlude" chapter for more on this.

The idea behind fingerprinting is that each of us in our individuality make decisions different from others; we thus produce a "fingerprint" different from everyone else in the same way that our actual fingerprint is distinct enough from others to convict us of a crime. If you were under threat by a state adversary you would have to take fingerprinting into consideration any time you connected to the Internet and it would become as important as anything else in this book. Consider the following examples of how your behavior online can be used to fingerprint you:

- A website sees your IP address and knows when you visit, when you return, and starts to attach your other actions on the website to this IP address. If you use you real IP address (not on a VPN), then they have an idea of who you actually are and where you live.

- Websites can detect how many fonts you have installed on your computer, so that if you downloaded that weird font that one time you are suddenly a much more distinguishable than everyone else who has not: you're the person with 43 fonts instead of 40.

- A website sees you are coming from Linux, and from a virtual machine (two things I've recommended in this book) and decides to ban your account or refuse to process your online payment because they consider these two categories to be suspicious.

- A website sees you hover over a video even if you don't click on it. They take that as tacit confirmation that you are indeed interested in that thing.

- A website can detect you use an adblocker and thus rejects you outright from accessing their material.

- A website detects that you have a combination of five browser add-ons that only .00000001% of people have.

- You type into a text box on a website and they detect your words per minute speed and your odd habit of pausing before the last word of each sentence. They track this identity over your many sessions on that website.

- You click on the Google CAPTCHA buses and chimneys at the exact same reaction speed every time, and in the same pattern counter-clockwise. Google is happy to see you again.

Note that any of these things can make another irrelevant. For example if you are the person with the 37 fonts and the specific combination of browser add-ons, your VPN isn't really giving you as much anonymity on that website as you thought.

What is to be done? The key here is behavior—consistent behavior. I believe behavior to be at the crux of all privacy, but especially of fingerprinting. Consider the following methods to fight fingerprinting:

- Use a VPN, always. Your real IP address is still the surest way to identify you.

- Use the Tor Browser for as much casual Internet surfing as possible. Tor is locked down with all kinds of privacy features but, most importantly, everyone who uses Tor is also using these features. So you get the privacy benefits without standing out. Just make sure to follows Tor's advice and not make any changes to the browser or to resize the resolution of the browser.

- Don't download any extra fonts. If you want to wipe your current fonts, you can reinstall your operating system to reset the fonts, and everything else, back to default settings. Avoid making changes to your computer.

- Don't type into text boxes on websites or on Google. Keep a text editor open; type your text, and paste it over. If you can't be bothered with that you could also type your text on the URL box and paste it over.

- Vary your spelling, punctuation, and writing style. Be as chaotic as possible. The same goes for Google CAPTCHAs.
- Don't reuse usernames, passwords, or email address across the Internet. Also fake names.
- For more extreme measures, use the Tails operating system as much as possible. In Tails all of your Internet activity, not just your browser, is protected by Tor. Most significantly, you start fresh with TAILS every time. So you don't have an operating system that has customization. Tails will really test your minimalism—in the best ways possible.
- Even more extreme and advanced users who are looking for a more stable experience (not a temporary operating system) might consider the Linux distribution Qubes. Not for the faint of heart, the main feature of this difficult-to-use operating system is that every program that you pull up is opened in a separate mini operating system that has no connection to the rest of your computer.
- Download and use the program BleachBit. This strip a number of temporary data from your computer and wipes out most internet activity. Use it as often as you like, including after each sensitive browsing session or once a day.
- Be cautious where your mouse goes on a browser. Add this to your website discipline; instead of being curious with the cursor, treat every website you visit as a static image. Use Page Up and Page Down.
- Choose common resolution screens for your laptop and desktop computers. Or at least avoid very uncommon ones. 1080 is one of the most common.

Becoming an International Nomad

If things have come to the point that you are stocking guns and dehydrated food, chances are that the place where you live is not treating you best.

- Andrew Henderson, the Nomad Capitalist

In 2018 the Australian government banned encryption: one of the most important means of privacy we have.[163] [164] Some companies were able to get around it by moving data centers to other countries, but the act speaks for itself: Australia has become (and not just in terms of privacy) the most authoritarian and privacy-despising regime in the Western world. Other legal jurisdictions are flirting with outlawing encryption, such as the European Union,[165] and places such as the US have laws in place—think of the unpatriotic 2001 PATRIOT Act—that are inimical to privacy. And things are only getting worse. Many of the countries in the West are joining the likes of China and, dare we say, North Korea in their desire to monitor their "subjects." For "national security" of course. I pick on the West, because they are supposed to be above this, but it's true that many non-Western countries are just as bad or worse about such things. And if they aren't yet, they probably just haven't gotten around to it.

The current book has taught you to do everything within the law to protect your personal privacy. But what if the law in your country doesn't allow you to pursue privacy? It is dangerous, Voltaire once said, to be right when your government is wrong.

You could hunker down. Fight the fight. Behave like V in *V for Vendetta*. Thump your chest and say that "this is my country and I'm not going to abandon it." I think we can all respect that. But the reality is that your actions are unlikely to change anything, and in the meantime you'll be supporting with your taxes and residence a regime that sees you as nothing more than a milk cow. Why not consider leaving?

When you live with a single passport and citizenship you have put all of your eggs into one basket. Conversely, by opening yourself up to travel, living elsewhere, and acquiring other residencies and citizenships you can achieve things that you simply cannot when you are rooted at home like a medieval serf. Andrew Henderson, the Nomad Capitalist, puts it this way:

> Having a second passport puts the power back in your hands by dividing that control between different governments and gives you the option to get rid of the one that serves you least if the need were

---

[163] https://www.nytimes.com/2018/12/06/world/australia/encryption-bill-nauru.html

[164] https://www.zdnet.com/article/australian-law-enforcement-used-encryption-laws-11-times-last-year/

[165] https://tech.newstatesman.com/security/the-eu-is-set-to-declare-war-on-encryption

ever to arise. ... Having a second passport is the ultimate escape hatch.[166]

This is a complex topic of which many words have been spoken. Let me give you the basic overview.

When you acquire a passport and travel to another country, you are beholden to its laws—laws (and culture) which might be more favorable than the country you were born in. Depending on a number of factors, you might be able to become a resident or citizen of that country. Residency is a step up from being a visitor, but a step below citizenship, where you would actually hold a passport, be able to vote, and have other privileges. Most new citizens begin as permanent residents.

Not all countries allow dual citizenship. In fact only eighty-five do. (If yours doesn't, then this could be your first sign that it's time to leave.)[167] This is important to keep in mind—you want to add to your passports, not subtract.

Many, though not all countries allow you to become a citizen of their country based on something you have that benefits them. You can gain residency or citizenship:

- By living there for a while
- By "investment"
- By heredity
- By special circumstances (you're an Olympic judo athlete in a country that would love to have a winner)

The most common way to gain residency or citizenship is simply to go to a country and live there, provided that country is open to foreigners and wants you as a resident (you're a young skilled worker, have a high level of education, no health problems, etc). Usually you'll have to be a student or hired by a company in that country. You might start as a resident and it may take many years to become a citizen—assuming you don't leave too often and make sure to follow other requirements. A few countries make this easy, such as Panama and Paraguay, and they require only minimal time spent in the country over

---

[166] From his book, *Nomad Capitalist*
[167] Some countries don't allow dual citizenship. There's the obvious collectivist states: China, Japan, India. But there are also some surprising ones: Austria, Netherlands, Norway, Singapore.

the course of a few years before you can qualify for citizenship. Not all countries are welcoming, obviously, and some have very stringent requirements to get on the citizenship path.

A more straightforward way to gain citizenship from the get-go is to gain citizenship by investment (CBI). If you have some money to throw around, several governments will hand you a passport in exchange for a donation or investment towards certain ailing sectors of their economy (real estate, out-of-work sugar workers.): usually $100,000 at minimum (but don't forget the several thousands it will cost to organize the whole endeavor). Some cost well into the millions, and don't expect to necessarily get this money back. The Caribbean countries represents most of the citizenship by investment programs, since they have tiny GPDs and produce little of their own products. St Kitts and Dominica are the two classic options. Some of these countries earn most of their money from selling citizenship to foreigners, so you can be sure that this process is legitimate and as efficient as government activities can be.

You should also look into citizenship by inheritance. If your parents, grandparents, and sometimes even great grandparents have citizenship from somewhere, you might have a chance to get citizenship from that country as well.

Unless you choose citizenship by investment, there is little guaranteed in any of these processes. Citizenship is one of the most significant gifts a government can give anyone. It is entirely their discretion to choose to give it to you, even if you technically qualify. Some people never hear back from "easy" countries like Panama, or they do ten years later when it's far too late. Your mileage will vary, which is why you should start the process now and become informed.

A passport is a powerful tool because it means the country can't reject you at the border. It's a little bit like Robert Frost's definition of family: it means when you knock they have to let you in. A passport also allows you to take part in certain aspects of that country—purchasing real estate, for example—that may have been excluded to non-citizens. It opens up new opportunities to invest in the country and arrange your life in a more favorable environment. As far as privacy, here are a few ways second citizenship might help you as regards privacy:

- You own real estate or various assets as a resident or citizen of one country that your previous country does not know about.

- You travel with your second passport and don't leave a trail on your other one.
- You pursue a "flag theory" lifestyle that involves owning a business in one country, banking in another, holding intellectual property in another, and living in another (or simply traveling constantly).
- You meet fascinating international people who offer you new ideas and business opportunities and might otherwise teach you about privacy and other techniques.

That's the process of expanding your residencies and citizenships, but what exactly should you look for in a new country? Here are a few criteria to consider:

- You enjoy living there and have spent *at least* several weeks visiting.
- You like the direction the country is going in in terms of freedom, privacy, economy, etc.
- They don't demand too much of you by way of taxes or regulations: a good sign that they stay out of your business.
- They have racial diversity so that you are accepted and don't stand out (this depends on region and city vs town, of course); or, they renounce racial diversity, but that means they are unlikely to own you or claim you as their own: think Japan, China, Korea.
- They don't have a history of travel or financial restrictions.
- They have favorable extradition policies, which means they won't send you back to your first country should you be demanded at court. See Brazil, Switzerland, Brunei, Russia, China, Ecuador.
- They have a decent legal system (common law is always nice where you can find it) that respects the individual, business, and does not allow for easy lawsuits.

If international nomadism appeals to you, I suggest you start becoming aware of the fascinating process. Start traveling as much as you can and start following international news. I hope to share research in upcoming projects comparing countries at length. An index of Privacy and Freedom, let's say. For now you'll have to digest some of this material yourself. Jim Rogers' books are essential for anyone who wants a comparative view of the world's regions, especially as they pertain to our interests. The Nomad Capitalist YouTube channel is also excellent, as is Escape Artist's website and The Expat Money Show. Doug Casey has books, articles, and videos of great insight.

You might just start reading news directly from the countries you're interested in. We get bogged down in our own country and surround ourselves with its own prejudicial view of the world. Even the "global" sections of news, such as the *Financial Times*, or from the *BBC* and the *Wall Street Journal*, give a pale imitation of what's going on. If you want to have a clearer (though by no means perfect) view of what's going on in Ireland, then start with *The Irish Times* and *The Irish Examiner*. If you want to figure out what's happening in Argentina, check their local news. I say "start" because mainstream media has proven to be severely lacking if not patently false too often, and these days relies more on unsubstantiated opinion rather than empirical journalism. Stay curious, rely on yourself, and travel widely.

LLCs, Trusts, and Other Legal Structures

Legal entities have been and always will be extraordinary privacy tools. Indeed, for a certain high-income demographic, the term "privacy" might *only* mean legal structures. You see, a legal entity can stand in for you, removing you and your identity from the equation. You don't own that house: The ABC Trust owns it. You don't own that vehicle, the Highway LLC owns it. You don't have anything to do with that occurrence, you're simply a member of that corporation. Legal entities can get extraordinarily complex. Countless millions are spent on lawyers for large corporations to hide what they can. The infamous "Double Irish With a Dutch Sandwich" technique involved Google sending profits in between Irish and Dutch companies, the last of which was headquartered in Bermuda to reduce taxes. While such techniques are arranged for purposes of escaping taxation, they can easily double as privacy techniques. Consider the following scenario:

> Three people own a company with equal share: one is American, one South African, and one Thai. They each travel globally, use multiple passports, and have no fixed abode. Their company is incorporated in Hong Kong but its owners are technically legal entities based in the Cayman Islands, Barbados, and Saint Kitts. It has its main banking merchant account in Dubai, and runs a websites whose servers are in Switzerland. It sells only digital items to clients across the world using a payment system run from Iceland

by a group of people equally as diverse as the three owners. Its "employees" are actually contractors working digitally largely from Eastern Europe.

Where could we say this company is centered and what could we possibly know about its real owners? I give you this very complex—though not at all unlikely scenario—to show you how legal entities can be extraordinarily useful at preserving your privacy.

Writing a book for a mass audience, I'm not in a position to give you legal advice. Nothing in this book is legal advice. Nor am I in a position to get into the complexity of all the variations of legal entities, especially as they vary by country and even by region (states within the US). I will, however, give you an overview of how you might start to think about the benefit of trusts and LLCs in a privacy lifestyle. You might then talk to your lawyer and ask more questions.

First, why would you want to hide ownership of something? Well:

- Owning a house in a legal entity can prevent people from looking it up in local property records to see who the owner is.
- It can also offer some liability protection in the event you are sued.
- Owning a vehicle in a trust can hide your name from license plate searches and require a second step for police searches.
- Purchasing an online service in the name of a corporate bank account instead of your name will keep you off that record.

Think of all the instances in which you must give out your name and address. Now imagine a legal entity replaces your name. Many things that a person can own or do, a legal entity can do likewise. The combinations are limitless but in all cases require careful consideration and proper legal advice.

Let's be clear about one other thing: piercing the corporate veil. If you own a Limited Liability Corporation (LLC) by yourself (the easiest way to do it), but you don't separate your personal expenses and activities from those of the business, then your liability can go out the window. A judge can deem that you and your legal entity are the same, pierce your corporate veil, and expose you personally to all of the liability of the entity. In order to achieve maximum separation between you and your entity, you should start by considering the following:

- Buy business-related items and services with business bank accounts only. Cash is acceptable as well and is desirable for our privacy reasons.
- Don't mix the streams! You might be tempted to buy something on your personal Amazon account with your business card, but that might not strictly be a separation of personal and business. Spend the time and money to create separate accounts for your business—it's not worth the risk to skimp.
- Make use of a registered agent service to separate your business address from your actual address.
- Always sign documents with the appropriate entity; if it's a business document, then the business should sign for it. For example:
  - Company X, LLC
    John Smith, member [if that is your designation]
- Insist that your company be the owner/primary user/recipient for any agreement, document, etc. Don't let them just put your personal name in by default. Say that "you are just a member of the company and cannot be put down personally."

Legal entities need not be fully-functioning business in order to be of use. You can create and hold an entity that does not have a tax ID number or a bank account and exists purely to be the owner of various things.

Following this logic you can escape the personal requirements of giving your name for a house rental or a house purchase. As a renter do your best to avoid large companies; find an independent house and offer to pay cash in advance. Ask them to waive any background or credit checks. A business entity might do the renting, especially since companies look more legitimate. You can even do something similar for a house purchase, which has some complexity and is beyond the scope of this book.

To learn more about these techniques I recommend talking to a lawyer who is willing to explain things, or to track down resources and slowly get into it. The NOLO series of books can be a great introduction to various legal topics and I'll also recommend the (somewhat advanced) book *Asset Protection ... In Financially Unsafe Times*.

Medical/Health Privacy

The sci-fi film *Gattaca* imagines a world of genetic discrimination where non-modified humans are not offered the same jobs, don't get the same sexual partners, and are otherwise treated as second-class citizens. Our non-modified protagonist has to hide his identity while working his dream job and ultimately succeeding immensely despite his "inferior" genes. *Gattaca* brought to the public's attention in a way that only fiction can how one's health and genetic data are often used to screen someone from opportunities. This will be especially important as genetic analysis (and even modification) becomes the norm in upcoming years and decades. Medical and health privacy is and will continue to be a serious issue.

Many people who are otherwise not interested in privacy will nevertheless work up a sweat protecting their medical privacy, and it's not difficult to see why. Not only can it be embarrassing for friends, colleagues, and partners to know about your health problems, but it can also be damaging to your career, your insurance premiums, and your relationships. Some basic tips will help you stay private in this regard:

- Take care to whom you share your health information, especially online forums, social media, and insecure messaging. Even to prove a point about being "open," you should question whether your health information should ever pass your lips—or your keyboard.
- If you take prescription drugs (most people do) then take care what your labels say about you in your medicine cabinet or kitchen. You might just remove the labels.
- Know that your medical information will never be fully secured. Despite laws in various countries to protect health privacy (think HIPAA in the USA), data gets exposed through breaches and blatant breaking of these laws—and powerful organizations find ways of obtaining it. Don't expect those "anonymous" counseling sessions to remain off the record.

There's another problem with medical privacy: that of the required information to even have an appointment. Walk into a doctor's or dentist's office and you'll likely be bombarded with paperwork. This is a difficult process to avoid, and in emergencies you won't bother with it. But so long as you have time to think about these encounters, set up some ground rules which you can follow in the heat of the moment. I have by no means solved this system, but here are some ideas to work with:

- First ask what sections are mandatory. They might say "all of it," to which you should point out you're only willing to give out basic information. You're going to have to be aggressive and stand your ground in most cases—this is key.
- Fill out what you're willing to fill out and return it to the desk person. If they tell you to do more say you won't and sit down.
- Ask the person to show you where in the law, or in the company's policies, you are required to give X information.
- Say you are a victim of identity theft (we all are via data breaches) and you have been instructed (I'm instructing you now) not to give anything but the basic information.
- Consider what information must be accurate. When it comes to an address, for example, one wonders why it is needed (spam, I would gather).
- It's obviously easier to pay with cash for medical visits, if it is within your power.
- Spend some time when you are not in need of medical attention to practice what you will say and determine where you will go. Visit or call some medical facilities and ask them what is expected of you, how you can pay, and how flexible they are with personal information.

Finally, consider taking care of medical issues outside of the highly bureaucratic systems. Glasses can be purchased online without giving any information besides an address to ship to, as can an increasingly large variety of medical care options. Stock up in advance in case these systems start to demand a lot of information from us in the future.

Virtual Machines

The entire digital realm and all cloud programs on the Internet exist at some point on physical devices. These devices, called servers, are simply computers that run specialized software to helps them store and share the text, images, and videos that will be used by any given website. Pretty straightforward, right? But virtual machines are changing all of this. A virtual machine is a computer that runs inside of a computer. Do you remember how we downloaded the Linux Mint and TAILS operating systems? Well, it's quite possible to perform that same process, not on a physical computer but within a program on your current computer. In other words, you can run operating systems within operating systems.

Why would you want to do this? Well, each new operating system works more or less like a separate computer. It has its own identity, including its own MAC address. People often talk about buying "air gap" computers: computers that never connect to the Internet and allow us to separate all of our business onto an uncompromised computer. A virtual machine does similar work. Let's say for example that you only have one computer that serves as your personal computer, your business computer, and your computer for a side-project that you don't want contaminating any of your life. Well you could simply create two virtual machines—one for business and one for the side project. Each of these machines would have their own storage, their own browser, their own password manager (if you want to go that far). There is a lot of opportunity with virtual machines for privacy and productivity.

I'll show you the basic way to go about this:

1. Download the program VirtualBox. This is the gold standard. It is free and open-source.
2. Find your downloaded copy of Linux Mint (.iso file), or return to their website and download the .iso file. You can choose any operating system you want. Let's say you use Mac but want Windows 10 running. You could download the Windows 10 .iso file. We'll stick with Linux Mint for this example.
3. Run VirtualBox, select "New," and follow the prompts.
4. Stick to the defaults except for RAM. I recommend at least 3072 mb (3 GB), but don't use more than half of your machine's total RAM. Also, for hard drive space, select what your computer can handle or what you need. Be aware that crappy computers (slow CPU or limited RAM) won't run virtual operating systems well.
5. Press "Create" a final time to finish the process.
6. Now double-click (or press "Start") on your new operating system. We're not finished yet—we have to install the actual OS.
7. While it's running, look above and click "Devices" > "Optical Drives" > "Choose a disk file." Select your Linux Mint .iso file.

8. You may have to restart, but now you can walk through the process just like you did in Chapter 4 to install Mint. This time, you can safely choose to "erase the disk" when installing, since you're installing within a folder of your computer.

That's all there is to it. You might want to adjust some settings to make things more comfortable. Shut down your virtual system and do the following:

- Go to "Settings" > "System" > "Processor" and bump it up to whatever you computer can handle (remember that you're sharing CPU cores between your main computer and the virtual one). I tend to own processors with many cores and so I assign three cores for my Linux virtual system. I find that this makes it run more smoothly.

- Go to "General" > "Advanced" and make sure the clipboard options are bidirectional. This will allow you to copy and paste between your virtual and real computer.

- Go to "Settings" > "Display" and max out the video memory; also select "Enable 3D Acceleration." If you have trouble running the OS, come back and undo these particular changes.

- Go to "Shared Folders" and click the folder icon on the top right. Name it, give it a location, and select "Auto Mount." This will allow you to share files between your virtual and real system.

- Finally, while running your virtual operating system, go to "Devices" and the top and select "Insert Guest Additions CD Image." Run it when prompted. This setting will allow you to view your virtual box in full screen, which makes it easier to see. Unfortunately this setting often encounters errors. If yours doesn't run right away, search for "Guest Additions Virtualbox" on YouTube and try a number of the solutions that people suggest until you can get it to work.

Now you can start to incorporate virtual machines into your routine. Just be aware that you're dealing with a second computer, and that means you'll have to update it, install programs you need, and change Internet browser settings just like you would for the first time on your main computer.

Fighting Facial Recognition

Facial recognition systems analyze the angles and shapes of your face and compare them against databases of photos of you that they already have to

195

have in order to accomplish this. The accuracy is very good and facial recognition is taking off across the world. Stadiums use it to analyze every face in the crowd,[168] churches use it to track attendance,[169] airports use it for speedy check-ins,[170] and companies and militaries use it to make sure people are who they say they are.[171] All for your protection, of course.

I hope I don't have to spell out the unintended consequences that all of this will bring about. If you have trouble imagining that dystopia, then I don't have much to say. On the topic of fighting against it, however, I have a few points to make. Let's start with the basics:

- Call out anyone and everyone who uses facial recognition and complain loudly.
- Do not participate in any of these systems. Forget the "easy check-in" at the airport that uses facial recognition.
- Keep your photos off the Internet and out of as many databases as possible. This is huge.
- Don't upload photos on social media. Facebook and Instagram are known for using *their* photos (you thought they were yours?) to train the AI of facial recognition.[172]

Watchman Privacy will have many more guides to warding off facial recognition in future editions of this book and on future podcasts and newsletters. For now, I'll leave you with a few more advanced ideas for fighting back:

- COVID face masks have been proven to disrupt (not completely mitigate) the tracking, and you should be able to use them for the next many years—if not forever (many people in Asian cities wear face masks regularly when in public).[173]

---

[168] https://onezero.medium.com/90-000-unsuspecting-rose-bowl-attendees-were-scooped-up-in-a-facial-recognition-test-18c843909858
[169] https://www.face-six.com/event-attendance/
[170] https://www.cnn.com/travel/article/airports-facial-recognition/index.html
[171] https://www.nextgov.com/emerging-tech/2021/04/army-wants-automate-base-access-facial-recognition-drive-thru-checkpoints/173113/
[172] https://www.forbes.com/sites/samshead/2018/05/03/facebook-used-3-5-billion-public-instagram-photos-to-train-ai
[173] https://www.independent.co.uk/news/world/americas/face-masks-facial-recognition-technology-us-agency-nist-a9642096.html

- The online service Fawkes alters pixels in photos ever so slightly so that they look nearly the same but are unrecognizable by many facial recognition systems.[174]
- One guy makes realistic printed masks of his own face that you can wear.[175] I suspect this would be for emergency situations only...
- A company called Reflectacles sells glasses that, through various means, repel facial recognition.[176]

Be aware of your surroundings and be familiar with the facial recognition laws in your region. Since concerts and other public gatherings increasingly use this technology, it wouldn't hurt to scan their websites to see if they participate in this nonsense. Above all, steel yourself against the numerous "but it's for your safety" arguments coming your way. Refer to Chapter 10 for said arguments and rebuttals.

---

[174] https://sandlab.cs.uchicago.edu/fawkes/
[175] https://leoselvaggio.com/urmesurveillance
[176] https://www.reflectacles.com

Chapter 9
Privacy and the End of the World

I know why you did it. I know you were afraid. Who wouldn't be? War, terror, disease. There were a myriad of problems which conspired to corrupt your reason and rob you of your common sense. Fear got the best of you, and in your panic you turned to the now high chancellor, Adam Sutler. He promised you order, he promised you peace, and all he demanded in return was your silent, obedient consent.

- V for Vendetta

A number of costly events have plagued the world from 2020 - 2022 and turned society on its head. The lingering COVID-1984 government lockdowns have tipped the scales in favor of authoritarianism, and in some cases there will be no looking back. New totalitarians come out of their rat holes every day, and as Milton Friedman once said: there is nothing so permanent as a temporary government program.

For the next months and even the next couple of years (maybe longer), the world is going to remain in this state of sickness hysteria. Fairly soon economies around the world will collapse as a result of being forced to shut down, infused with unprecedented fake money (inflation),[177] and having business and supply chains destroyed. Joblessness, homelessness, violence, theft, hard policing, and military intervention will make the few killed by COVID look like a rounding error. Indeed, one study in August of 2020 (early on in the lockdowns) suggested that Americans had already lost ten times as many human years of life as COVID had wiped out in the same

---

[177] https://www.aier.org/article/the-everything-bubble-and-what-it-means-for-your-money/

period of time.[178] That number should have been (and certainly is now) much higher.

Another seeming-apocalyptic trend has been than of cancel culture—defined momentarily—which can with the snap of its fingers end your job, destroy your business, or send you to prison. The tenants of a privacy life can help you to have backup options and other ways of staying out of the range of this monstrous death ray.

Privacy is going to be your greatest asset in the upcoming decade. Sure, wealth, investing knowledge, survival skills, and network are important. But what does your seven-figure checking account matter when the government wipes it out, Cypress-style?[179] Or when the extensive Bitcoin you "own" in a Coinbase account is made illegal overnight? Or when the network of libertarians in New Hampshire that you've gathered are rounded up by an anxious military with weapon-enabled drones capable of eradicating towns in a matter of minutes? Everything is secondary to privacy.

This chapter is broken into three sections: privacy during COVID-1984, privacy from cancel culture, and privacy as regards socioeconomic collapse. See also my podcast episodes on privacy during economic collapse.

Privacy During COVID-1984

We must also be alert to the equal and opposite danger that public policy could itself become the captive of a scientific-technological elite.

- Dwight D. Eisenhower, "Farewell Address"

I'm not going to insult your intelligence by telling you to make your own decisions for your health and all of that self-righteous rubbish. Instead, I'm going to show you how to protect your privacy during these times. Let me first list some of the main ways in which privacy has been compromised during the forced lockdowns of 2020 - 2022:

1. Geo-tracing apps—government mandated in some cases.

---

[178] https://www.revolver.news/2020/08/study-covid-19-lockdowns-deadlier-than-pandemic-itself/

[179] https://www.reuters.com/article/us-cyprus-parliament/cyprus-banks-remain-closed-to-avert-run-on-deposits-idUSBRE92G03I20130325

2. Working from home: increased online conversations and business dealings instead of face-to-face private meetings. Personal devices becoming work devices.
3. Mandatory testing (DNA extraction) to return to work, school, or to travel.
4. Extra identification (testing results, passports)
5. Refusal of cash. Coin "shortages."
6. Reporting from peers for not wearing masks or "social distancing."
7. Social scorn and in some cases arrest for selling items at too high a price ("price gouging"), or for "hoarding."

We'll break these down one by one. Contact-tracing or geo-tracing we have discussed in previous chapters (such as Chapter 5), but I'll reiterate a few points. If you want privacy you will *not* participate in any contact-tracing whatsoever. In May of 2020 Apple and Google jointly—*shivers*—created the "Exposure Notification" system. It was forcibly installed on iPhones and for Android phones it is an optional app to download. Is all of this anonymous as the tech companies say? Here's what Google has to say:

> Neither Google, Apple, nor other users can see your identity, but public health authorities may ask you for additional information, such as a phone number, to contact you with additional guidance.[180]

In other words, while Google and Apple claim not to see this identification, the state (your real enemy in privacy) can. There is a record being kept and if you are interested in privacy you will not be participating in these systems.

Here's the basic line of defense against contact-tracing:

- Don't sign up for it. If you have an iPhone, "Exposure Notifications" will have appeared under your settings. You might click on it to make sure it is not running.
- If you've already downloaded or signed up for some kind of tracking, uninstall immediately and wipe your data as best you can. If necessary, resetting your phone always done the job completely.
- If you live in a country where contact tracing is mandatory, then say you don't have a phone, or start carrying your phone in a Faraday bag

---

[180] https://www.google.com/covid19/exposurenotifications/

when you're not using it. (Keep in mind that as soon as you pull it out of your bag, you will be transmitting your location.) The long-term solutions for private phone usage I discuss in Chapter 5 and begin with purchasing a new phone and phone service in cash and not in your name.

- Start leaving your phone at home more often and rely on a laptop with private messengers such as Wire, Session, and Signal to communicate with friends and colleagues.
- Do the full MySudo-iPod Touch plunge as I describe in Chapter 5.
- Don't send messages through insecure channels (SMS, email, standard phone calling) talking about your health.
- Take care in responding to questionnaires at work, school, or anywhere else saying you have a cough or any kind of symptoms.
- Speak out loudly against mandatory contact-tracing, protest, and otherwise make it clear that you will not be going along with this.

Also re-read Chapter 5 for some harrowing consequences of revealing your location during COVID-1984.

Contact-tracing as of now depends entirely on your phone. If you're like me and regularly travel without a phone, then you're automatically in good shape. But contact-tracing may become mandatory in your country, and at that point you will have to take seriously my recommendations about phone use that I describe in my chapter on phone privacy. And to rehearse some really good reasons why you don't have your phone on you.

Let's talk employment privacy. COVID-1984 has proven that the lifestyle I advocate in this book is incredibly useful. Being a digital nomad and running your own business means you don't have to comply with any of the various regulations, mandatory health checks, and mandatory vaccinations that you would at an office, or a school, or in a large city. You're not bound to any region. I encourage you to pursue that lifestyle now more than ever. Digital work is basically the norm right now, and you can quite reasonably get a job using your laptop while sipping piña coladas in Barbados. Indeed, many countries whose tourist economies have been devastated by the lockdowns have started inviting people in with offerings of preferential tax treatment, generous temporary residencies, and the like. Such countries have also begun to relax their restrictions on gatherings. You would do well to consider these options. Now is the time more than ever. Start by checking the Caribbean countries.[181]

The previous chapters of this guide have prepared you for all the security you should need for employment privacy, but I'll outline again some of the concepts with emphasis on a few others:

- If you work at a job that is now "from home," consider purchasing a computer strictly for business or insist on your employer providing you with one. It's very important to separate your work life from your personal life. If you don't want to purchase a whole new system, check out my section on *virtual operating systems* at the end of Chapter 8, which will allow you to have a separate computer within your computer—for free.

- Be very skeptical of Zoom and Skype as platforms. Insist that your colleagues or clients migrate to a product like Jitsi Meet (great alternative, no account needed), Wire or Signal, which allows conference calls under the zero-knowledge encryption conditions that we favor at Watchman Privacy.

- If your coworkers simply won't budge, tell them that you don't feel comfortable having your camera on and talking about confidential topics. It's possible they'll get the message at that point, and also possible that you can keep your face off the record. I know some people who have never used their cameras and simply say if challenged that something is wrong with their equipment.

- Similarly, ask your colleagues to send all correspondence via a Signal group, a Wire group, or other services that feature end-to-end encryption and expiring messages (to the extent that this works for you). Now is the time to give up Google, Discord, and other insecure platforms.

- Be on high alert for email scams. Identity theft is at an all-time high right now because the bad actors out there know that people are on their computers twelve hours a day—including people who don't normally use computers. Reread Chapter 3 and practice its techniques.

---

[181] Just make sure to keep up with the news if you go to an island. You can easily get trapped. In April of 2021 the prime minister (murderer?) of St. Vincent and the Grenadines prohibited unvaccinated people from evacuating amidst a volcanic eruption: https://www.youtube.com/watch?v=2kEvMwsHFG0

- If you are a student or employee required to have a camera on you at all times—consider quitting? Otherwise explain that you don't have a camera. Michael Bazzell has suggested using a clear piece of tape to distort the picture while also showing that someone is clearly there—shout out to him for that idea.

Traveling. I performed considerable travel in the last year and have a few thoughts on the landscape. As contact-tracing becomes more popular and more regulated at the government level, it might be prudent to not leave a GPS trail. You'll recall from Chapter 5 the activist group who tracked lockdown protesters by their phones.[182] (Notice also how *The Guardian*, supposed defenders of privacy, stops caring about it when it cuts against their hard-left politics. Cowards.). These protesters are considered bio-terrorists. I wish I were exaggerating. In short, your GPS trail *matters*.

A refresher on hiding GPS coordinates:
- Credit card use, phone use, and geo-tracing digital technology use while traveling will reveal your location. Cash and only cash is your solution for purchases, including fueling up your vehicle. Don't leave a trail of where you've been.
- Don't forget your phone. Get a new phone in cash and pay for service anonymously. Leave it off unless absolutely necessary. For driving instructions, use maps or rely on dedicated GPS units such as Garmin.
- Make use of your VPN to seem to be where you are not. If your job or government mandates that you work from a particular country or be in a particular place, then a VPN can help you make sure you always appear to be there. Be consistent.
- Travel by private car as often as you can. Even Uber is reporting and banning people who don't follow their demands or who remove their mask for a moment.[183]
- Use this opportunity to get as far away from cities as you can and to diversify your citizenship and accommodations. Get working on it today.

---

[182] https://www.theguardian.com/us-news/2020/may/18/lockdown-protests-spread-coronavirus-cellphone-data
[183] https://www.usatoday.com/story/tech/2020/09/24/uber-banned-1-250-riders-not-wearing-masks-app-says/3514508001/

- Start practicing private accommodation. Start building a network of people you can stay with, start exploring couch-surfing groups online, and find ways around traditional hotels and their requirements (Chapter 7).

COVID restrictions are moving rapidly. Vaccines have now been issued and in some contexts made mandatory. This includes countries, regions, and most troublingly universities and job offices. For people who do not wish to give up DNA for testing or to receive a vaccine, these will be trying times. If you are such a person, start surveying the global scene and see which countries might be on board and which might not be. As a warning, remember that people who skirt COVID restrictions are increasingly being compared to murderers, so any attempt to fake a certificate, or to PhotoShop one, or to purchase one on the Dark Web could have serious consequences if you are exposed. We will have more to say about this topic in the Watchman Privacy newsletter in upcoming months.

Cancel Culture and Censorship

Some people don't believe in "cancel culture," claiming that this simply describes people getting what they deserve. I would ask you, as you have throughout this book, to challenge your assumptions. I will keep the phrase cancel culture, even as I entertain a broad definition that encapsulates the following: actively shutting people down whose politics one disagrees with, good old-fashioned government censorship, soft or shadow banning (where a person is not banned but becomes invisible on a platform), and everything in between. Allow me to share just a few examples of the kinds of things our fellow humanity has been up to in the last couple of years (indeed, last few months):

- The President of the United States was kicked off of various social media accounts
- A study shows that 60% of Americans now make purchases (or not) based on politics[184]

---

[184] https://www.edelman.com/sites/g/files/aatuss191/files/2020-06/2020%20Edelman%20Trust%20Barometer%20Specl%20Rept%20Brands%20and%20Racial%20Justice%20in%20America.pdf

- Amazon has banned certain books critical of LGPTQ lifestyles.[185] [186] Meanwhile, it still sells Hitler's *Mein Kampf*, among many other hate-filled books.
- eBay stopped allowing the sale of certain used Dr. Seuss books after they were banned from their publisher for supposed racism.[187]
- The free-speech platform Parler was banned from even its web service in a sudden blitzkrieg of Big Tech shutdown.
- A podcaster was visiting by police for criticizing an American congresswoman.[188]
- Countless people, including doctors and politicians, have been censored and banned from numerous websites and social media for contradicting health claims by the Center for Disease Control (CDC) and the World Health Organization (WHO).
- Disney Plus has begun to restrict classic cartoons for supposed racism,[189] and to edit others to remove nudity and other material deemed questionable.[190]
- A New York Times columnist called for the establishment of a "Reality Czar" to police "fake news" across the country.[191]
- In 2020 there were 29 countries that shut down the Internet for parts of the country,[192] in many cases during or preceding protests.
- Scottish Parliament have been pushing for a "hate speech" law to punish speech inside one's private home.[193] Numerous other governments have pushed through "hate speech" laws in the past year.

---

[185] https://www.wsj.com/articles/amazon-wont-sell-books-framing-lgbtq-identities-as-mental-illnesses-11615511380
[186] https://s.wsj.net/public/resources/documents/Amazonletter0311.pdf
[187] https://www.wsj.com/articles/dr-seuss-books-deemed-offensive-will-be-delisted-from-ebay-11614884201
[188] https://www.msn.com/en-us/news/us/police-visit-the-home-of-podcaster-after-he-criticized-aoc-on-twitter/ar-BB1fvttt
[189] https://www.the-sun.com/news/2479490/disney-pulls-iconic-movies-dumbo-the-aristocats/
[190] https://www.newsweek.com/disney-plus-censorship-movies-series-edited-splash-racist-nudity-censored-1498006
[191] https://www.nytimes.com/2021/02/02/technology/biden-reality-crisis-misinformation.html
[192] https://www.accessnow.org/keepiton-report-a-year-in-the-fight/
[193] https://www.thetimes.co.uk/article/hate-crime-bill-hate-talk-in-homes-must-be-prosecuted-6bcthrjdc

As a privacy consultant I've found myself surprisingly well equipped to deal with cancel culture. Privacy deals with matters of diversification and decentralization, two concepts which offer the only tools we have to escape the power brokers of the world. Big Tech companies have shown again and again that they can take someone down when the raging mob demands it. Even Dr Seuss is not immune. Maybe you're in the favorable political winds today, but that wind might change tomorrow. Also remember that services come and go, accounts get banned mistakenly, algorithms change, and accidents happen.

Your new rule is simple: redundancy, separation, and redundancy. Expect to be kicked out of your account at any time. Fight it, of course, and wield your boycotting power and loud voice, but also be prepared to fall back to Plan B. Each step along the way hide as many personal details as you can so as not to become a target in the first place. Let's get into it.

If your business or brand relies solely on Facebook for its messaging and advertising, you're doing business on the razor's edge. You should first develop a way to reach your audience outside of a single system: especially a Big Tech system. Get a newsletter service (not the censorious MailChimp[194]) and start collecting those valuable email addresses of customers—which can never be taken from you. Don't stop there. Download these addresses on your physical computer regularly in case you ever lose access.

Don't reject Big Tech options offhand, but make sure to replicate everything you have on their services to a friendlier alternative. If you're on Facebook, duplicate your material on Locals or Rumble. If you have a YouTube channel, get on BitChute, DTube, or LBRY. If you rely on writing then get on Medium and Substack as well as your website. Start a podcast and replicate your material there. These diversifying options can ensure your survival and flexibility.

Speaking of your website, that should be a top priority. Website hosts rarely kick people off their service. Many of those people you've heard of getting banned still have their website alive and kicking. Alex Jones, who runs Info Wars, saw traffic to his website skyrocket after he was banned during a Big Tech blitzkrieg in 2018.

---

[194] https://spectator.org/mailchimp-censorship-terms-of-service/

Still, as can be seen with the Parler case, you are vulnerable from web hosts. In defense, make sure when building websites to use free and open source (FOSS) services like WordPress instead of walled-garden services like Squarespace and Wix, which present an extra vulnerability. These companies essentially own your website content (at least the design), so that when they kick you out you lose all of that. Poof, gone. By contrast, WordPress is inert software that you own. Consider this: should your hosting service ban you, you could back up your WordPress website onto a hard drive and upload it to another host provider in a matter of minutes. Everything just as it was. By contrast, if Wix bans you then your website design is stuck permanently behind that ban wall. Just remember to back up the website often—weekly, if you can.

A website host is simply someone who provides space on one of their computers (called servers) for the images and files that make up your website to be shared on the Internet. I have hosts that I prefer, many of them free speech promoting services based in Iceland, Romania, and the Netherlands—where they also have the added benefit of requiring your local government to get international privileges to snoop on your account. Some of these services allow you to get up and going with as little as an email address and a bit of Bitcoin (should you desire to pay in that way). And their service and reputation can be pretty good as well. I'm speaking of services like Orange Website, EuroVPS, LibertyVPS, and others.

Other host and domain providers, such as Njalla, are run by principled anarchists who refuse to comply with any requests for take down and offer absolute privacy—in exchange for you trusting them with ownership. That might be too high a cost, but still, I bet you never realized this was an option? Whichever route you take make sure to buy multiple domain names and be sure to keep your domain service separate from your hosting service. If either your hosting or domain service should ever drop you then you can swap one for the other and continue on without compromising the whole website.

All of these strategies can be replicated across your digital life. Most things you rely on are probably services and not things you own. For example, you don't own that Gmail address; Google can take it from you with the snap of their fingers—or simply have a technical error—and you would never see/send/receive emails again. Reduce this reality as best you can. In this case, buy a domain name and create an email address through it: yourname@your website.com.

And if you're feeling more extreme (and tech-savvy), host your own server or get someone to do it for you. With an old laptop and some free software you can build your own physical server which could house your website and your email. A self-hosted server is the surest way to get rid of services and own your property. This is quite extreme and I don't expect the average person to try it.

At this point, who's going to stop you? Your Internet Service Provider? Have a back-up provider and a third option via mobile service. And if you use a VPN (as you should be), then they won't be able to see a single thing you're up to.

The only other main thing is money. As any businessperson knows, a business is nothing without a bank account. And yet, even financial institutions have decided to play politics instead of process transactions. When MasterCard,[195] PayPal,[196] and HSBC (who said they would close accounts of those who did not wear masks in their branches[197]) remove clients on a political whim, they expose an emotionalism that is unfitting for any financial partner. Use them while you can, but arrange for support in other ways. Have multiple financial accounts, including one in another country if possible. Try the VISA-MasterCard competitors in Discover and American Express. Try a local credit union in addition to a big bank. Then get out of banks. Collect money from fintech solutions such as TransferWise and Revolut. Accept digital currencies such as Bitcoin. Use trusts, LLCs, and otherwise hide your identity as much as you can throughout this process.

Find additional ways to collect money. Always allow direct support such as donations on your website. Type up a book and sell it on Amazon: a miraculous process that cuts out the traditional publishing agencies. Get on Patreon, but don't trust it.[198] Get on Locals. Get on Rumble. Share an Amazon wish list with your audience and have them send you gifts, mail, and gift cards (to a PO Box far from your house). On second thought—maybe not that last one. You don't want people waiting for you to pick up your mail one evening. But my point is to simply never lack for imagination. Stay on your

---

[195] https://finance.yahoo.com/news/mastercard-activist-shareholder-vote-ban-payments-far-right-groups-224513648.html
[196] https://thefederalistpapers.org/us/paypal-targets-conservatives
[197] https://www.fnlondon.com/articles/hsbc-threatens-to-close-accounts-for-people-who-refuse-to-wear-masks-in-branches-20210113
[198] https://www.businessinsider.com/sam-harris-deletes-patreon-account-after-platform-boots-conservatives-2018-12

toes and realize that when people and companies are making decisions based on politics and mob threats, you simply have to do your research and build antifragile systems.

The Upcoming Socioeconomic Collapse

In case you don't understand economics, it's not possible for societies to stop manufacturing and working for even a few days without consequences. We've now been at it for more than a year. Once the infusion of fake government money into the system hits a point of no return you can expect enormous financial collapse—if not tomorrow then in the upcoming few years—and such crises always carry with them more danger to your privacy and security. When books titled *In Defense of Looting* (2020) are published to tepid acceptance, you better expect that civilization is headed down the drain.[199]

Here's what you can expect:

1. Looting, rioting, and otherwise increased aggressions against you and your property.
2. Eradication of cash payments and cash storage (via a central bank digital currency).
3. Price controls, capital controls, and other restrictions on using money and moving it out of the country.
4. Banning of or required reporting of precious medals and cryptocurrency ownership.
5. Mandatory contact-tracing and other surveillance based on your phone, DNA, face, and gait.
6. Military or police checkpoints to enter or exit cities, states, or regions.
7. Recording of your travel anywhere outside of your house.
8. Mandatory proof of vaccination and possible DNA records.

In short, it will not be fun: economically, politically, socially, and certainly in terms of privacy. But just in case you're not convinced about the direction of the world right now, allow me to share a few bullet points to chew on:

---

[199] One "hard-hitting" *NPR* article treated the author—advocating violence and theft—rather sympathetically: www.npr.org/sections/codeswitch/2020/08/27/906642178/one-authors-argument-in-defense-of-looting.

- World government debt approaching 300 trillion dollars.[200]
- Stock market bubble preparing to burst and wreak havoc.[201]
- Housing bubble preparing to burst and wreak havoc.[202]
- Developing economies being crushed.[203]
- Unparalleled computer chip shortage shutting down entire companies.[204]
- Food shortages and price increases already beginning: a death sentence for people in many countries, and a national security threat for others.[205]
- Homicides up by 33% in American cities for 2020.[206]
- Mass shortage of goods and business activity because of the reduced-rate of many shipping ports.[207]

I'm sorry to say that this is the time to begin prepping. Here are a few thoughts regarding your privacy and safety in the upcoming disaster years:

- Start practicing how to own real assets and study how you might get around capital controls (see Chapter 6).
- In particular start learning how to use cryptocurrencies. Monero is especially useful as it is the most private coin—it does not reveal its blockchain. Just remember that the privacy of cryptocurrency depends entirely on how you acquire it.
- Acquire physical precious metals now. Once you have a few in hand, try to secure some more in private vaults in other countries.
- Diversify within precious metals. Silver coins could be great for bartering given their low cost per ounce. Gold on the other hand,

---

[200] https://www.bloomberg.com/news/articles/2021-02-17/global-debt-hits-all-time-high-as-pandemic-boosts-spending-need
[201] https://www.forbes.com/sites/steveforbes/2021/03/23/stock-market-bubble-will-burst-and-inflation-will-follow/
[202] https://www.wsj.com/articles/house-prices-are-inflating-around-the-world-11616932846
[203] https://www.wsj.com/articles/as-u-s-economy-roars-back-life-in-many-poor-countries-gets-worse-11617874201
[204] https://www.bloomberg.com/news/articles/2021-04-05/why-shortages-of-a-1-chip-sparked-crisis-in-the-global-economy
[205] https://www.msn.com/en-us/money/markets/the-grocery-price-shock-is-coming-to-a-store-near-you/ar-BB1fZDaC
[206] https://www.cnn.com/2021/04/03/us/us-crime-rate-rise-2020/index.html
[207] https://www.wsj.com/articles/americas-imports-are-stuck-on-ships-floating-just-off-los-angeles-11617183002

which is as much as eighty times more valuable per ounce compared to silver, will be easier to transport wealth. Half ounces of precious metals might help you slip through security since they look like regular coins.

- Try to get a second citizenship or residence in the next year or two—as soon as you can. Consider staying in a country that you trust more than your own.
- Move to a part of your country where you feel protected, have natural resources, and are far from danger. *Strategic Relocation* by Joel Skousen is a great book to begin your study in this area.
- This will be more serious than previous world events in part because of the nasty trend of urbanization in the last century: one in eight people live in just 33 cities of the world.[208] Avoid cities as best you can.
- Open up a bank account abroad and put some money in there now before it's too late. Have your home currency but also foreign currency.
- Be careful what you invest in these days. This is not investing advice, but I would be very afraid of the stock market and the major currencies (Dollar, Pound, Euro).
- Prepare a boat for departure. Learn how to use it.
- Consider seasteading and the sea houses made by fascinating companies such as Ocean Builders.
- Prepare a private jet for departure if you have the money. Get a pilot's license. Combine wealth with others to afford one.
- Start reading the news in other countries to see how they handle things. *Trends Research* is a handy news source.
- Find community; form relationships with your neighbors and friends.
- Learn some martial arts and how to handle various weapons.

Things might not get apocalyptic and may instead test your resolve as first-world amenities are stripped away. During the early months of COVID-1984 the Internet systems were strained as everyone used their computers religiously during the day and streams videos at night. YouTube and Netflix in

---

[208] https://www.dw.com/en/un-68-percent-of-worlds-population-to-live-in-cities-by-2050/a-43818167

2018 accounted for twenty-five percent of the world's Internet bandwidth.[209] And that was two years ago. Governments have also been increasingly talking about their ability (and prerogative) to shut down internet services, and have been particular aggressive in de-platforming anyone who speaks out against the conventional COVID narrative. Russia and Belarus have recently tested shutting down their Internets nationwide[210], and in total 29 countries in 2020 shut down Internet service.[211] You would be wise to consider what your options are and to take time to think deeply about what the Internet means to your life.

Here are a few ways to plan for internet collapse:

- Increase your phone's data plan.
- Learn to use radios.
- Migrate to offline software so you don't have to rely on the cloud.
- Start learning about decentralized messaging apps that can send information from phone to phone without a traditional data signal.
- Practice downloading archives of online material that you might enjoy if the Internet were to ever go down. You can download the entirety of Wikipedia in around 15 GB of compressed data.[212] That's more than six million articles—some of them the length of novellas—of choice information, including any survival data you might need.
- Start listening to survival podcasts and otherwise make yourself informed about SHTF planning (start with a solar-powered generator). My favorite resource on this topic is the book *Patriots: A Novel of Survival in the Coming Collapse*. You'll find plenty of options once you start getting into this world.

Good luck and stay dangerous.

---

[209] https://www.pcmag.com/news/netflix-and-youtube-make-up-over-a-quarter-of-global-internet-traffic
[210] https://www.bloomberg.com/news/articles/2020-08-28/belarusian-officials-shut-down-internet-with-technology-made-by-u-s-firm
[211] https://news.trust.org/item/20210303140415-x16mh
[212] https://en.wikipedia.org/wiki/Wikipedia:Database_download

Chapter 10
Defending Privacy

Had I not once lived under the dictatorship of Spain's Generalissimo Francisco Franco, I would not be working in the field of privacy today.

- JJ Luna

To conclude this book I want to arm you with arguments about the fundamental importance of privacy. I have found that most people who disregard privacy simply haven't spent enough time in historical and philosophical examination. Please consider the following arguments and their rebuttals.

Argument One: We Can't Define Privacy

Maybe not, but so what? We all have an idea of what we mean by privacy: the kind of climate that allows an individual to be left alone and participate in society at his choosing. And just because we can't precisely define something doesn't mean that thing isn't exceedingly important. Let's continue to work out its meaning—if we need to—and not settle for the kind of academic masturbation perpetrated by groups like the Surveillance Studies Network, which sees surveillance as "complex and multi-layered." Whenever you hear that kind of drivel, run far in the other direction. There is nothing "complex" about the way governments crush people across the planet with the aid of their fascist lackeys in the private sector.

Argument Two: Privacy Hides and Protects Bad Guys

I was surprised to be reminded that fully 50 percent of the Bill of Rights were intended to make the job of law enforcement harder.

- Edward Snowden

Former Google CEO Eric Schmidt once said that "If you have something that you don't want anyone to know, maybe you shouldn't be doing it in the first place."[213] The cleverest response was from the website CNET, which published Schmidt's home address and other personal information. Another authoritarian, former Attorney General John Mitchell, put it this way: "any citizen of the United States who is not involved in some illegal activity has nothing to fear whatsoever." Assuming these arguments are genuine and not simply bored trolling by sociopaths, Schmidt and Mitchell have it completely backward.

The purpose of privacy is to protect people from the whims of the punitive systems around them, which 99.9% of the time means the government. What is legal today might be illegal tomorrow. Tomorrow you might be a "bad guy" for doing the same things you were doing yesterday. Take the following examples:

- COVID. Overnight you could suddenly be punished for not wearing a piece of fabric across your face, and many have been punished for breaking that order.

- In recent years Canada made it illegal to suggest that there are two human sexes, punishable by discrimination laws.

- In the United Kingdom, which doesn't have a constitution, a girl was arrested for posting Snoop Dog lyrics on Instagram ("hate speech"). Hate speech is a made-up term that was created on the whim of closet dictators. It is entirely subjective—I consider Schmidt, Mitchell, and most government officials to be espousing hate speech according to my own more principled definition.

- In the United States Constitution, only three federal crimes are listed (all controversial); today there are many thousands of federal laws that have been created by bored or malicious legislators.

The laws of governments sway according to which direction the evil people in charge want them to go. In Nazi Germany it was illegal to hide Jewish people from extermination. I suppose Schmidt would say Germans hiding Jews shouldn't be doing it in the first place.

---

[213] https://www.youtube.com/watch?v=A6e7wfDHzew&feature=emb_logo

But really: of course privacy protects bad guys, just like it protects good guys. One wonders first who is defining "good" and "bad." But as they say: I'm a freedom fighter, you're a rebel, he's a terrorist.[214] Privacy is a tool used by everyone. The same could be said of roads, utility knives, cash, and oxygen. All of these things technically assist bad people who do bad things. Does that mean we should ban them all?

It's funny how hesitant police and intelligence agencies are to becoming more transparent: i.e give up *their* privacy. I wonder why? Alan Westin has noted that "the modern totalitarian state relies on secrecy for the regime, but high surveillance and disclosure for all other groups."[215]

After Snowden leaked his information the White House went after him, saying that what he released was "a critical tool in protecting the nation from terrorist threats." The irony is laughable. Governments demand privacy for themselves, but don't allow it to the people.

If I knew that my advice on privacy was specifically reaching bad people— those who coerce others (in all forms)—then I would do anything in my power to stop it. But the nature of privacy is that I don't have vast data on the people I write for. I don't have any information at all. That's how it should be.

The toxic underlying conviction of this argument is that the purpose of society is to remove all danger from existence. This kind of Utopian thinking has been responsible for almost every instance of evil in human history. Tyrannical governments have always used the jingle "it protects bad people" to erase human freedom little by little. The nature of freedom is that bad actions will happen, and that it is our first duty as neighbors and social creatures to build a social ethical fabric that discourages such behavior, and to right our own moral compass. Then we can punish coercion against us or deter it in the moment. To reverse this process, or to offload it to institutions that have an ever-expanding monopoly on coercion (governments) is to disbelieve in the concept of freedom entirely.

Let's put it a different way. Privacy is similar to freedom. It is said that freedom and security are incompatible. That's not true, since freedom allows one to have security—it is the means to the end. Even if we had to pick one, which we don't, the purpose of society is not to be more secure, but to be more free.

---

[214] Or as Doug Casey says.
[215] See his book *Privacy and Freedom*

There will always be danger in human existence. Danger actually increases the more top-down authorities want to make societies more secure. How often do we forget Benjamin Franklin's words? "Those who would give up essential liberty to purchase a little temporary safety deserve neither liberty nor safety."

Rules should be determined by collective agreement (at the local level) about the few things not allowed: namely theft and violence. Outlawing any tool such as privacy at the governmental level for the sake of security is coercive (evil), doesn't work, and in fact often has the opposite effect.

Argument Three: I Have Nothing to Hide

If you give me six lines written by the hand of the most honest of men, I will find something in them which will hang him.
- Cardinal Richelieu

Show me the man and I'll show you the crime.
- Lavrentiy Beria, Soviet Politician

Congratulations on being a boring, cookie-cutter drone who lacks any semblance of an imagination. To be perfectly honest, I don't really care if you think you have nothing to hide. Here's Snowden: "Ultimately, saying that you don't care about privacy because you have nothing to hide is no different from saying you don't care about freedom of speech because you have nothing to say."[216] It's irrelevant to me whether you think you have nothing to hide. That fact does not give you the right to support coercive authorities that will strip *me* of *my* privacy.

I've also never met a person who actually meant this. You really have nothing to hide? As a member of the cybersecurity community I have seen people who have the ability to sabotage your life with just a single email address. With minimal information and a bit of moxie, a hacker can gain access to your phone number, wipe out your financial accounts, devastate your relationships, erase all files you have ever created, and much more. With an IP address angry online gamers have sent in SWAT teams to their rivals houses to have them gunned down ("swatting"). Reread the introduction of this book if you can't think of any reasons why you would need to hide. Then again, we've already established your imaginative deficiencies.

---

[216] *Permanent Record*, page 208.

Argument Four: Privacy is About Hiding from "Surveillance Capitalism"

One afternoon I came across someone who on a major privacy community website said that he was looking for advice to hide "not from governments but from tech companies." This line of thinking puts the cart before the horse.

First of all tech companies cannot harm anyone. All that a company can do is offer you a good or service which you can choose to have or not. This is voluntary exchange. When I stopped liking Google and Facebook I gave them up the next day.

By contrast, your relationship with government is mandatory and coercive. You take what they offer or they will kill you. You think I'm exaggerating? Try not paying your taxes and then resisting arrest when they come for you. Mao Zedong once rightly said that all governmental power flows through the barrel of a gun. Exactly. It is estimated that in the last century governments killed 170 million people, not including world wars.[217] How many people has Facebook killed?

The concept of "surveillance capitalism," popularized by a limousine Marxist whose name I won't even mention here, is on its face ridiculous. Companies are nothing more than the enlarged ethic of their user or customer base. Google has taken your information because you have given it to them. Jeff Bezos is a trillionaire because you gave him your money voluntarily. I don't like Google and don't support them. I recommend throughout this book to avoid all of the big tech companies as much as possible. But suggesting insipid nonsense like so-called capitalism (an inaccurate bogeyman term popularized by Karl Marx) is what you should be afraid of is ridiculous.

That's not to say that large corporations are incapable of doing harm. But they only do harm when their work is used by the entity that has the monopoly on force: the government. Like when IBM helped the Nazis tabulate the Jews sent away in cattle cars. Or when Peter Thiel's surveillance company Palantir Technologies starts to go after whoever the US government considers its enemy on any given day. Or even when candy companies get government-approved "heart healthy" labels on their "foods" and lobby to have the real food producers excluded by government order. This system is precisely called fascism (a form of socialism) and it is a problem not of industry or free exchange or "capitalism" but of government, whose power sustains it all.

---

[217] See R. J. Rummel, *Death by Government*, for example.

Argument Five: Privacy is Holding Back Humanity

Joe Rogan is a proponent of this argument. His biologically deterministic thinking assumes that the future of humanity is to connect with AI and to become a kind of a hive mind where sharing is the norm and identity and individuality no longer exist. Nor does privacy. As is often the case with bad logic, the argument is self-defeating. Rogan is an independent figure whose refined idiosyncrasies are a big reason for his success. In a world with AI, Joe Rogan would not exist, nor would his argument about the future of humanity.

This argument also begs the question: holding back humanity from what? Many futurists, from Rogan to Ray Kurzweil, fetishize some grand world in which humans have moved beyond their nature and solved all individual and social problems. They have merged with AI, filled their bloodstream with life-extending nanobots, uploaded their minds online to download into a different body on a different planet, and perfected through careful science the perfect socio-political environment.

I'm happy for people who can look at these futures and smile. But the reality is that these are dystopias. The political thinker Edmund Burke once said that there is no progress to be made in ethics.[218] Humans are special by virtue of what they are. In these altered future states we will have scrubbed out everything that makes us special.

The other aspect that futurists miss is the belief that society can be perfected. Rogan seems to think that in the future we will be so advanced in our thinking that major ethical and social problems will all be solved. Really? My study of history has shown that, if anything, we have devolved in terms of ethics over the millennia. As far as I'm concerned, the great ethical debate of human history is the balance between coercion and individual freedom. I fail to see how freedom will be preserved in a world in which we are all linked. Technology and the scientific method cannot and will never be able to solve ethical problems. No, I'm afraid all the familiar ethical and all-to-human questions will be the same in any future time.

---

[218] See his *Reflections on the Revolution in France*

Argument Six: By Hiding We Reinforce Surveillance

Here is a nuanced argument worth thinking about. Nomad Capitalist Andrew Henderson in his book puts the argument like this:

> If you really are living the Nomad Capitalist lifestyle, why do you need to hide your money? You want to put up an extra layer of protection between you and the government, sure; but *freedom means having nothing to hide.*

This is an argument not so much against privacy, but against the way we currently pursue it. This entire book has focused on hiding things from other people and from institutions. Privacy extremists will go so far as to tell you never to vote since it exposes your name to various databases. But the more privacy supporters stop participating in civic life, the more privacy itself retreats to the shadows. Why not simply say that we're going to search for "bomb making" simply because it might be an interesting topic—surveillance systems be damned? By unabashedly exposing ourselves and saying "Yes I'm going to do something 'suspicious:' what are you going to do about it?" we cultivate a society in which such behavior is acceptable and not relegated to shady back alleys of the Internet. Just as the physical health of a society becomes worse the more people think about healthfulness,[219] so too does privacy seem to vanish the more we discuss it.

The argument is not air-tight, but instead of poking holes at it I prefer to leave it as a parting thought.

---

[219] See *In Defense of Food* by Michael Pollan

Resources

Literature

1. *The Machine Stops*, E. M. Forster
2. *Nineteen Eighty-Four*, George Orwell
3. *Brave New World*, Aldous Huxley
4. *Childhood's End*, Arthur C. Clarke
5. *The Circle*, Dave Eggers

Privacy

6. *Nothing to Hide*, Glenn Greenwald
7. *Permanent Record*, Edward Snowden
8. *Data and Goliath*, Bruce Schneier
9. *Privacy: A Manifesto*, Wolfgang Sofsky
10. *Future Crimes*, Marc Goodman
11. *How to Be Invisible*, JJ Luna
12. *Asset Protection ... In Financially Unsafe Times*, Arnold Goldstein
13. *Extreme Privacy*, Michael Bazzell
14. *The Hitchhiker's Guide to Online Anonymity*, AnonymousPlanet
15. *The Police and You*, Boston T. Party
16. The Privacy, Security, & OSINT Show (podcast)
17. The Hated One (YouTube/Bitchute channel)
18. Privacytools.io (website)
19. The Watchman Privacy Podcast

Red Pilling

20. *Discipline and Punish*, Michel Foucault
21. *Totally Incorrect: Volume 1*, Doug Casey
22. *A History of Western Philosophy*, Bertrand Russell
23. *The Abolition of Man*, C. S. Lewis

24. *The Rational Male,* Rollo Tomassi
25. *IN-SHADOW* (YouTube video; I interviewed creator)
26. *The Present Age,* Soren Kierkegaard
27. *UNSCRIPTED,* MJ Demarco
28. *V for Vendetta* (film)
29. *The Fountainhead,* Ayn Rand
30. *Against Intellectual Property,* Stephan N. Kinsella
31. *The Sovereign Individual,* Davidson and Rees-Mogg
32. *Anatomy of the State,* Murray Rothbard
33. *The Origins of War in Child Abuse,* Lloyd deMause; (audiobook)
34. *Without Conscience: The Psychopaths Among Us,* Robert Hare
35. *The Devil Drives: A Life of Sir Richard Burton,* Fawn Brodie
36. *The Real Crash,* Peter Schiff
37. *Crisis Investing for the Rest of the 90's,* Doug Casey
38. "The Culture Industry," Theodore Adorno
39. *In Defense of Food,* Michael Pollan
40. *Battlefield America,* John W. Whitehead
41. *AI Superpowers,* Kai-Fu Lee
42. *Digital Minimalism,* Cal Newport
43. *Antifragile,* Nassim Taleb
44. The Rebel Capitalist Show (podcast)
45. Radical Personal Finance (podcast, start with early episodes)

International Living and Preparedness

46. *Nomad Capitalist,* Andrew Henderson (also YouTube channel)
47. *Adventure Capitalist* and *Investment Biker,* Jim Rogers
48. The Expat Money Show (podcast)
49. *Strategic Relocation,* Joel Skousen and Andrew Skousen
50. *Patriots: A Novel of Survival in the Coming Collapse,* James Rawles

Newsletters

51. The Watchman Privacy Newsletter (https://watchmanprivacy.com)
52. International Man (https://internationalman.com)
53. The Sovereign Man (https://www.sovereignman.com/)

Everything Else

Credit Reports/Score/Freeze

You should keep your credit reports frozen until the moment you're ready to use them for a credit check. The US passed a law making this free to the user after the 2017 Equifax data breach. Visit Equifax, Experion, and TransUnion to freeze each report. Recently these companies have started demanding account creation and phone numbers to process the transactions. Be persistent and mail in requests if you have to.

You should also check your credit reports at least once a year. You can check each of the three for free once per 12 months, and the official website is AnnualCreditReport.com, but if you don't trust that, then go to https://www.usa.gov/credit-reports and follow the link from there. You'll have to fill in some sensitive data, including your social security number, but they already know all of that and it's simply what you have to do.

Identity Theft

Continuing from my ideas at the end of Chapter 3. Identity theft can occur if someone collects enough information about you that they can apply for some kind of credit account under your name. Keep your credit reports frozen until you need them and check them regularly (minimum once per year). Look for any accounts you did not create. Unfortunately a lot of the information needed to steal your identity is already online in the form of hacked or leaked databases. For that reason some experts advocate "planting your flag" on any credit-related account. So you might create an account at each of the credit boroughs (an online account—separate from your actual credit report), and possibly in your state/region's unemployment system so that no one else can take them and fake unemployment under your name. These kinds of unemployment scams have increased tremendously during the COVID lockdowns as governments have made it highly lucrative to be unemployed. Other examples of the plant-your-flag technique include creating an online account for any financial service you have (even if you only use their services with a physical branch) and creating accounts for online utilities if you've not yet done so. Basic identity theft protection involves never giving out your ID to be scanned and collected (tell them you are a victim of identity theft), never using cards to pay at restaurants (where you can be scammed), and otherwise keeping your information out of as many systems as possible.

Most identity theft happens within businesses as employees (disgruntled or malicious) target employers or other employees. Don't hire employees if you can help it! Be very careful typing in your pin number at an ATM (jostle the keyboard around to see if it is a fake). Don't leave any personal items face-up in your car. Avoid babysitters. Shred all paper documents.

Security Questions

Think about it. Security questions exist largely to make sure you can reset your password. In other words, they are the weak link for a hacker. Use security questions the same way you would use a password: randomly generated numbers and symbols. Save the question and answer in your password manager. Never give a "real" answer to an insecurity question.

Private Utilities

Utilities are the most difficult thing to set up privately: see the end of Chapter 7 for basic advice. However, alternatives to utilities companies do exist. Solar panels and batteries such as Tesla's Powerwall make that somewhat possible (Tesla, however, demands a monitoring app for most of their services, which is unfortunate). If you have water underneath your property, consider having a well dug and a water tank installed. Solar panels might be tempting, but consider that most towns and cities make it immensely difficult to get off the grid. In many cases you will be forced to stay on the grid. To attain off-grid utilities you'll have to live outside of city limits, for starters. Finally, Elon Musk's backyard satellite internet service Starlink could be the first step to greater internet independence.[220]

---

[220] https://www.wsj.com/articles/elon-musk-and-amazon-are-battling-to-put-satellite-internet-in-your-backyard-11616212827

Police

There's a popular YouTube video called "Don't talk to the police." Watch it. Anything that you say can and will be used against you. Officers are trained to psychologically exploit you and this is made worse by the badge or gun in front of you. Listen to what they say, never touch them, and never respond to more than basic questions. Don't let them search your vehicle ("My lawyer told me not to permit searches without a warrant"). Learn the laws of your country and area regarding what you can and should say. Take some time to study these as they could be a life-changer. Read Boston T. Party's *You and the Police*.

Fourteen Eyes Countries

This is a group of allied countries with an agreement to share surveillance data that they accumulate on their citizens—and anyone else. They include the United States, Canada, United Kingdom, Australia, New Zealand (the Five Eyes) as well as Denmark, France, Netherlands, Norway, Germany, Belgium, Italy, Sweden, Spain. These nations are also known for performing more surveillance than other countries, as you might imagine.

Notice this is largely Europe and North America, leaving South America, the Caribbean, Asia, and Africa out of the system. These parts of the world can be less interested in pursuing you (obviously not China, etc.), and you might consider them for your next habitation. Asian countries rarely cooperate with each other for cultural reasons and you can find great independence in that environment. You'll also encounter many privacy services (VPNs, email, messaging) that are outside of Fourteen Eyes countries. These kind of services are great, though if your service is performing "no logging" and has an audited "zero knowledge" policy, there shouldn't be any data to be compromised anyway.

Extradition

Extradition involves your home government having you kidnapped at the behest of a foreign government (where you currently are) so they can funnel you through their own legal system. Then you can be tried and sentenced for whatever perceived injustice you have done. For some people like Glenn Greenwald, who received the documents from Edward Snowden in Hong Kong, extradition is a serious threat. I suspect for this reason Greenwald lives in Brazil, which has laws against extradition to the US. It wouldn't hurt to make yourself even vaguely aware of countries and their extradition traditions. I recall Jeffrey Epstein's friend Ghislaine Maxwell spending time in France for a similar reason, though she bizarrely traveled to the US where she was caught.

See Brazil, Switzerland, Brunei, Russia, China, Ecuador, and France.

5G

You don't need to participate in any conspiracy theories to know that 5G technology is going to make privacy a lot more difficult. At a basic level 5G simply enhances the speed at which data can transmit through cellular towers. We will only start to fathom the consequences of this in upcoming years, but you can expect video recording to become a lot easier as well as location data to become more accurate. Soon most of our lives will be on camera. Because 5G is so strong and its towers so close together, it can more easily penetrate walls to note your location or to even theoretically be used to map out the inside of your house. A company called Safe Living Tech offers bed coverings, paint, and other tools to reject 5G and other signals entering your home. You can also choose a house that has no cellular signal in the area and rely on VoIP services (see Chapter 5).

Website Hosting and Domain Service

First, separate your domain service and your hosting service. Pick a hosting service in a privacy-friendly country such as Iceland. For your domain name, things get trickier. The ICANN, who regulates these matters, must have some real information on you. So if you use fake information and they ask you to prove that you are "John Doe," you won't be able to do it. Thus, you could lose your domain name, as unlikely as this is. This isn't the end of the world, as you can direct to another domain, but it can certainly hurt your business. The company Njalla buys the domain for you in their own name and requires no information from you. It is risky offloading your ownership, but very private; Njalla is reputable. Gandi.net requires the usual data, but is known for limiting and protecting this information. When you register for your domain service, you should be able to get away with your initials instead of your name. For address, you can select something that you can at least prove should the need arise (a hotel?). If you run a WordPress website make sure it is updated daily. Remove any plugins that you don't need. Basically keep everything as simple as possible. Consider writing your own basic HTML website which, if kept simple, is as good as it gets for privacy and security.

Homelessness, Living as a Bum

Quite possible and can definitely get you off the grid. Dumpster diving is an art and there is no reason to starve or beg. I suggest reading the book *Rough Living* by Chris Damitio. Fantastic story of a man who lives high off the hog while being a bum. Homeless shelters are a great resource for privacy since these people don't have all the expected data of the average person: address, phone number, employment status, etc. In the upcoming decade when the West and the world becomes poverty-stricken, this will be helpful knowledge. You might try to live like a bum for a few days to improve yourself, as self-help guru Tim Ferriss advocates.

Being Stateless

Not as romantic as it sounds. You would think that not being owned by a slave master would make you free; unfortunately it makes you free in the same way an escaped slave was free in antebellum America. You can also get caught in a Catch-22 kind of scenario where you can't leave and you can't stay—you can't get citizenship again either. By all means look into the consequences of this, and then consider settling instead for multiple citizenships where you can play one country against the other. And renounce one if it becomes necessary.

Blackmail, Revenge Porn, etc.

Or other unsavory things about you online. It's a tricky situation and you wouldn't be out of order getting in touch with a professional or (possibly) law enforcement. Though law enforcement likely won't be able to help. Withoutmyconsent.org and cybercivilrights.org are two resources. The thing to realize is that if you pay these people, they'll either ask for more money or post the things anyway. Instead you might want to avoid all communication and prepare to mitigate the damage. Indeed, the standard advice is not even to acknowledge any messages from the person. Get in touch with the websites they post to and ask to have them taken down. Play every card in the book: child porn, privacy laws in your region (or not in your region), copyright, DMCA, etc. You can block the first page of search results by creating social media accounts in your name (LinkedIn, Twitter) and creating a WordPress blog under a domain of your own name. Few people look beyond the first page of search results. It's not a bad idea to reserve these ahead of time before something bad does happen. Follow the advice of this book strictly to ensure this never happens to you.

Sending Things Through the Mail

To be fair, mail delivery has often been surveyed, such as in the United States when the US Postal Service was actually the main arm of censorship and obscenity examination in the country (late nineteenth and early twentieth centuries).[221] First, use some common sense. In many countries you're not required to put a return address. Why advertise to the world who is sending this thing? At the very most just put your initials or some code word that your family would recognize. If sending cash, send it in between the pages of an old book. The risk of losing cash in the mail is fairly slim. Some recommend special sprays to hide the contents of a package, but that could simply draw suspicion if someone is watching. When looking for alternatives keep in mind that the shipment of items is strictly regulated by governments. I hope more private delivery options crop up in the future.

Right to Privacy

The concept of "rights" has been greatly perverted in recent decades. Today most people mean "government goodies" when they use the term. That's actually the antithesis of what a right is, which is something that, by virtue of your humanity, the universe, or God, no earthly thing (government) can take away from you, nor grant to you. Think of Jefferson's language in the *Declaration of Independence*: "Granted by their Creator with certain unalienable Rights, that among these are Life, Liberty..." I suppose people may have a right to privacy, but if that's the case it means it's your duty to protect it at all costs from government and anyone else who is forcibly trying to take it from you. That is some serious responsibility.

I find the most moving and correct definition of a right in the Ancient Greek play *Antigone* by Sophocles. The protagonist Antigone says:

>... [I]t wasn't Zeus at all
>who proclaimed them, nor did Justice who lives
>with the gods below make laws like these for men,
>nor did I think your decrees so formidable

---

[221] See *The Most Dangerous Book*, Kevin Birmingham

that you, mere mortal as you are, could override the laws of the gods, unwritten and unshakable. They are not for now and yesterday, but live forever...[222]

Computer Hibernation

Hibernation is a weird anomaly that shouldn't exist. Shutting off your computer turns it off. Sleeping your computer saves your current session in your RAM. Hibernation saves your current set-up on your hard-drive. With today's SSDs hibernation provides no benefit. More pressing for our concerns is that a hibernating computer is uniquely vulnerable. Unlike sleep or shut down, your hard drive can be copied and your information taken when it is in this mode. Disable or don't use hibernation, and shut off your computer fully when it's not being used.

Firearms

Very few countries are civilized enough to not punish people for acquiring the most useful tool for self defense. We'll speak of the United States for the moment. Gun purchasing laws varies by state. Your best bet by a wide margin is a private gun sale: a friend or a friend-of-a-friend. Some people at gun shows allow private sales, but not all of them. If you go through a regular shop they will run a background check. You will be marked down, make no mistake. As for ammo, make sure to buy it in a place where you don't have to show ID. Cash should go without saying.

Especially as guns become forbidden items in upcoming years be careful where you store them and keep your mouth shut if anyone (friends included) asks you if you have one. Also (not legal advice) note that transporting guns in your car is usually acceptable provided it is in a locked container out of your reach. And that in some cities you are not allowed to have a gun on you at any time, usually including your car. Indeed, in some states guns of "high" clip sizes (such as a standard Glock) are also illegal. Store firearms in innocuous containers such as musical instrument cases. Note that pre-1898 guns are not considered legal guns in many cases. Consult Boston T. Party's *Gun Bible* for the ultimate resource on all things gun-related.

---

[222] Mary Lefkowitz and James Romm - *The Greek Plays* (2016), *Modern Library*, lines 450 - 457

Reputation Management

Don't bother messaging Google or a news company to take down a story about you—they won't comply. Fill the first page of search results with your own accounts and website. Create a Google Alert for keywords about you or your business. Contact me via my website for consulting and service on this topic.

Census

A legal obligation in many places, including the United States. Around half of Americans never respond to the census, and the last person to be prosecuted for not filling it out was half a century ago.

Employment Privacy

A Wisconsin company asked employees to install an RFID chip in their bodies to track their movements and behavior.[223] Need any further motivation to be self-employed? When filling out a job application provide only the information that you are willing to give. State ID numbers, for example, should be avoided; instead put something like "Can provide upon offer of employment." PO Boxes and burner phone numbers come in handy. Avoid downloading any company applications on your own electronic devices. Ask for a company device, or say you are unable to do it because you don't have a smart phone, etc. It might not hurt to ask this before signing a contract.

EBay, PayPal, and Selling Online

PayPal reports to the IRS after $20,000. The new payment system at eBay, Ayden payment processing, which they instituted slowly throughout 2020 and 2021, by default sends details to the IRS and expects you to explain that your old items are not being sold at profit. This is a deal-breaker for many eBay sellers, though unfortunately there aren't many good alternatives. When selling online process your photos through the Signal app or through something like Ver Exif to strip out its GPS coordinates. EBay does this for you, but it never hurts to get in the habit. Take care selling anything attached to a Facebook account, and with Craigslist be sure to meet in neutral

---

[223] https://www.usatoday.com/story/tech/nation-now/2017/07/24/wisconsin-company-install-rice-sized-microchips-employees/503867001

locations, use a burner phone, don't reveal personal details, and don't make exceptions to this system.

Online Dating

Should be used as a backup option. Get a burner phone number—this is where MySudo comes in handy—and be careful what photos and information you give out. Do basic online research to find out about the person. Always meet in a neutral location for the first time, and in public. Don't get picked up at your house, or if you do, walk down the road a bit. Don't let him or her hold your phone or give them any information about where you live or that can expose you on (at least) the first date. Most importantly, do not compromise on your rules. No exceptions.

Index

5G: 97, 228
Alternatives to digital services: 23, 56
Amazon: 10, 39, 129-131
Android: 104
Apple: 81, 104, 201
Asset protection: 122, 137, 152, 189
Assets: 137
Banking: 120-121, 151, 152
Browsers: 23, 58-62
Cancel culture/censorship: 10-12, 55, 88, 205-208
Car registration: 160-161
Cash: 24, 123-129
Central bank digital currencies: 55
Civilizational collapse: 210-214
Cloud storage: 23, 164
Cookies: 59-61,
COVID: 10, 107, 199-205, 225
Credit reports and credit freezing: 77, 225
Cryptocurrencies: 136, 138-147
Data breaches: 16, 168
Disinformation: 173-174
DNA: 48, 192-193
Doxing: 27-28, 32-33
Email: 23, 66-70
Encryption: 91-93, 163-164
Extradition: 227
Facebook: 9, 27-30, 207
Facial recognition: 196-197
Family: 175
Fingerprinting: 182-184
Fourteen Eyes: 227
Gold: 133-136
Google: 22-23, 105, 201
GPS: 158-159
Guns: 231

Homeschooling: 176
Hotels: 168-169
Identity Theft: 77, 225
International living: 46-47, 162, 184-189, 202, 229
Internet browser: 58-59, 62
Internet of Things (IoT): 12, 89-91
Legal-Industrial Complex: 11, 42, 105, 122
Linux: 80-85, 180-181
LLCs: 148-151, 189-191
Mail: 230
Medical: 192-193
Moving: 170-171
Offshore banking: 121, 152
Passwords: 71-76
PayPal: 110, 132, 232
Physical solutions: 54-57, 89-91
Police: 10, 161-162, 210, 227
Prepaid debit cards: 148
Privacy.com: 129-132
Private messengers: 25-27, 101
Rental culture: 89-91
Revenge porn: 168, 229
"Right to privacy": 230
RVs: 166
Seasteading: 166
Self-employment: 21, 148-151, 189-191
Social media: 27-30, 32-33
Surveillance: 79, 106, 227
Swatting: 33
Taxation: 152-154, 184
TOR: 93-95, 180-181
Torrenting: 85-91
TVs: 18-19, 37
Uber: 162
Utilities: 48, 226
Virtual machines: 193-195
VPN: 63-65, 179-180
Website/domain hosting: 207-209, 228

Stay tuned for more:

The Watchman Privacy Podcast
Available on most podcast platforms
or at Bitchute.com/privacy

Private Cryptocurrencies:
How to Buy, Own, and Use Bitcoin Like a True Radical
bitcoinprivacycourse.com

The Watchman Privacy Newsletter
watchmanprivacy.com

Printed in Great Britain
by Amazon